W9-CYZ-485

LONERGAN'S CHALLENGE TO THE UNIVERSITY AND THE ECONOMY

Philip McShane

University Press of America™

81051817
Copyright © 1980 by

University Press of America, Inc.
4710 Auth Place, S.E., Washington, D.C. 20023

Library of Congress Catalog Number: 79-3809

For Bernard Lonergan,

on his seventy-fifth birthday,

December 17th 1979,

"perched on giant stilts,....
taller than church spires,
constantly growing",*

with affection and gratitude,

       Phil and Fiona McShane.

* Marcel Proust, <u>Remembrance of Things Past</u>,
                             conclusion.

CONTENTS

INTRODUCTION

> "What more do they want?   She asks this
> seriously, as if there's a real conversion
> factor between information and lives. Well,
> strange to say, there is.   Written down in
> the Manual, on the file at the War Depart-
> ment. Don't forget the real business of
> War is buying and selling. The murdering
> and the violence are self-policing, and can
> be entrusted to non-professionals".[1]

And what is the real business of peace, what is the
real business of the university?

Eric Voegelin recently remarked on Pynchon's novels as
expressive of contemporary paranoia.[2]   Laurens van
der Post, with African heart, reflects, in the conclusion of his book Jung and the Story of our Time, on
the schizophrenia of modern western man.[3] Victorino
Tejera, looking back on the aesthetic integrity of
early Greece, speaks of our contemporary culture as
anaesthetized.[4]   Maslow and Aresteh find adult growth
uncomfortably rare: 99% of us are dwarfs.[5]

Now I find little evidence for exempting the university,
breeding ground of economists, lawyers, politicians,
educators, from this numb daft dwarftness.   There is,
then, the possibility of a challenge to alert lucid
academic adulthood: a slim possibility[6] for the challenge within each of us in the university is anaesthetized.
It is the challenge of finding a conversion[7] factor
between information and life which is not in the faculty
manual but in the faculty member's bones, feelings,
loneliness.   It is the challenge of an odyssey in growing
old and up, alone, as a community, as a history.   It
has the risk of a Jung discomfortingly seeking at the age
of 38 the threatening freshness of a dream with the words,
"Well Jung, here you go".[8]   It requires a stand on being
a beginner such as Husserl expressed on his 45th birthday in a letter to Brentano.[9]   It becomes, with the years,
a Proustian habit which is not the habit that is "the
guarantee of a dull inviolability"[10] but the blossoming
of a quest.   It blooms into the autumn hope for the
integrated incompleteness described by Bachelard: "Late
in life, with indomitable courage, we continue to say
that we are going to do what we have not yet done: we
are going to build a house".[11]

Yet further: the adult academic growth that I envisage
goes beyond the reachings of these great men towards
a fivefold differentiation of consciousness meshed with
a threefold conversion factor.(12) So it is that its
present possibility is slim. Our generation's
challenge, then, would seem to be to reach indeed, but
more to point, to encourage, so that a later generation
might live a more improbable dream.

When I wrote chapter one of this book in 1976 I was
considering the title The Structure of an Academic
Revolution. Echoing, as it does Kuhn's title of some
years ago, it brings to mind immediately the difficulty
of fundamental paradigm shifts. The title I have
chosen, however, serves a more complex purpose. It
indicates clearly, honouring his 75th year, the initiation by Lonergan of what I regard as a profound
cultural shift. It specifies his challenge as being,
not to small groups of philosophers or theologians,
but to the academic community. It leaves no doubt
about his concrete concerns. Finally, if it locates
the challenge in the context of an academic perspective
that goes beyond Newman, of a paradigm of economic
thinking that goes beyond Mark, of a cultural transformation going beyond Jasper's view of an axial shift,
then one may expect that we have here a novel and
unacceptable[13] paradigm.

The unacceptability is perhaps most immediately and
uncomfortably apparent to many of my readers in their
spontaneous reaction to the table of contents. Most of
the contents are outside their discipline, as presently
conceived. But the paradigm requires a revolution in
the conception of any discipline. The issue, in the
end of this century and beyond, is procedure. We proceed
in our living and thinking as academics, either in
dulled contentment with the opaqueness of that proceeding or in a twisting reaching for a luminousness
of that proceeding.

But here indeed is the paradox and the slim possibility.
To seriously notice that spontaneous human procedure
is indeed opaque is the beginnings of the conversion
factor that is so necessary and so absent. Such
advertence can blossom into an adventure of understanding
feelingfully the proceedor that is me, alone and in
history, into a seeking for a modern odyssey, within an
Illiad, continuously redefining that odyssey and
Illiad.[14]

The present book is a set of pointers towards the
pursuit of that adequate personal story. It is
continuous with previously published pointers,[15]
and indeed emerged alongside of them, since the essays
here span twenty years of searching mediated by
Lonergan's achievements.

The first chapter, on academic psychological presence,
gives a compact indication of the structure of the
quest for that presence, and that indication is comple-
mented by the first two sections of chapter six.

Chapter two, on mathematical procedures, previously
published[16] was originally given at the Dublin Institute
for Theoretical Physics in the winter of 1960. I still
recall with pleasure the response of that delightful
theoretician, Cornelius Lanczos, to my unorthodox presentation: "I too am an intuitionist!". The paper does
indeed draw attention to parallel's between Lonergan's
strategy and Brouwer's program, but whereas Lonergan's
strategy leads to an understanding of the mathematician,
Brouwer's program leads to a particular version of
mathematics.

The third chapter, outlining the relevance of Lonergan's
work for the elucidation of biological procedure, was a
contribution to the Festschrift in honour of Lonergan's
sixtieth birthday.[17] Parts of that sketch were filled
out later by the book Randomness, Statistics and Emergence, and by chapter one (on botany) and chapter three
(on zoology) of The Shaping of the Foundations. A major
work still remains to be done on the complex procedures
involved in understanding plant and animal development.

The fourth chapter, written for a conference already
referred to,[18] seeks to throw redeeming light on the
confusion of procedures in contemporary literary criticism. It parallels a previous effort to do the same for
musicology,[19] and the strategy, of course, is relevant
to any other field of art.

Chapter five faces the issues of academic modernity in
a manner that complements previous indications. It was
written for a conference on religious studies in Carleton
University, Ottawa, during October of 1978, and while
it is addressed here to academics in general it is still
most urgently addressed to students of religion within
the christian tradition. The evident chasm between
contemporary academic Christian thinking and the living
of life is not just a chasm between enlightenment and

bad will.   It involves a chasm between such Christian
thinking and modernity.   Lonergan has made this
point regularly: "I have been indicating in summary
fashion a series of fundamental changes that have cone
about in the last four centuries and a half.   They
modify man's image of himself in his world, his science
and his conception of science, his history and his
conception of history, his philosophy and his conception
of philosophy.   They involve three basic differentiations of consciousness, and all three are quite beyond
the horizon of ancient Greece and medieval Europe.
These changes have, in general, been resisted by churchmen for two reasons.   The first reason commonly has
been that churchmen has no real apprehension of the
nature of the changes...."20   Even in those thinkers
who are attracted by Lonergan's challenge I find all
too frequently an absence of such a real apprehension.
We are back at the issue of slim probabilities.

In the context of a consideration of such improbable
Christian thinking chapter six raises the issues of
economic thinking and practice, and chapter seven continues the reflection.   Since Lonergan's work in this
area is still unpublished the treatment here of his
economic thinking is sketchy.   Some account of his
views is given through descriptive modelling, through
comparisons and contrasts with present systematic macroeconomics and through broad suggestions regarding the
dialectic of economic theorizing in these past centuries.
These indications of Lonergan's novel perspective in
economics were made possible by his continued generosity,
during this past decade, in making available to me both
his early manuscripts and the directions of his present
reading and thinking.   It is hoped that the chapters
will provide a context aiding towards the understanding,
acceptance and implementation of his own analysis when
it emerges in public.

The final chapter, "Lonergan's Quest and the Transformation of the Meaning of Life" was delivered this spring
as a lecture at the new Lonergan College of Concordia
University.   It fittingly concludes this book and this
set of pointers to adult academic growth, since it spells
out these pointers in terms of Lonergan's own long quest,
and, further, spells them out in a manner that highlights
their concrete relevance.

A concluding remark regarding psychology is in order.

A contemporary psychologist, on glancing at the table of contents, might well claim that this stuff has little or nothing to do with his or her discipline. Now I might simply reply that there are not a few explicit indications regarding a renewed psychology in the following pages, as there are also in Lonergan's own work. But I wish to make a larger, and perhaps less acceptable, point. It is, that the entire book is a book on data intrinsic to psychology.[21] Chapter one evidently asks about psychological presence. But chapter two is not about mathematics, but about the minds of mathematicians. And so on.

And if this view of the book is considered far-out and far-fetched, perhaps it is because 99% of contemporary psychologists are paranoic, schizophrenic, anaesthetized, or truncated?[22] For they too are part of our present time. Nor do I claim exemption.

> "All I know is that I have learned to
> interpret the whole of life in terms
> of conspiracy. That is the sword I
> have lived by, and as I look around me
> I see it is the sword I shall die by as
> well. These people terrify me but I
> am one of them".[23]

Philip McShane
Visiting Fellow, Lonergan College,
        Concordia University, Montreal:
Professor of Philosophy,
        Mount St. Vincent University,
        Halifax.

August, 1979.

CHAPTER I

THE PSYCHOLOGICAL PRESENT OF THE ACADEMIC COMMUNITY

Preface

If there is to be a massive shift in public minding
and kindliness and discourse in the next century,
there must be a proportionate shift in the mind and
heart of the academy and the arts at the end of this
century, with consequent changes in operating schemes
of recurrence from government to kindergarden. This
two-part essay deals in preliminary fashion with
elements of the academic shift.[1]   The first part
was written for a Halifax Lonergan Conference on Interdisciplinary Philosophy, October 1975. Distributed
through that part there are seven section headings
(A - G) which were the original summary of that paper.
That summary, in fact, indicated that the problem
was larger than one of interdisciplinary philosophy,
and so, the seventh section of the summary (see page
16 below) leads naturally to the problems of the second
part.

I append here immediately three texts from the writings of Fr. Lonergan which I selected as keynote texts
for the original three sections of the present paper.
As the paper emerged, they turned out to be surpris-
ingly more apt than I had originally envisaged.

Part I The Psychological Present of the Inter-
        disciplinary Philosopher.

        "Philosophy is the flowering of the individual's
        rational consciousness in its coming to know
        and take possession of itself. To that event,
        its traditional schools, its treatises, and
        its history are but contributions; and without
        that event they are stripped of real signif-
        icance. It is this aspect of personal devel-
        opment and personal commitment that the
        scientist turning to philosophy is, perhaps,
        most likely to overlook".[2]

Part 2   The Psychological Present of the
          Contemporary Academic.

          "The goal of the method is the emergence
          of explicit metaphysics in the minds of
          particular men and women.   It begins from
          them as they are, no matter what that may
          be.   It involves a preliminary stage that
          can be methodical only in the sense in which
          a pedagogy is methodical, that is, the goal
          and the procedure are known and pursued
          explicitly by a teacher but not by the pupil.
          The preliminary stage ends when the subject
          reaches an intelligent and reasonable
          self-affirmation.   Such self-affirmation
          is also self-knowledge".[3]

Part 3   The Psycholgical Present of the Contemporary
          Theologian.

          "In both Barth and Bultmann, though in differ-
          ent manners, there is revealed the need for
          intellectual as well as moral and religious
          conversion.   Only intellectual conversion
          can remedy Barth's fideism.   Only intell-
          ectual conversion can remove the secularist
          notion of scientific exegesis represented
          by Bultmann.   Still intellectual conversion
          alone is not enough.   It has to be made
          explicit in a philosophic and theological
          method, and such an explicit method has to
          include a critique both of the method of
          science and of the method of scholarship.[4]

I.   The Psychological Present of the
          Interdisciplinary Philosopher.

A.   A first context is the mood of Husserl's
          search for "intentional origins and unities of
          the formation of meaning", of Jasper's "stand-
          point of the encompassing", of Heidegger's
          stress on mindfulness of, care of, being.

In this first part I would like to share a mood of
inquiry and also to indicate general and specific
directions of solution to contemporary problems of
methodology. The mood I wish to share is one which
I find most sympathetically present in the German
existentialist tradition. In so far as one has
shared that tradition, not merely in scholarly stance
but in the resonance of carefilled reading which
Bachelard so well intimates[5] one needs no more than
this hint. In so far, however, as one fits into
the general mood of the contemporary academy with its
less than encompassing stance,[6] not a hint but a
horizon-shift is required. And if it is a horizon-
shift that is required, I have no illusion about
specifying it for, and in, a reader in the introductory remarks of a paper or a conference. Fichte's
"Sun-clear statement to the Public at large concerning
the true nature of the Newest Philosophy. An attempt
to force the reader to an understanding,"[7] has the air
of such an illusion. Sun-clarity in the present issue
results only from a life-long self-attentive climb out
of the prevalent cultural cave. What is it to care
for, to be mindful of, being? The answer is a
mustard-seeded personal history of adult-growing
anamnesis and prolepsis which may be mainly before
one.[8] I recall here, as symbol, the recollected "man
on giant stilts" at the conclusion of Proust's novel.[9]
I recall, as model, Husserl's life work.[10] Husserl,
in his last great incomplete work, specifies the problem
with which my paper deals, that of the psychological
present of the interdisciplinary philosopher, in terms
of recollection as a strategy of reaching "the intentional origins and unities of the formation of meaning".
"Recollection, above all, exercises the intentional
function of forming the meaning of the past .... Like-
wise, in expectation or anticipatory recollection, again
understood as an intentional modification of perception
(the future is a present-to-come), is found the meaning-
formation from which arises the ontic meaning of that
which is in the future. And the deeper structure of
this can be revealed in more detail. This represents
the beginnings of new dimensions of temporalization..."[11]

Successfully incarnated, the new dimension of temporalization grounds what Jaspers would term a contemporary
axial shift,[12] what Lonergan speaks of when he discusses

the two times of the temporal subject.[13]   Therein is
grounded the possibility and probability[14] of an epoc-
hal shift in the control of meaning,[15] and part of
that probability is the concrete possibility of asking
and answering with contemporary precision Jaspers'
basic question: "Beyond asking: 'what is Being?',
he asks: 'How can we and how must we think Being if
we want to speak of Being?'"[16]

B.   A second context is the Popper-Kuhn controv-
          ersy regarding normal and revolutionary science,
          as paradigmatic of contemporary normal meta-
          science.   (Cf. Criticism and the Growth of
          Knowledge, edited by Lakatos and Musgrave,
          Cambridge, 1970, where Popper, Kuhn, Toulmin
          etc., revisit Kuhn's The Structure of
          Scientific Revolutions).

The previous context, mounting to that final carefilled
question, is remote from the controversy to which we now
turn, and it is deeply foreign to most of English-speak-
ing philosophy. But I would note that this large
community unavoidably speaks about being, and speaks
about speaking about being, even as they rule out such
speech. What Lonergan remarks about Leslie Dewart
is a generally valid thesis. I quote at length
because, I would suggest, it is an extremely good
starting point for tackling the opaqueness regarding
truth mentioned in the fifth section: Tarski too is
strangely silent on judgments. [17]

"I have no doubt that concepts and judgments (on
judgments I find Dewart strangely silent) are the
expression of one's accumulated experience, developed
understanding, acquired wisdom; and I quite agree that
such expression is an objectification of one's self
and of one's world.

I would urge, however, that this objectification is
intentional. It consists in acts of meaning. We
objectify the self by meaning the self, and we objectify
the world by meaning the world. Such meaning of its
nature is related to a meant, and what is meant may or
may not correspond to what in fact is so. If it corresponds, the meaning is true. If it does not correspond the meaning is false. Such is the correspondence
view of truth, and Dewart has managed to reject it
without apparently adverting to it. So eager has
he been to impugn what he considers the Thomist theory
of knowledge that he has overlooked the fact that he
needed a correspondence view of truth to mean what he
said.

Let me stress the point. Dewart has written a book
on the future of belief. Does he mean the future of
belief, or something else, or nothing at all?"[18]

The question of a correspondence metaview of truth
coterminus with a basic position on being[19] will
occupy us later. Immediately however I wish to note
a more evident parallel. The contributors to the
volume Criticism and the Growth of Knowledge have
written a book about the past, present and future of
science and indeed of scientific belief. Do they
mean the past, present and future of science? Or
what do they mean? Of what, from what, do they speak?
The questions point to the key implicit problem of
the volume we are considering, and of the Kuhn-Popper
tradition of the philosophy of science. It is the
problem around which this present book spirals. Here
I continue to be impressionistic, descriptive.

Margaret Masterman, in an illuminating contribution
to the volume in question, notes a certain aggressiveness in the various contributions, and permits herself
"A little pro-Kuhn aggressiveness".[20] I too feel that
I might indulge in what may be called a little honest
aggressiveness.

I first came across Kuhn's The Structure of Scientific
Revolutions when I was in Oxford in the mid-sixties.
The book failed to impress me. That failure was
related to the fact that I had come to it from a background of mathematical science and of a mode of meta-
scientific reflection related to the third context.
I could of course sympathize with Kuhn more that I could
with Popper, and here I would echo Masterman's delightful aggressiveness: "the one thing working scientists
are not going to do is to change their ways of thinking,
in doing science, ex more philosophico, because they
have Popper and Feyerabend pontificating at them like
eighteenth-century divines; particularly as both
Popper and Feyerabend normally pontificate at even more
than eighteenth-century length".[21] I sympathize with
Kuhn because, as Masterman indicates, "Kuhn has really
looked at actual science"[22] just as "Lakatos, in Proofs
and Refutations has introduced a new complexity and
realism into our conception of mathematics, because he
has taken a closer look at what mathematicians really
do".[23] Yet my sympathy is limited to the degree that
the manner of 'looking at', 'talking about' of this
genuinely struggling tradition has the radical[24] limitations to be specified by raising such questions as are
already raised above: of what, from what, are they

talking? in what sense are they looking?

Kuhn asserts that his and Popper's views of science "are very nearly identical. We are both concerned with the dynamic process by which scientific knowledge is acquired rather than with the logical structure of the products of scientific research".[25] From the first context I would raise the issue of the measure of their concern; anticipating the third context I would question the seriousness of their focus on the dynamic process. One might perhaps describe their handicap as that of a deeply embedded tradition of detached conceptualism. Toulmin describes well one facet of that limited care: "The term concept is one that everybody uses and nobody explains - still less defines. One the one hand, the word has a familiar currency in twentieth century history and sociology, psychology and philosophy alike. For many twentieth-century philosophers, indeed, concepts provide their central subject matter, their very bread and butter ... Many of them would even describe the central task of philosophy itself as being that of conceptual analysis. Yet, despite all their scrupulous care in the actual practice of conceptual analysis, the precise meaning of the terms 'concept' and 'conceptual' is rarely made explicit and frequently left quite obscure".[26]

The limitation runs deep through European intellectual history by way of Plato, Neo-platonism, and the pervasive influence of Scotus.[27] Such an influence leads with a narrowing cogency to the mistaken identification of the task of philosophy as conceptual analysis. The struggling tradition I speak of is limited by the near-dogmatic presence of the mood of that mistake, but it is gradually bringing forth the possibility and probability of locating the task of philosophy as an elucidation, not of concept, but of process, not of 'Whiteheadian' process, but of intellectual process.[28]

Lakatos describes his own development of interest in a manner that usefully intimates that emerging probability,[29] and so I quote the description at length:

"The problem of continuity in science was raised by Popper and his followers long ago. When I proposed my theory of growth based on the idea of competing research programmes, I again followed, and tried to improve, Popperian tradition. Popper himself, in his (1934), had already stressed the heuristic importance of 'influential metaphysics', and was regarded by

some members of the Vienna Circle as a champion of
dangerous metaphysics. When his interest in the
role of metaphysics revived in the 1950's, he wrote
a most interesting 'Metaphysical Epilogue' about
'metaphysical research programmes' to his Postscript:
After Twenty Years - in galleys since 1957. But
Popper associated tenacity not with methodological
irrefutability but rather with syntactical irrefutability. By 'metaphysics' he meant syntactically
specifiable statements like 'all-some' statements
and purely existential statements. No basic statements could conflict with them because of their logical
form. For instance, 'for all metals there is a
solvent' would, in this sense, be 'metaphysical', while
Newton's theory of gravitation, taken in isolation,
would not be. Popper, in the 1950's, also raised
the problem of how to criticize metaphysical theories
and suggested solutions. Agassi and Watkins published several interesting papers on the role of this
sort of 'metaphysics' in science, which all connected
'metaphysics' with the continuity of scientific progress.
My treatment differs from theirs first because I go
much further than they in blurring the demarcation
between (Popper's) 'science' and (Popper's) 'metaphysics': I do not even use the term 'metaphysical'
any more. I only talk about scientific research
programmes whose hard core is irrefutable not necessarily because of syntactical but possibly because of
methodological reasons which have nothing to do with
logical form. Secondly, separating sharply the descriptive problem of the psychologico-historical role of
metaphysics from the normative problem of how to distinguish progressive from degenerating research programmes, I elaborate the latter problem further than
they had done".[30]

Lakatos focuses his attention on the methodology of
scientific research programmes, such programmes con-
sisting "of methodological rules: some tell us what
paths of research to avoid (negative heuristic), and
others what paths to pursue (positive heuristic)".[31]
In such focusing, and in the wish to "only talk about
research programmes whose hard core is irrefutable"
there is certainly an advance. But there remains
that central opaqueness which calls for the question,
of what, from what, does he talk and mean? What is
his psychological present?

C.   A third context is the emergence (1928-79)
       of the psychological present of Lonergan.

"Numberless experiences extending over several years
are gradually co-ordinated .... and the total synthetic
whole finds expression, it may be, on some particular
occasion .... A genius may be defined as a man who is
exceptionally rich in recoverable contexts".[32]

I quote, not without purpose, from Sullivan's account
of Beethoven's spiritual development: the quotation
grounds an evident and fruitful parallel, but also a
reaching for a less evident twist of meaning related
to the twist of Jaspers' axial period.   The twist of
meaning will be specified somewhat better in the next
sections, but we must begin that specification immediately.

I speak in this present section of a third context,
and that third context has to do with the spiritual
development of "a man who is exceptionally rich in
recoverable contexts".   But this third context cannot
personally be glimpsed unless one seeks within oneself
for "a needed clarification of the notion of the
spiritual".[33]   That clarification is reached by grasping that "the adjective, intelligible, may be employed
in two quite different senses.   Ordinarily, it denotes
what is or can be understood, and in that sense the
content of every act of conceiving is intelligible.
More profoundly, it denotes the primary component
in an idea;   it is what is grasped inasmuch as one is
understanding;   it is the intelligible ground or root
or key from which results intelligibility in the ordinary sense.   Moreover, there is a simple test for
distinguishing between the ordinary and the profounder
meaning of the name, intelligible.   For the intelligible in the ordinary sense can be understood without
understanding what it is to understand;   but the
intelligible in the profounder sense is identical
with the understanding, and so it cannot be understood without understanding what understanding is".[34]
That clarification in turn gives rise to some little
appreciation that while the spiritual development of
Beethoven did not require, much less pivot on, the
presence of a similar clarification in Beethoven, in
Lonergan's spiritual development the reaching and
ever-fuller reaching of that clarification was the
centre-piece of that development.

I have used, in the previous sentence, the words "some little" in relation to our appreciation. In doing so I take a stand which puts me out of sympathy with the predominant mood of the contemporary academy. That mood would expect here a summary, instead of a set of pointers. Whereas, indeed, I have no intention of giving a clear set of pointers here - they are available elsewhere[35] - my intention is to intimate, to raise the question of, a counter-mood. It is a counter-mood only secondarily relevant to the study of Bernard Lonergan: primarily it is relevant to one's own adult growth. The incarnate questing of that counter-mood might well initially be focused, by student or professor alike, in such elementary existential questions as, what is a doctoral dissertation, a beginning or an end? Is contemplative intellectual growth an accelerating accretion of insight to habitual insight, mediated by an axial shift, so that grown wisdom's articulation is little more than an invitation to ascent, or is intellectual growth a matter of diminishing returns, the addition of grey-haired footnotes to a tired world view?

Sympathy with the counter-mood is easier to win in the field of music than in the field of mind: it seems easier to admit the feebleness of our resonance with a great composer than to admit it in relation to a great thinker.[37] Yet it is not foolish but human to make that admission in the second case. Is what Sullivan says of Beethoven in the realms of music only implausibly applied in the realms of mind? "The human mind may be likened to some kind of multiple plant, here in full bloom, there still in bud. Different minds have flowered in different ways. Beethoven had reached relative maturity in directions where those of us who respond to him are still in the stage of embryonic growth. And in some people, it is obvious, there is no germ of consciousness akin to the state of awareness manifested by the late Beethoven".[38]

I may usefully recall now some of my own earlier gropings towards what I would now name as the psychological present of the elder interdisciplinary philosopher or theologian - normatively speaking. There is the fact that "all we know is somehow with us; it is present and operative within our knowing, but it lurks behind the scenes...."[39] There is the eccentric achievement of James Joyce: his friends of the 1930's

recorded their impression of him at work and bore
witness to the fact that "he held an incredibly
complex form of the Wake in his mind as a single image,
and could move from one section to another with complete freedom".[40]   And, to return to the field of
music, there is the manner in which a temporally
structured composition challenges our 'disposition
to the present', to use a phrase of Schenker: "We
know how difficult it is to grasp the meaning of the
present if we are not aware of the temporal background.
It is equally difficult for the student or performer
to grasp the 'present' of a composition if he does not
include at the same time a knowledge of the background.
Just as the demands of the day toss him to and fro, so
does the foreground of a composition pull at him.
Every change of sound and figuration, every chromatic
shift, every neighbour note signified something new
to him.   Each novelty leads him further away from the
coherence which derives from the background".[41]   I
recall, further, that in the composition Method in
Theology there is a Background and a Foreground, and
that the Background is a set of instrumental acts of
meaning inviting the thinker towards a self-constitution
which would redeem him or her from trivialization of the
novelty in the Foreground.   Finally, to come full
circle - in good joycean Viconesque fashion! - I would
recall F. E. Crowe's remark regarding the two parts
of Insight, that the first part is liable to be neglected and the second part disputed,[42] and give that remark
this new context.

What I am touching on here is the concrete possibility
of absentmindedness or presentmindedness, the meaning
of both of these depending on the meaning of 'psychological present'.   What, then, is the psychological
present?

The psychological present "is not an instant, a mathematical point, but a time-span, so that our experience
of time is, not a raceway of instances, but a now
leisurely, a now rapid succession of overlapping time-
spans .... whether slow and broad or rapid and short,
the psychological present reaches into its past by
memories and into its future by anticipations".[43]
Such is Lonergan's indication of the nature of the
psychological present.   One may recall here my earlier
quotation from Husserl. Yet the psychological present
achieved by Lonergan leaves clearly behind the opaqueness concerning fact that haunted the mind of Husserl.

Constitutive of the spiritual that is the kernel of
mind is understanding, and in particular that reflective understanding by which we grasp the unconditioned,
"and inasmuch as we are grasping the unconditioned, we
are attaining the lucid, fully rational factualness
that contrasts so violently with the brute factualness
with which instances similar in all respects still
are different instances, with which the multiplicity
of the continuum is non-countable because non-ordinable,
with which actual frequencies diverge from ideal frequencies in any manner provided it is non-systematic.
But if insight and grasp of the unconditioned are
constituted quite differently from the empirical residue, so also are the inquiry and critical reflection
that lead them and the conception and judgment that
result from them and express them".[44]   But the
lucidity, the constitution, the psychological present,
and the spiritual development related to it, which
are our concern here, are of a different order. It
is a lucidity for which and from which the content of
the previous quotation is habitually lucid.   It is
a lucidity, a psychological present, which emerges
from the slow shift from presence to self to knowledge
of self.   It emerges from the habituation, with
incarnate resonances, of the conception, affirmation
and implementation of the heuristic that is the kernel
spiritual self.   Through that development the "position
on being" becomes a present, serene and carefilled
answer in the interweaving of questions and answers
which is an actual context.[45]

There is much more to be said in regard to such a
psychological present, whether in regard to Fr. Lonergan's spiral,[46] or in regard to the vortex of its
genesis in ourselves.[47]   But perhaps enough initial
indication has been given.   I may note in conclusion
that the lucid reaching into the past by memories and
into the future by anticipation of the human subject
may take on all the subtlety of complexly differentiated consciousness[48] and of functional specialization.[49]

D.   The three contexts are related dialectically
        by a speaking of, and from, an actual context
        (cf. Method in Theology, 163) regarding
        actual contexts.   This relating and speaking
        is identified as meaning, with third stage
        meaning, (cf. Method in Theology, 94-99) a
        psychological present of the interdisciplinary
        philosopher.

How can one relate these three contexts? Obviously this is the question of the present section. Yet I would note that if I indicated a twist of meaning[50] in the previous section, I move forward now in the actual context of that twist of meaning. The question of the present section is not one of actually relating but of the context and strategy of relating. The twist is most nearly indicated by the fact that I identify the metaunderstanding of context as the central issue of the relating of the contexts.

"But what precisely is meant by the word, context? There are two meanings. There is the heuristic meaning the word has at the beginning of an investigation, and it tells one where to look to find the context. There is the actual meaning the word acquires as one moves out of one's initial horizon and moves to a fuller horizon that includes a significant part of the author's.

Heuristically, then, the context of the word is the sentence. The context of the sentence is the paragraph. The context of the paragraph is the chapter. The context of the chapter is the book. The context of the book is the author's opera omnia, his life and times, the state of the question in his day, his problems, prospective readers, scope and aim.

Actually, context is the interweaving of questions and answers in limited groups".[51]

Actual context is in a mind, and the relevant actual context here must be one from which comes forth adequate dialectically-relating speech regarding all contexts. Nor do we have here some shadow of the problem of the class of all classes. We have here, not the problem of avoiding with Russell the semblance of conceptual self-inclusion, but the much deeper issue of reaching asymptotically towards intentional luminosity, of achieving a dynamic perspective[52] on science, scientists, and perspectives on science in the weave of history. It is the issue of context raised and heuristically contextualized by the author of the book Insight: "There is the noêsis or intentio intendens or pensee pensante that is constituted by the very activity of inquiring and reflecting, understanding and affirming, asking further questions and reaching further answers. Let us say that this noetic activity is engaged in a lower context when it is doing

mathematics or following scientific method or exer-
cising common sense. Then it will be moving towards
an upper context when it scrutinizes mathematics or
science or common sense in order to grasp the nature
of noetic activity. And if it comes to understand
and affirm what understanding is and what affirming is,
then it has reached an upper context that logically is
independent of the scaffolding of mathematics, science,
and common sense. Moreover it can be shown that the
upper context is invariant...."[53]

We may recall Lakatos' "focusing of attention" on
method and his desire to "talk about" research programmes. I may now specify my claim regarding the
limitations of his project briefly and accurately as
an absence in Lakatos of the adequate actual context,
a context which can be mediated only by the serious
admission of generalized empirical method[54] as the
strategy of attention-focusing and the source of more
than descriptive "talk about". "Philosophy finds its
proper data in intentional consciousness. Its primary
function is to promote the self-appropriation that cuts
to the root of philosophic differences and incompre-
hensions. It has further, secondary functions in
distinguishing, relating, grounding the several realms
of meaning and, no less, in grounding the methods of
the sciences and so promoting their unification".[55]

Yet not 'it', not 'philosophy', but you and I and the
tradition struggling with science's history and method
that must focus on that data, so that later generations
may emerge, in a developed third stage meaning, to mean
and speak, with adequate presentmindedness, of the past
and future of science in history.

E.   Issues relating to the truncated (cf. Lonergan,
      A Second Collection, 73) interdisciplinary
      philosophers' neglect of meaning and of the
      anthropological turn in the higher sciences
      and the arts are left to the other speakers.[56]
      Essential elements in the genesis of the
      adequate psychological present of any inter-
      disciplinary philosopher are indicated by
      reference to the two lower and the two middle
      sciences. Such essential elements are contra-
      sted with contemporary metascientific opaque-
      ness regarding truth, hierarchy theory,
      statistical science and the heuristics of
      evolution.

I can be legitimately brief here, for my indications
are, fairly literally, by reference. What is at
issue is a genetico-dialectic specification of the
life of the interdisciplinary philosopher, and the
mediation of his or her adult growth through the
appropriation of the lower and middle sciences, and
these are topics I have already dealt with at some
length.[57]

Still, I would like to lay further emphasis on the
"necessary beginning",[58] however long it may take one,
[59] which is the personal reaching of a coherent position on truth. Kuhn sees Popper's acceptance of
Tarski's semantic conception of truth as a fundamental
difficulty,[60] and rightly so. That fundamental difficulty lies at the heart not only of the Kuhn-Popper
traditional discussion of verification and proof, but
of the main stream of contemporary theological, philosophical and scientific confusion. One does not easily
move out of that main stream.

The opaqueness regarding truth clouds all other meta-
scientific issues, in particular those mentioned in
the summary statement above. The most obvious way of
handling the problem of the evident hierarchy of
sciences and things is to deny through reductionism
its ultimate relevance. But one may not be willing
to settle for that cluster of errors. Then one joins
forces with such systems theorists as Ludwig von
Bertalanffy.[61] Evidently there are layers of systems
corresponding to levels of science: but the meta-
evidence is as opaque as the systems theorists' view
on truth. How, they may ask, are these layers linked?
"Although the world appears to function as a whole
there should be some complex, multilevel representation
possible. The design of such a multilevel construct
depends on a methodology for the valid organization
of systems into suprasystems. Whereas the inverse
problem of analytic resolution of a system into
subsystems is readily treated by such top-down approaches as deduction, and single level systems are
amenable through induction or statistical procedures,
there is no corresponding technique for vertical
bottom-up organization. This lacuna is a task for a
new epistemology".[62] But the new epistemology requires
as centre the conception and affirmation of the iso-
morphism of knowing, with its term truth, and being.
Only from this centre can one think and speak with

metaprecision of things, real things, entities, aggregates of entities, and the manner in which "a concrete plurality of lower entities may be the material cause from which a higher form is educed":[63] clearheaded non-reductionism.[64] And only on the basis of that heuristic clarity can one build a precise and powerful principle of evolution.

F. Against this background one may move to a more precise specification of the adequate psychological present of the interdisciplinary philosopher, and the community of interdisciplinary philosophers, in the third stage of meaning.

If the reader is to some extent with me at this stage the meaning of the phrase "against this background one may move" will not be lost. The precise specification in question is the term of a decade and more of adult philosophic growth. Undoubtedly the basic possibility of the specification is rooted in the solitary searcher's anamnesis and prolepsis. But the more than random recurrence of successful search requires the linkage of community, and the basic shift in schedules of probability of adult philosophic growth requires the emergence of complex supporting schemes of recurrence.[65] Such schemes are remote from present schemes. The scattered community of interdisciplinary philosophers in this immature period of the third stage of meaning is in the main characterizable by what Lonergan says of "undifferentiated consciousness in the later stages"[66] of meaning. As Berger remarks in his recent book, "it is, in principle, impossible to 'raise the consciousness' of anyone, because all of us are stumbling around on the same level of consciousness - a pretty dim level".[67] His book, with the seventh section of the summary of this paper with which I presently conclude, provides an indicative context for the issues to be dealt with in Part 2. The book is a "Political ethics - in quest of a method",[68] but the quest lacks basic strategy, and the method does not emerge. He does, however, focus attention on the need for intermediate structures: "The paramount task, as Durkheim saw, is the quest for intermediate structures as solutions to this dilemma of modern society - structures which will be intermediate between the atomized individual and the order of the state".[69]

Undoubtedly, in the short run, various partially
adequate intermediate structures of living may emerge.
But for the long run, the longer cycle,[70] the task and
the quest must be itself incarnate in an intermediate
structure. That paramount task is not one for some
community of interdisciplinary philosophers: it is the
evident task, it seems to me, of the academy. It is
a task of academic self-definition and self-constitution.[71] What is involved is a sophisticated
functionally-differentiated Wendung zur Idee that,
quite precisely, goes beyond present dreams.

G.   At this stage interest is shifted to the
      community of academics, in their commitment
      to, and pursuit of, their particular dis-
      ciplines. The question of their interpret-
      ation of their special fields to themselves,
      to their colleagues, to their students, is
      raised.

      There emerges the suggestion that a personal
      and communal cultivation of the third context,
      above, in the mood of the first context, is
      vital to 21st century adult growth. Without
      that cultivation by the professional
      non-philosophers, normal science and scholar-
      ship will remain under the muddled influence
      of a personal consciousness which is relatively
      compact, and of a normal metascience which is
      paradigmatically determined by a long-surviving
      tradition of what may be precisely defined as
      an absent-mindedness of professional philoso-
      phers.

II   The Psychological Present of the
      Contemporary Academic.

"The emancipation of the methods of the other sciences
and philosophies from trivialization or fanaticization
is not done by any direct intervention in their methods
by theology. Rather it is done indirectly and
heuristically inasmuch as political theology would
succeed in interrelating the intellectual praxis of
science with the moral praxis of political social life
and the religious praxis of ecclesial institutions.
Theology would thereby be an instance of socio-critical
concern within the academic world just as the church
should be one within the political world. For it
would oppose any conceptualism that would separate
theory from praxis."[72]

The quotation from Fr. Lamb's work gives a tone to
our present enterprize and also adds a further problematic context. One might shift from the sciences to
the arts to add further contexts: neither literary
criticism nor music criticism are in good health.[73]
But I must leave such additions to the interests of
different readers. The broad issue is the psychological present of academics.

Moreover, that broad issue increasingly manifests
itself as an issue, not just of knowledge, but of
values. As Joseph Haberer remarks, "For science, the
age of innocence is over. That innocence to which
J. Robert Oppenheimer alluded in his famous, if somewhat enigmatic, remark that 'scientists have known
sin',[74] began to disintegrate some decades before the
blinding flash of Alamogordo...."[75] Peter Berger's
book, already cited, makes the point with factual
vigour, and his final thesis gives us yet another point
of departure: "We need a new method to deal with
questions of political ethics and social change
(including those of development policy). This will
require bringing together two attitudes that are usually separate - the attitudes of 'hard-nosed' analysis
and of utopian imagination".[76] What I wish to do in
this part is to add two more interlocking ongoing
methodological contexts of Fr. Lonergan, under the
titles "Generalized Empirical Method" and "From Implementation to Praxis". These contexts add a new
precision to the meaning of "the growth of knowledge",
but more particularly to the meaning of "criticism",
and so we move in a brief penultimate section to a
discussion of criticism. It is in that section that
we spiral back into metatheological discussion, but
perhaps the topic deserves a word here.

I do not think that a high percentage of contemporary
theologians are psychologically present in the twentieth
century. The same, of course, could be said of a
large number of other academic sub-groups such as
generalist historians or students of literature.
Herbert Butterfield is of the view that the scientific
revolution of the sixteenth and seventeenth centuries
"outshines everything since the rise of Christianity
and reduces the Renaissance and Reformation to the rank
of mere episodes, mere internal displacements, within
the system of medieval Christianity".[77] Fr. Lonergan
repeatedly draws attention to the mediation by science

of adequate interiority: "The Greek achievement was
needed to expand the capacities of commonsense
knowledge and language before Augustine, Descartes,
Pascal, Newman could make their commonsense contributions to our self-knowledge. The history of mathematics, natural science, and philosophy and, as well,
one's personal engagement in all three are needed if
both commonsense and theory are to construct a scaffolding for an entry into the world of interiority".[78]
Below I note the possibility of a growing respect for
empiricality, a respect which mediates a growing
incarnate authentic nescience. I think that such
adult growth is normally greatly mediated by the type
of prolonged inquiry one has to do, say, in the most
elementary science, physics, to arrive at the limited
contemporary understanding of the electron. The
contemporary theological community may not have both
time and talent for such footholds on modernity, but
surely there might be fostered some shift in statistics
of educational schemes of recurrence of later generations of theologians.

Generalized Empirical Method

In Insight, generalized empirical method stands to the
data of consciousness as empirical method stands to the
date of sense.[79] In "Aquinas Today: Tradition and
Innovation", Lonergan remarks that "Insight sets forth
a generalized empirical method that operates principally on the data of consciousness to work out a cognitional theory, an epistemology and a metaphysics".[80]
A little further on, he speaks of method's reversal of
the priorities of logic: "Method reverses such priorities. Its principles are not logical propositions
but concrete realities, namely, sensitively, intellect-
ually, rationally, morally conscious subjects".[81]

In the three lectures, Religious Studies and Theology,
[82] Lonergan returns at greater length to the topic of
generalized empirical method. In the first lecture,
it is defined as a method, "a normative pattern of
related and recurrent operations that yield ongoing
and cumulative results" and one may recall the slightly
different definition of method in Method in Theology.[83]
But now "generalized empirical method operates on a
combination of both the data of sense and the data of
consciousness: it does not treat of objects without
taking into account the corresponding operations of the

subject; it does not treat of the subject's operations
without taking into account the corresponding objects".
It is a generalization of the notion of method, going
behind the diverse methods of natural sciences and of
history and hermeneutics, to discover the ground of
their harmonious combination in human studies. Its
appeal is "not to the individual subjectivity that is
correlative to the world of immediacy but to the individual subjectivity that is correlative to the world
mediated by meaning and motivated by value".[84] And
finally, in the context of a discussion of authentic
and inauthentic traditions, Lonergan points out that
"since disintegration and decay are not a private
event, even generalized empirical method is experimental. But the experiment is conducted not by any
individual, not by any generation, but by the historical process itself".

Now what seems to be going forward here is a growing
respect and care, and a thematization of that respect,
for adequate and balanced empiricality. It is a many-
faceted growth and respect and its tracing in the
thought of Lonergan is a task beyond our present effort.
Fr. Crowe remarked in 1970, in an article very relevant to the present issue of ongoing learning, "there
is no doubt that Lonergan's thinking has undergone a
profound reorientation in the last five years, and
that in a way which bears directly on the present
question. If we take his De Deo Trino to mark a
kind of term in the prior phase and compare it with
some of his later work, we find extremely significant
differences. In the trinitarian treatise we read
the assertion, like a kind of refrain, that theology
rests on truths and not data..."[85] In his reply to
Fr. Crowe, Fr. Lonergan acknowledges a shift from
truths to data, adding "this raises a complex issue
that cannot be treated fully at once" and spelling
out some aspects of the shift. The reorientation of
Fr. Lonergan's thinking of the last five years would
seem to be no less remarkable.[87] A casual following
up of indices of recent volumes[88] reveals a growing
emphasis on the relevance of method over that of static,
though essential, logic. Again, there is the regular
recalling, with growing detail,[89] of the shift from
the Aristotelian notion of science to the modern notion:
and here too I would note the difficulty of a serious
appreciation of that shift without some personal involvement in the modern activity. "One may easily use
the phrase 'Newtonian mood" but to enter into serious

metadiscussion of the topic requires as a minimum
some familiarity, e.g., with the integration of the
Newtonian equations of motion".[90] But now I would
note an inverse difficulty: serious involvement with
the equations of physics, or with any endeavour of
science, scholarship or art, requires, in the modern
problematic context, a personal thematization of the
grounds of the shift. And both these difficulties
are related, it seems to me, to what I have called
Lonergan's growing respect for adequate balanced
empiricality.

There are two aspects to this respect, the first being
contextual to the second, and both being contextualized,
as we shall see, by Praxis.

The first aspect is very much like a thematization of
Aquinas' "It is all straw". What alone is invariant
in mind is the concrete structure of intentionality
in human subjects.[91] The suprastructure that is the
ongoing and cumulative result of that dynamic structure, despite its present popular titleing as an explosion of knowledge and technology, is predominantly a
frail network of elementary suspicions the most
palatable[92] of which are overhastily objectified in
history's constructs and schemes of recurrence. In
the article by Fr. Crowe already cited he puts forward
a useful metaphor: "The dogmas are not a continent but
a beachhead, not the sea of infinity but little islands
scattered on the sea".[93] But the respect I am noting
goes beyond the theological zone into all realms of
human knowing and doing:[94] we are each of us vortices[95] of quest of very finite achievement in an
infinite ocean.

The second aspect emerges when one considers that the
respect is for an adequate and balanced empiricality.
The respect is a subtle methodological respect, whose
thematization expresses a strategy relevant to the
"cultivation of the third context, above, in the mood
of the first context"[96] by the community of academics.
Generalized empirical method, one might say, is academic
method for the twenty-first century. How else can
science and commonsense be reoriented and transformed
by metaphysics?[97] How else can there emerge a
harmonious interlocking of the searchings and findings
of sciences, scholarship and the arts in human
sciences?

The problems of such reorientation, transformation and interweaving are enormous, but let me note here just one small aspect of them, which is present below the level of study of meaning as well as within it: the aspect of aggreformic expression, an expression to be born of clear-headed non-reductionism or aggreform-ism.[98]   I have indicated this problematic aspect of expression in some detail in sample areas of botany,[99] zoology[100] and musicology.[101]   Present language there is in the main reductionist, mechanist, even cyber-netic.   Are we to expect a transformation of such language[102] ab _extrinseco_, by encyclopedists of a new enlightenment? or should we not hope that the academic be at the level of his time?

At all events, generalized empirical method invites him or her to be thus at the level of the times.[103] "It does not treat of objects without taking into account the corresponding operations of the subject; it does not treat of the subject's operations without taking into account the corresponding objects".   It requires a balanced adequacy of empirical interest: otherwise one is, so to speak, walking through modernity with one overgrown leg in a cultural gutter.[104]   That requirement and strategy grounds the cultivation of the mediation of interiority by science, scholarship, art: and vice versa.   It is a strat-egy generative of Jaspers' "standpoint of the encom-passing", and of a more radical care.

But the question of the care of being leads us to our next topic, the pragmatic thematization of communal care.

From Implementation to Praxis

The book _Insight_ was an implementation of a conception of metaphysics: "I would contend that the conception of metaphysics that has been implemented in the present work yields unique results".[105]   The conception was constitutive, to a certain level of development,[106] of the writing subject.   Moreover, the conception included a conception of implementation: "Explicit metaphysics is the conception, affirmation, and imple-mentation of the integral heuristic structure of proportionate being",[107] features of that implementat-ion being the transformation of commonsense and sci-ence,[108] of theology,[109] indeed of history both written[110] and lived.[111]   Moreover, the conception of implementation included all the heuristic complexity of schedules of probabilities ranging over actual, probable, and possible schemes of recurrence, things, environments, some of which possible schemes and environments included things that conceived of such implementation.[112] Neither the implementation, however, nor the conception of implementation, were as fully mediated, rendered luminous, by the heuristic conception of the notion of value as they are by Lonergan now.[113]

In a previous paper,[114] I took up briefly this issue of the inclusion of implementation within metaphysics and noted that, since the metaphysical enterprize was sublated in the new enterprize of Method in Theology, there would be a refinement of the task of implementation. Indeed, the second phase of theology seemed likely enough to involve a distribution of labour ranging from categories of implementation to strategies of communication and execution. But I do not think that this does justice to Lonergan's ongoing methodological context. I suspect, indeed, that there is an altogether more profound shift involved, and I will attempt here to trace out lines of this shift. The pure notion of value[115] puts us in open indeterminate harmony within the passionate finality[116] of the universe. "The levels of consciousness are united by a single transcendental intending"[117] and the intending of the good sublates all other intendings. Also "just as the notion of being intends, but, of itself, does not know being, so too the notion of value intends, but does not know value. Again, as the notion of being is the dynamic principle that keeps us moving toward ever fuller knowledge of being, so the notion of value is the fuller flowering of that same dynamic principle that now keeps us moving towards ever fuller realization of the good".[118] Furthermore, let us recall the previous section on generalized empirical method, where there emerged some leads on the appreciation of just how limited our knowledge of being is, and recall that such limited knowledge is itself an instance of the limited achieved good. In so far as one labours over, spirals round, these clues, I think there comes forth a new context which I call conveniently Praxis-weltanschuung.

The finite functioning of our notion of being, a segment of our dynamism, generates in itself a puny limited knowledge. Reflection on that reach and its limited achievement indeed grounds a heuristic notion of being, but it is a dwarf achievement. The fuller truth is beyond, the fullness of truth infinitely remote, and what counts is, not so much the notion of being as the notion of value, what counts is not so much Thomas' natural desire to know God as Augustine's restless heart.[119]   And what counts is the praxis-thematization of what counts.

Let us return here to Insight's discussion of meta-physics: "Just as the notion of being underlies and penetrates and goes beyond all other notions, so also metaphysics is the department of human know-ledge that underlies, penetrates, transforms and unifies all other departments".[120]   But now what underlies and penetrates and goes beyond all other notions would seem to be the notion of value.   What then becomes of metaphysics?

We are not here dealing with a deductive system.   What becomes of metaphysics is an ongoing discovery, with Method in Theology expressing a stage in its genesis.

But there is an ambiguity here.   As "metaphysics is something in a mind",[121] so one may say that method in theology is in a mind such as Lonergan's.   But more properly one has to say that method in theology is in a community.   And just as one can note the gap between adequate metaphysics as in an implementing mind and its implementation in others' minds and lives, so one may note the gap between Method in Theology as ade-quately conceived and its realization in community.

But the gaps are different, and related to that diff-erence is a discontinuity in statistics of emergence and survival.

We are speaking here of the concrete process of the meshing of the history of ideas with history, but the envisagement of details of that process must be left to the reader.[122]   In popular terms, Insight is an invitation to modernity and intellectual self-trans-cendence which can be, has been, too easily dodged, or reduced.   Its strategy might be adequate for an age of innocence which does not exist: the restless heart has its mix of stone.   But with Method in Theology there emerges such an ongoing praxis-thematization of the mix of restlessness and stone in human hearts as can twist, with a new statistics,[123] the actual selection from the manifold of series[124] in the prob-able seriation of schemes of recurrence towards the fuller realization of the impossible dream.

In place, then, of the optimism of an invitation to intellectual self-appropriation and of "implementation", there is an unavoidable "use": "the use of the general theological categories occurs in any of the eight functional specialties";[125] and there is the spiralling interplay[126] of the specializations contributing to a genetic and dialectic development of categories and their use. That spiralling is, normatively, shot through with the new heuristic notion of value and a genetic-eschatological view of man's development. The entire set of operations is praxis, and foundations is Praxisweltanschauung.[127]

Criticism

Praxis is critical, and continually brings forth a new definition of criticism. Underpinning it is "the transcendental principle of all appraisal and criticism, the intention of the good".[128] The direction of development here is given in some detail by Fr. Lonergan in reply to a question from Fr. Tracy - is the functional specialty foundations dogmatic or critical?[129] Fr. Lonergan replies that foundations consist in a decision, an operation of the level on which consciousness becomes conscience:

"Operations on this level are critically motivated when the deliberation has been sufficiently comprehensive and when the values chosen and the disvalues rejected really are values and disvalues respectively. But the sufficiently comprehensive deliberation is secured through the functional specialties of research, interpretation, history, and dialectic. The value-judgments are correct when they occur in a duly enlightened and truly virtuous man and leave him with a good conscience. Due enlightenment and true virtue are the goals towards which intellectual and moral conversion move. Conscience, finally, is the key, and its use by humble men does not encourage dogmatism in the pejorative sense of that word.

Is this critical? On views I consider counterpositions it is not critical. On views I consider positions it is critical".[130]

Just as in Insight, so in Method in Theology, Lonergan takes his stand on the dynamism of the human spirit. Just as in Insight, he presents a strategy which can facilitate the subject's ongoing thematization of the subject's cognitive dynamism, so in Method in Theology

a strategy emerges which facilitates the community's
ongoing objectification of authenticity.   The latter
strategy broadens[131] the meaning of criticism just
as the notion of value goes beyond the notion of being.
The strategy is intrinsically critical, and the criticism is grounded in the open dynamism of the human
spirit.   Fr. Tracy recognizes the strategy as methodological, facilitating collaboration.   But he main-
tains that "it does not, however, provide critical
grounds for the enterprize itself - more precisely,
for the truth value of the claims to ultimacy of
religious and explicitly theological language".[132]

I would make two brief points.   First, the enterprize
itself is grounded in the concrete critical (in the
wider sense noted above) spirit within the sublating
dynamism of religious experience: the critical
spirit "cannot criticize itself";[133]   the sublating
dynamism finds in itself "its own justification".[134]
Secondly, the previous statement expresses a foundational claim, a complex component in a Praxisweltanschuung, intrinsic to that claim being a claim to
its truth and value.

Conclusion

The new view of criticism places the Lakatos volume
on criticism, and the Kuhn/Popper debate, in a new
context.   The history of science finds itself bracketed between other functional specialties, and the
use of inadequate categories spiral into a context
of a hermeneutics of a deeper suspicion and a more
vigorous recovery.

The new view of praxis would seem to locate more
precisely Fr. Lamb's discussion of the role of political theology and to meet Berger's quest for a method
meshing 'hard-nosed' analysis and utopian imagination:
an invariantly structured critical multi-vortexed[135]
praxisanamnesis blossoming into a strategy of ongoing
policy-making, planning and execution umbrellaed by
a Praxisweltanschuung that includes concrete finite
fantasy[136] and an Eschaton.[137]

The new view of generalized empirical method places
a burden of modernity on academics.

That burden should be most evident to theologians:
"A theology mediates between a cultural matrix and
the significance and role of a religion in that

matrix".[138]   For this "the theologian needs the
alliance of fuller enlightened scientists"[139] and
of fuller enlightened scholars and artists.   But
such an alliance cannot remain at the level of
commonsense exchange: indeed the only level of
exchange adequate to our times is an exchange within
interiority mediated by strategic insights and incarn-
ation[140] in the relevant area.

The fundamental issue for the academic is being in the
world but not of it: the issue of psychological
absence.

I come finally to comment on, to sublate, the text from
Insight which I selected for this part:

"The goal of the method is the emergence of explicit
metaphysics in the minds of particular men and women.
It begins from them as they are, no matter what they
may be.   It involves a preliminary stage that can be
methodical only in the sense in which a pedagogy is
methodical, that is, the goal and the procedure are
known and pursued explicitly by a teacher but not by
the pupil.   The preliminary stage ends when the
subject reaches an intelligent and reasonable self-
affirmation.   Such self-affirmation is also self-
knowledge".[141]

We have reached perhaps, some glimpse of a new meaning
of "men and women as they are", for we have noted a
larger and more concrete pedagogy than was involved,
invited to, in Insight.

But that larger pedagogy includes and sublates the
strategy of Insight.   It contextualizes the invitation
to modernity and cycles its fruits through eight
specialties in an ongoing genesis of the psychological
present.   But far from removing the need to reach the
end of the preliminary stage of intellectual self-
transcendence, it places that need in an epiphanal
context as a circulating opaqueness,[142] a recurrent
topic,[143] a focal feature of public academic discourse.
That need was noted as a problem of conversion as
early as 1951,[144] not alluded to as such in Insight,
and more recently spoken of by Lonergan as intellectual self-transcendence: "Intellectual self-transcendence is taking possession of one's own mind".[145]   The
opaqueness for those who never investigate their adult
cognitional procedures is asserted with a new vigour

of metaphor: "What goes on between the input from
sense and the output in language, that is obscure,
vague, unconvincing.   To them the human mind is just
a black box.   The input is clear enough.   The output
is clear enough.   But the inner working is a mystery".
The core strategy of achievement remains the same, but
in so far as the attempt is not made the character of
one's cultural input and output is left in no doubt:

"For intellectual self-transcendence a price must be
paid.   My little book, Insight, provides a set of
exercises for those that wish to find out what goes
on in their own black boxes.   But it is only a set
of exercises.   What counts is doing them.

Should one attempt to do them?   As long as one is
content to be guided by one's commonsense, to
disregard the pundits of every class whether scientific
or cultural or religious, one need not learn what goes
on in one's black box.   But when one moves beyond the
limits of commonsense competence, when one wishes to
have an opinion of one's own on larger issues, then one
had best know just what one is doing.   Otherwise one
too easily will be duped and too readily be exploited.
Then explicit intellectual self-transcendence becomes
a real need".

CHAPTER 2

THE FOUNDATIONS OF MATHEMATICS

The following article presents the results of an investigation on various levels into the nature and foundations of mathematics. The basic level I may call the methodological level, the precise nature of which will be determined more fully as we proceed. Other levels involved are that of mathematics proper, that of metamathematics where this is not restricted to finitary methods, the pedagogical level, and the level of scientific applicability. The presentation will be in a somewhat popular nontechnical form, and this for two reasons. First, specialization has separated the levels in question, and a presentation on any one of them would be meaningful only to those familiar with that particular viewpoint. Secondly, researches on any but the basic level already mentioned have failed to yield genuine clarity; and since this methodological level has a touch of novelty about it, familiarity with it can neither be presupposed nor generated here.

Now, a successful clarification should meet squarely six major requirements. First, it must account for the historical development of mathematics. So it must face up, for example, to the transition from prime numbers to polynomial ideals, the extension of the notion of parallelism and of metric from Euclid to Riemann and beyond, the developments in integration theory, in topology, and in lattice theory.[2] Secondly, it must account for the process of evolution of mathematics in the individual mind, as experienced and described by pedagogues and psychologists. Thirdly, it must account for the happy interplay of the experimental sciences with mathematics. Fourthly, the successful clarification must account for the various other views on the same subject. Fifthly, it must say just enough, not so much as to appear to solve genuine mathematical questions, not so little as to leave mathematics without a future. The significance of this requirement will appear in the conclusion.

Sixthly, the clarification must square with the personal experience of the individual mathematician, and I place this demand last not because it is least but

because it is the basis from which clarification
springs.   No doubt the notion that one might clarify
the foundations of mathematics by introspection is
distasteful to many others besides Gottlob Frege.[3]
However, the introspection in question is not the barren
or helpless looking into oneself popular with some
Scholastics and many existentialists.   It is rather
the process of catching oneself in the act of doing
both mathematics and metamathematics.   It goes beyond
Hadamard's effort in his little book,[4] yet it is not
unrelated to it.   In this connection I quote the
following comment on Hadamard's reflections on the
working of mathematicians' minds:

"Such things may strike us strange and rather fascin-
ating, a strand of queerness enlivening the dull
desert of scientific thought, arid stretches of logic.
We may dismiss them lightly and pass on to the
serious consideration of what thought and understanding are in terms of the words that philosophers have
been accustomed to use.   But we may be quite wrong in
this.   We may miss the turning leading to an understanding of understanding".[5]

It is precisely this turning leading to an understanding
of understanding that I have taken;   and before I go on
to discuss the results I should like to remark that the
understanding of understanding in question is reached
only insofar as one moves through personal acts of
understanding to an appreciation of one's own experience of understanding.   For this reason what follows
may on mere reading ring hollow and not true.   If,
however, it is to be judged fairly it must be judged
not by comparison with other theories but by comparing
it with one's own personal experience of mathematics.

Generally, when the nonscientist asks me what understanding is, I try to give the experience of understanding by some simple geometry.   With mathematicians
such a method is not so sure to succeed, for the simple
problem in geometry is usually no problem at all -
the solution is too obvious.   However, I will take
here one simple example, the significance of which will
not be missed, and I will make some comments on the
processes it involves.

In a circle of, say, unit radius, we draw two perpend-
icular diameters.   Taking any point P on the circum-
ference, we drop perpendiculars PR and PS on the two

diameters.   Joining R to S, I ask my nonscientific
friend (or in the present case the reader), What is
the ratio of RS and the radius?   At this stage my
friend looks puzzled and perhaps tries calculation.
Eventually I draw an extra line.   I simply join P
to the centre, and my friend utters his own version
of Archimedes' "Eureka!"   Now, while the element
of surprise is absent for the geometer, a few
interesting remarks may be made on the process.
First, the act of understanding or insight involved
in the solution was dependent on the diagram, and
indeed even on the modification of the diagram for
the nongeometer.   Secondly, what was grasped in the
insight was a relation, the relation between RS and
the radius.   Thirdly, that grasp can be formulated
or thrown into syllogistic form - and here some light
is thrown on a feature of Aristotelian logic often
misrepresented.   The question raised was one concerning the relation of RS to the radius, OM, say.   The
question indeed was one of finding a middle term, and
the middle term was supplied as soon as one adverted
to the significance of OP.   Only then is the syllogism
constructed.   To coin an expression for this, let us
say that the insight is crystallized into a syllogism.
The points raised in this simple example will recur
later, and their importance will become evident.
While on the topic of crystallizing insights, however,
let me give two examples of insights crystallized
not into syllogisms but into axioms.

The first example is a casual insight which occurs
regularly in Euclid, the insight that a line which
contains a point of one side of a triangle must contain
a point of one of the other sides.   The insight was
formulated as an axiom of order by Pasch (1890), and
its effect is to liberate us to some extent from
diagram.

The second example is an assumption occurring in
Cantor's work,[6] which was first formulated by Zermelo
(1904), the famous axiom of choice.[7]   This axiom is
concerned with the possibility of selecting a definite
representative element from each nonvoid subset of a
given set.

Now, what I illustrated by simple example can happen
on a larger scale, and then what is formulated is not
just a syllogism or an axiom but, for example, the
whole of Euclidean geometry.   Further, insofar as
one eliminates casual insights and merely nominal
definitions such as are present in Euclid, one achieves

the ideal of proper axiomatization aimed at by Peano
and his followers.   If I might venture a definition,
I should say that an ideal axiom system is a related
set of terms and relations, in which the relations
determine the terms and the terms the relations.
This definition may be seen to include Hilbert's
notion of implicit definition.   Yet it does more,
for it lays emphasis on the fact that the terms are
defined precisely by the relations and vice versa;
and in doing so it excludes the notion of what might
be called "absolute definitions", a notion that has
had such an adverse effect on both philosophy and
science in past centuries.   The false notion is both
present and partially rejected by Pasch in the following remark:

"If geometry is to be deductive the deduction must
everywhere be independent of the meaning of geometrical concepts, just as it must be independent of
diagrams;   only the relations specified in the propositions and definitions employed may legitimately
be taken into account".[8]

Pasch rightly laid emphasis on the significance of
the relations, but he was a child of European philosophy in not identifying the meaning of the geometrical
concepts with the relations.   The most important
example of such oversight and confusion concerns
"quantity".   On the present view quantity is anything
that can serve as a term in a numerical ratio;   and
inversely a proportion is a numerically definable
ratio between quantities.   Quantities and proportions
are terms and relations such that the terms fix the
relations and the relations fix the terms.

Modern mathematics is rich in examples of axiom systems
which tend towards the above idea.   As a very powerful instance one might mention the axiomatic presentation of lattice theory,[9] in which the terms are not,
as some authors would have it, meaningless but are
precisely defined by the relations.

While it would be logical to discuss at this stage the
analytic nature of basic propositions, the manner of
generating axiom systems, and the process of selecting
relevant ones, such a discussion would take us too far
afield.   I cannot, however, omit a brief treatment of
the nature of the deductive expansion by which one
passes from the basic axioms to the theorems in any

patricular branch. I cannot agree with the common
view that this process is a mere logical expansion of
conceptual premises. Let me illustrate the point
with a simple and obviously imperfect axiom system.
While I use the words "point", "line", and so on,
they are not to be taken at their face value.

Axiom 1. Every line is a collection of points.
Axiom 2. There exists at least two points.
Axiom 3. If p and q are points, then there exists
one and only one line containing p and q.
Axiom 4. If L is a line, then there exists a point
not on L.
Axiom 5. If L is a line and p is a point not on L,
then there exists one and only one line cont-
aining p that has no point in common with
L.

One reason why I use this axiom system is that it can
have a real model which will serve as an illustration
later. One need only add a sixth axiom restricting
the number of points to four, and then the real model
is provided by four eccentric old gentlemen who form
six clubs, two men in each club. Axiom five for
the model then states that there exists one and only
one club containing the gentleman p which contains no
member of a specific club not containing the gentleman
p. However, our immediate concern is the deduction of
Theorem A, "Every p is on at least two Ls". We
consider two lines to be different when they are
different collections of points.

The proof is more or less obvious according to one's
mathematical ability. Thus if p is any point, we
have a second point q by Axiom 2. Axiom 3 gives us a
containing line, say L^1, for p and q; and Axiom 4 a
further point r not on L^1. By Axiom 3 there exists
a line L^{11} containing p and r; and since L^1 does not
contain r, we conclude that L^1 and L^{11} are different
collections of points and so different lines.

It is to be noted first that the theorem is not proved
without symbols. Secondly, the proof involves a series
of insights into the relations of terms, relations and
axioms. Thirdly, these insights can be crystallized,
all assumptions made explicit, and the whole cast into
deductive form. Lastly, the proof is understood properly only when it is grasped as a whole and when it can
be explained intelligently and not just repeated
mechanically.

In what we have so far discussed of mathematics, one basic type of question has continually recurred, the type of question which I call the "what" question. So, for example, we had the questions, "What is the relation between the line RS and the radius?" "What relations hold between the axioms?" and so on. The "what" question is a question for direct understanding, and the answer is some form of definition or relation.

There is, however, a second fundamental type of question which I call the "is" question; for example, "Is it true?", "Is it an axiom?" "Is it consistent?" The proper answer to this type of question is yes or no, a judgment. Furthermore, the answer, to be of value, must be an intelligent one; and so it too must spring from understanding, an understanding which may be called reflective to distinguish it from the direct understanding of the "what" question. Now, in mathematics, while judgments undoubtedly do occur, still the stress is on the "what" questions. On the other hand, in metamathematics, while there is an abundance of theory, the stress is on the "is" questions. So there are the three basic metamathematical questions regarding any axiom system:

(a)   Are the axioms independent, or is one axiom derivable from the others?

(b)   Is the system consistent?   If I persevere long enough will I arrive at a contradiction, P and not-P?

(c)   Is the system complete;   that is, does the system enable me to prove one out of each two contradictory statements, R and non-R, legitimately expressed in the terminology of the system?   "Legitimately" here means according to rules for the formation of formulae, rules, for example, which govern the distribution of parentheses.

Before further discussion it will be helpful to note that we have so far distinguished seven basic components of cognitional structure which I may designate as experience (on the sensible level, diagram, and so on), the what-question, direct understanding, formulation, is-question, reflective understanding and judgement.

Judgment - or more precisely the reflective understanding leading to judgment - can be centrally involved with one or other of the components. Thus one may ask, "Am I seeing, hearing, imagining, this or that?" and then one's concern is with the first component.

One may ask, "Have I understood properly?" and then
it is direct understanding that is being scrutinized.
Thirdly, one may ask, "Does my theory hold together?"
This is the type of question central to metamathematics.
It is centered on formulation; and if one visualizes
the theory cast into deductive form, then it is
scanned from top to bottom by the questions (a), (b),
(c), mentioned already.   So one examines axioms,
deductive processes, and the extent of the theory.
This, of course, is simplifying the situation somewhat,
since the three basic questions are in fact interrel-
ated.   Fourthly, one may ask, "Is my theory true?"
This is the question which occurs primarily in
science; it is answered in the affirmative only insofar as a given theory is verified.

Let us return to the question of consistency which is
obviously the most pressing.   There are three main
approaches to the problem. The first approach is to
search for an actual model.   If one is found, then
one has verified the theory, and one concludes from
the existence of the real model that the theory must
be consistent.   So, for the simple axiom system
which we discussed earlier, I pointed out that there
could be a real model insofar as any four people might
form the required six clubs.   This method is clearly
related to the fourth type of judgment mentioned above.

The second method is to produce what I call a semi-
imaginary model.   Examples are the models of Poincaré
and Beltrami for hyperbolic geometry, these two models
being neatly brought together by Klein as projections
of a sphere on different planes.[10]   I call these semi-
imaginary, since, while they make use of an imagined
model, they refer back to a second theory - in the
examples to Euclidean geometry.   One might consider
the stress in this method to be on the first and
second types of judgment mentioned above, though
none of these distinctions is rigid.   This method,
moreover, yields only relative consistency.

Thirdly, one can tackle the problem of consistency
more or less according to the Hilbert program.[11]
This last method is closely connected with the third
type of judgment mentioned above.   One is heading
for success here insofar as one generates an ideal
axiom system, grasps the axioms as analytic, and
makes explicit the deductive procedures allowed, so
that one has ensured that all casual insights have

been crystallized. By doing this one is casting the
theory into a form in which one can grasp the evidence
for judgment on its consistency. One may even
formalize one's grasp of the evidence, and then one has
a formal metasystem. So, for example, one formulates
a consistency proof for propositional logic by using
a mapping onto a domain of two objects. Again, Gödel's
first incompleteness theorem may be described as
demonstrating that, in a system broad enough to contain
all the formulae of a formalized elementary number
theory, there exist theorems that can neither be
proved nor disproved within the system. The manner
in which he arrived at his theorem involved a formal-
ization of the metasystem within the arithmetic. This
was done essentially by a judicious use of prime numbers
which gave to each formula a unique number, called its
Gödel number, and to relations in the metasystem
definite relations between Gödel numbers. I cannot
go into Gödel's work further here, but I wish to relate
his second theorem to the present methodology and thus
also highlight a definite limitation of the Hilbert
program.[12]

Gödel succeeded in producing a formula of the arithmetic
which, when interpreted in the metasystem, meant "A is
consistent", A being the arithmetic. He then showed
that if A is consistent, then the formula corresponding to "A is consistent" cannot be proved in A. The
proof program thus receives a setback in that a
consistency proof of a given system will presuppose a
stronger system than the one under examination.

Consider now the Hilbert program from the methodological
point of view. From that point of view what is required
is a formulated judgment falling on the formulated
theory, A. The evidence for this judgment lies in a
grasp of the analytic nature of the axioms, of the
reliability of the allowed deductive processes, and
so on. The problem of systematically formulating a
consistency proof is that of formulating the grasped
evidence for consistency. Grasping the theory A is
only a part of this evidence, and so we cannot expect
a full formulation of the evidence within A. In
making this methodological comment I am not of course
implying that it is independent of the work of Gödel.
The methodology and the metamathematics, or mathematics,
should indeed always move forward together in a complementary fashion. To this I will return in the
conclusion.

Having given some account, by means of a schematic
presentation of cognitional structure, of the general
movement in both mathematics and metamathematics, I
would like to discuss briefly a few of the other
schools of thought in terms of that account.
Although there is a large range of opinions, both
Scholastic and non-Scholastic, I restrict myself
here to three of the modern tendencies: logicism,
intuitionism, and formalism.[13]

Logicism, roughly, would have mathematics cast into
a _logica magna_ in which one can pass by deduction to
all the theorems of mathematics.[14] Clearly the
stress in logicism is on the third component in our
schema, on formulation or fully axiomatized mathematics.   Its failure, which could be traced historically, lies in not recognizing the role of insight
in formulation, in considering deduction to be merely
a conceptual, even tautological, expansion, and in
not sufficiently acknowledging the openness of mathematics.   Known mathematics at a given stage may well
be thrown onto a _logica magna_, where deduction is
understood correctly.   But the process would demand,
as remarked earlier, the "crystallization" of all
"casual" insights; and unless mathematicians are
silenced, the latter will always run ahead of the
former.

Next, a few remarks on Brouwer's intuitionism.[15] It
is interesting to note that the maxims of the intuitionists re-echo to some extent our own methodological
principles.   For example, intuitionists would claim
that it is not possible to penetrate the foundations
of mathematics without paying due attention to the
conditions under which the mental activity proper
to mathematicians takes place.   The program was not
followed up successfully, however; instead, the
school has developed its own version of mathematics.
Intuitionism lays stress, for example, on the need
for constructive proofs, on the inadequacy of the
principle of the excluded middle, and on the notion
of absurdity as basic in mathematics.   These stresses
spring from the fact that the intuitionists' attention
is on the insight prior to formulation, its incompleteness and its presuppositions.   This is borne
out, for example, by considering the manner in which
the principle of the excluded middle is limited on
this level.   On the level of judgment the principle
of the excluded middle enjoys definite validity;

if a judgment occurs it must be either an affirmation
or a denial.   On the level of direct understanding,
however, there are not two but three possibilities
with regard to any formulated proposition;   for not
only can one accept or reject, but one can also go
on to seek a better understanding and so a more
adequate formulation.

Hilbert and his proof program have already been fav-
orably mentioned in relation to the ideals of axiomatization, of implicit definition, and of casting
mathematical theories into a form suitable for some
judgment on consistency.   Needless to say, we could
not enter into any of the details of the actual
achievements of the program or its modifications.
The fact that theorems like those of Gödel and
Church[16] put limits to the program does not deprive
the method of its value as contributory to the understanding of mathematics.   Weakness on the nature of
deduction and on the meaningfulness of terms betrayed
by this as by other approaches are points which have
already been discussed.

I add some brief methodological comments on the various "paradoxes".   These I divide into five groups
in order of ascending complexity.   I will, however,
omit the fifth group, which includes paradoxes
springing from metamathematics such as the Skölem-
Löwenheim model paradox, since their discussion would
be too technical.[17]

The first group may be classed as paradoxes of
denotation.   For example, consider the inference:

>   343 contains 3 figures,
> $343 = 7^3$,
>   therefore 7^3 contains 3 figures.

Here, as in the case of many of the paradoxes, there
are various solutions formulated by different authors.
These solutions, I would claim, are correct insofar
as they crystallize the casual insight which provides
the solution on the methodological level.   On this
level the casual insight consists in grasping the
distinction between properties which pertain to
numbers on the experiential level and properties
which pertain to them insofar as they are understood.
Furthermore, the solution is adequate, in this as in
other paradoxes, insofar as it excludes by means of

axioms and notation the reoccurrence of similar paradoxes, removing thus the burden from the casual
insight to the symbolism.

The second group may be classed as dictionary paradoxes, and I will take as example the Berry paradox.
Consider the finite set P of sentences which contain
at most fifty words from a given dictionary. Consider
further the subset Q of these which define a natural
number. Since the set Q is finite, there are natural
numbers not defined in Q. The first of these, taking
the numbers in their natural order, we call the Berry
number. Now consider the sentence:

> The Berry number is the first number, in
> accordance with the usual arrangement of
> natural numbers, which cannot be defined
> by means of a sentence containing at most
> fifty words, all of them taken from our
> dictionary.

This sentence contains only thirty-seven words, but
it defines the Berry number. So the Berry number is
defined in Q.

Again, while elaborate solutions can be presented,
to be correct they must take account of a basic
distinction which is as important as it is apparently
trivial. It is the distinction between description
and definition or explanation. The thirty-seven-word
statement does not in fact define the Berry number;
it merely describes it. To bring out the importance of this distinction in other fields, it is worth
noting that one can describe electrons as particles
or waves; but if one wishes to define or explain
them - which is what the physicist seeks to do - one
must have recourse to mathematically formulated and
verified equations.

The third group of paradoxes includes what are called
semantic paradoxes. The simplest example is the
"liar paradox". Somebody makes the statement, "I
am a liar". Is the statement true or false? If it
is true, then he is a liar; and so it is false. If
it is false, then he is not a liar; and so it is true.

Tarski's discussion of this paradox does not seem to
be adequate, nor, as far as I know, has a clearly
formulated systematic solution appeared.[18] Methodologically the basis of the solution is as follows.

First, the statement "I am a liar" can be written
down, represented on the sensible level; and then,
while it has meaning for the reader, it is still
merely so many black marks ordered against a white
background. Again the reader may think the statement "I am a liar"; he may merely consider it, as
he is doing now, without judging. But he cannot
go on to make it a judgment, for judgments proceed
from intelligent grasp of evidence; and evidence
for the present proposition is lacking unless one
has actually lied, in which case the correct judgment is "I have lied". However, one can also utter
aloud the sounds "I am a liar", but then these sounds
are on a level equivalent to that of print on paper.

The fourth group of paradoxes consists of the paradoxes of set theory. The most familiar example is
perhaps that of Russell: Is the set of sets which
are not members of themselves a member of itself
or not?[19] Here again I restrict myself to a
methodological comment.

There are two ways of "defining" a definite set,
either by identifying the members (real or imagined)
individually or by defining the set intelligently.
The first method presents no basic difficulty. As
regards the second method, however, paradoxes may
emerge if in fact particular sets are not intelligently
defined. The problem is to crystallize, or axiom-
atize, the insight by which one grasps this, so as
to exclude systematically further occurrences.
Various solutions have emerged, the most familiar
perhaps being that of Zermelo, at least in one of
its modified forms.[20] In each of these some
restrictions are imposed on the type of class that
can be condensed into a set. The present state of
the discussion of the notion of set in general,
however, is not a very happy one. Methodologically
speaking, I should say that some obscurity would be
removed if more emphasis were laid on the notion that
the set and its members are relation and terms in
which the relation fixes the terms and the terms
fix the relation.

My account has been necessarily sketchy, and if I
claim that the solution presented meets all six
requirements listed at the beginning, I must do so
without justifying that claim here. That justification would indeed entail a systematic discussion of

for example, the findings of a historian such as E.
T. Bell,[21] of a psychologist such as J. Piaget,[22]
of a mathematician such as J. Hadamard.[23] Sufficient indications have been given, however, to show
that the claim is not groundless. I will conclude
with a word about the background of this work,
adding references to enable the interested reader
to complement what has been here discussed, and
some remarks on the broader significance of the
methods here used.

The fundamental element in the solution presented is
of course the methodology which I have all too
briefly described. For this methodology I am
indebted to the works of Bernard Lonergan, especially his book Insight,[24] and to his articles "The
Concept of Verbum in the Writings of St. Thomas
Aquinas".[25] Many points which I should have
discussed here have in fact been omitted because they
are adequately treated in these works. Such points
are the object, nature, and heuristic definition of
mathematics,[26] the nature of relations,[27] the genesis
of basic propositions and their analytic nature,[28]
the nature of probability,[29] the process of mounting
generalization,[30] and the interplay of mathematics
with science.[31]

Lastly, a few remarks on the broader significance
of the present approach. Three levels have been
successfully distinguished: mathematics proper,
metamathematics - in which I would like to include
also a substantial section of logic - and methodology
of mathematics. The distinction between mathematics
and metamathematics is not strict; the domain of
methodology is, however, more clearly defined. This
methodology is such that it gives expression to something which (a) is basically the same in, for example,
Euclid, Eisenhart, and Einstein, (b) can be more fully
formulated as mathematics advances, (c) is scientific,
since its scientific formulation is constantly check-
able in the changing data of cognitional fact.

I would content that this methodology is identifiable
with the philosophy of mathematics. Hence I would
consider as inadequate various other approaches,
ranging from theories that treat philosophy as an
abstract deductivism to the view that considers philosophy to be a matter of commonsense discussion. I
would exclude also systems which enthrone philosophy

over science as omniscience guiding ignorance, or
which profess mysterious insight into the nature of
number and of the continuum which the mathematician
cannot attain.   Further - and this is the point of
most interest to physicists - I would consider that
it is precisely the absence of this methodology in
the role of philosophy of physics that is at the root
of current confusion regarding the nature of both
relativity and quantum theory.

No doubt there will be those who resent my restrictive
and exacting delineation of the philosopher's task.
But it would seem that the goal of the philosopher,
of the lover of wisdom, should be wisdom.   Further,
it would seem that the history of philosophy is the
history of a dialectic movement towards that wisdom.
And if I go on to call this basic methodology "critical
wisdom" I do so in order to lay emphasis on the claim
that, as a fundamental component of human wisdom, this
continual explicitation of cognitional structure,
forced on us by science and mathematics, supplies
a genuine answer to Aristotle's question regarding
the wise man who should know yet not know all
science,[32] to Descartes' quest for a method of rightly
conducting reason, and to Kant's search for a science
which should determine a priori the possibilities,
principles, and extent of human knowledge.[33]

CHAPTER 3

INSIGHT AND THE STRATEGY OF BIOLOGY

"What we have to do is not to regard ourselves as
being outside the system of things we are studying,
but to take as our material for study the system of
ourselves studying things. We have to find conceptual models for our logical processes, and test the
hypotheses that these lead to against the observable
features of our mental activity".[1]

The moving force in contemporary biological investigation is essentially a cluster of questions centered
on the genetic material. What is its nature? How
does it act in determining the course of specific
development? How do its nature, action and mutation
account for the spatio-temporal distribution of
organisms? Progress towards the solution of such
problems depends on the refined techniques of protein
chemistry, on the power of the electron micro-scope,
on elaborate breeding experiments. But, rather
obviously, it depends too on the intelligence which
grasps what questions can be tackled immediately, how
technological advances can be exploited, what experimental set-up will test a plausible hypothesis or be
the source of a better one. It is intelligence which
appreciates the possibilities for biological research
of radio-isotopes. It is intelligence which correlates
a particular diffraction pattern with a possible chromo-
some structure. It is intelligence which weighs the
evidence for the correlation of the survival rates of
varieties of the British Peppered Moth with industrialization. However, that the obvious role of intelligence in such matters should become the centre of attention in a discussion of biology may, at first sight,
appear neither profitable nor even possible. While
questions of profit and possibility may be decided on
performance, some preliminary remarks on possibility
will throw light on what follows.

Each of us has his own experience of the activities
of intelligence, of looking for clues, of catching
on, of weighing up the pros and cons. Some have
had the experience within the field of biology, but
all are capable of extending their experience into

that field.   Such experience of biology can be the
starting point of a science, for science is man's
response to wonder about his experience.   Admittedly
a science having as subject matter the experience of
doing biology will have its peculiarities.   Still,
it will be found to follow the essential cycle of
scientific inquiry.   Just as the biologist seeks
to understand growth by examining, not one, but
many and varied instances of if, so the metabiologist -
if we might so call him - seeks to understand the
development of biology in himself by adverting to
his experience of a range of biological insights.
Just as the biologist must carry his investigation
into the lower sciences to get beyond descriptive or
even anthropomorphic notions, so the metabiologist
must have recourse to instances of insight in mathematics and physics to deliver himself from vague and
even mythic notions.[2]   Just as the biologist is
satisfied with his theory only when it stands the
test of crucial experiment, so the metabiologist is
satisfied only when his theory squares with the
experience from which it took its origin.   And so
on.   Briefly, metabiology, like biology, moves from
data through insight and formulation to a third level
of verification, but the data of metabiology includes
all three levels of biological inquiry.[3]   In contrast
with biology, the mode of understanding of metabiology
is not direct, but indirect, or introspective.   By
introspection is meant, however, not some strange
process of looking into oneself, but rather a shifting of attention.[4]   Both biologist and metabiologist
engage in doing biology, but while the biologist's
attention centres on the content, the metabiologist's
attention centres on the activity - for his goal is
not merely biological understanding, but an understanding of biological understanding.

It is clear that one cannot reach metabiology without
biology, and so I will try here to engage the reader
in elementary biological insights.   Obviously,
however, such elementary instances are no more
adequate for metabiology than some random observations
are for biology.   Ideally, the reader should be led
through a sequence of biological insights of growing
complexity so that he would actively appreciate the
need for, and nature of, the various complementary
types of investigation which belong to biological
method.   In so short an essay, however, he can only
be led to vaguely appreciate how the present view

meets the facts in plausible fashion. Undoubtedly
discussion might have been restricted to one particular problem. Still, a general survey seemed in
place, not only because it best reveals the relevance
of Lonergan's work, but also because it may lead some
competent biologist to attempt the more extensive
treatment clearly called for.

Paradoxically, however, the reader who is also a
biologist may well be handicapped here, at least
initially, by the temptation to assert that he knows
quite well what biological understanding is. Perhaps
he may best counter the temptation by recalling that
non-biologists, even philosophers, at times call his
science in question by their claim that they know
quite well what a dog or a daisy is.

Again, the reader may have his own views on the nature
of biology. I would ask only that he check the
present view, not against that theoretical account,
but against his experience of doing biology.

Finally, there are questions concerning reality,
objectivity, etc., to which answers might well be
expected. These questions are, however, laid aside
here. The present task is restricted to trying to
understand correctly what is going on when one is knowing biology. Perhaps we might say that, unlike the
prisoners in the Republic, our problem is, not to come
forth from the cave, but to advert to what is in it.

Let us now turn from theory to practice. We join
the scientist at his microscope. Within the field
we distinguish a small blob. Careful observation
reveals to us that it remains together, that it moves
slowly about, that small particles in the surround-
ings are able to get into it and eventually pass
through it. Our growing curiosity about the blob
and its peculiarities may lead us soon to ask the
question, "Is it alive?" where life means nothing
more than an obscure correlation with the class of
animals and plants. Perhaps indeed, if we are
chemists, we will be slower to raise this question,
for we are aware of the odd properties of drops of
chloroform or of alcohol-injected clove oil. But
eventually the question will be seriously entertained,
and we move into the circle of empirical inquiry.
For convenience we give the data a name: let us call
it Chaos.[5] The obscure correlation of life is an
hypothesis to be tested. Relevant tests quickly
suggest themselves and are carried out. We find,
for example, that only one part can be properly said

to survive dissection. Again, further observation
reveals that Choas divides into two of its kind.
And so on, until we grasp that we have sufficient
evidence to conclude that it is alive. But this
is only a beginning, a process of generic classification which no more than determines the relevant
investigator. It is for the biologist to raise
the significant question, "What is Chaos?" "Why
is Chaos alive?" in a more methodical fashion.

At this stage no one will doubt but that our questions are raised regarding sensible data.[7] To
answer such questions one may well have to have
recourse to images as well as data, but without the
data or the images there is no understanding, and
this no matter how far into abstract theory one has
advanced.[8] Like much else that we treat of here,
this is a question for personal reflection, the answer
to which might well echo Waddington's remark regarding his own model of the developing system: "Although
the epignetic landscape only provides a rough and
ready picture of the developing embryo, and cannot
be interpreted rigorously, it has certain merits for
those who, like myself, find it comforting to have
some mental picture, however, vague, for what they
are trying to think about".[9]

It is not, however, what he imagines, but what he
sees, experiences, either directly or through instru-
ments, that the biologist wishes to understand. He
values only those insights that are verified, or at
least have sensible consequences for which he can
look. Thus, if he seeks to understand amoeboid
motion he finds no place for the hypothesis of a vis
vitalis, but he is willing to consider an hypothesis
involving protein foldings, or diffusion forces. The
search for these sensible consequences may well
require the finest of microscopic and biochemical
techniques, and perhaps wonder might fade into
frustration were it not that besides pure science
there is also applied science to foster research
and to foot the bill.

At all events, the biologist is not allowed to fall
short of the goal of his science, which is one of
complete explanation. He cannot remain satisfied
with description on any level. The goal of complete
explanation requires that one take the clear step
from description, which relates the data to us, to

correlations verified in the data.   Explanation,
then, is not merely refined description: between
it and description there is a clear discontinuity.[10]
One can see a spectrum, or register a diffraction
pattern, but what is verified scientifically is a
set of equations.   Again, in our present example,
the contractile vacuole may be described as a clear
globule which grows within Chaos and gradually finds
its way out.   Then through a variety of experiments
involving, say, changes in the medium, and by appeal-
ing to theories of osmosis, etc., we would gradually
move towards an explanation, through a sequence
of systematic correlations, of the varying geometry,
physics and chemistry of the vacuole.   But the vacuole process is also grasped as playing some obscure
role in the life of the organism, and here too the
transition from description to explanation must occur.
By means of the lower level correlations the biologist must move towards an understanding of the role
of the process in the life-pattern of Chaos, and
explanation on this level requires that one grasp
the total process not only as correlated with other
functions within the animal but as related to
similar processes in a range of animals.

This description of biological investigation runs
counter to a currently popular view which in fact
stresses, not the sequence of insights involved,
but the corresponding images.[11]   This view gives
the impression that if we had better equipment,
small enough eyes, or big enough amoebae, we would
be able to have a good look at the structure of
chromosomes and the sequence of aminoacids; indeed,
even to read off the genetic code in some mysterious
way.   Modern physics should help in driving out such
illusions: no more than the atom is the gene a
complex of small balls.[12]   While the error may
suffer exposure on the micro-level, it has its origin,
so to speak, on the macro-level.   Thus, when studying the heart, the anatomist "studies it chiefly as
a visual object and owing to our preferences for
visual experience and our persistent naive realism
it is extremely easy to fall into the error of
thinking of the visual heart as the very concrete
heart itself".[13]   If indeed one can see the real
heart, then one can see its parts, and the parts of
its parts.   Clearly, a better strategy would be to
meet the error on a wider front.   Since, however,
that would demand another essay,[14] we content ourselves here with calling attention to the alternative,

a verified insight into data. Thus, at an earlier stage we raised the question, "Is it alive?" with regard to the blob called Chaos: implicitly we were asking, "Is it a thing?" Now to ask is, obviously, to admit that we do not know: but we had been led to conceive Chaos as a thing, and we eventually satisfy ourselves that it is, not by taking another look, but by experimental verification.

Finally, we may ask in general what type of explanation is reached. We have described it as an explanation to be had from the immediate data of sense, and to be expressed by a complex of verified correlations. Just as the first obscure correlation contained in the question, "Is it alive?" was a grasp of possibility based on the data, an hypothesis to be verified, so will any of the correlations be. If verified, they form part of the slow scientific transition from the obscure notion "the nature of Chaos" to the still unknown goal of a definition of Chaos. If we here associate the Aristotelian form with that goal, we must insist that it denotes precisely a goal, what is to be known by scientific insight. It does not denote some deeper reality in the amoeba which philosophers alone can intuit.[15]

Our next example takes us, so to speak, into the fields. We raise the question, "What is a buttercup?" A first step towards an answer is to replace everyday description by scientific description.[16] Spontaneously we expect a difference of insight when data are significantly different, and so sensible differences give rise to preliminary classification. Thus, variation in sepals, flower stalk etc., leads us to group buttercups into three types. These in turn are related to a larger group of similar plants to form the genus Ranunculus. The genus in its turn finds its place within a general classification of plants. Now while this classification is based on more than sensible similarity, nevertheless the clear transition from descriptive to explanatory classification requires the implementation of such a basis of classification as is provided by an evolutionary theory.[17] We postpone for the present a discussion of the nature of such an evolutionary hypothesis, but its role in biology as a principle of explanation is worth emphasizing at this stage. One might compare the significance for biology of Darwin's insight with that of Mendeleff's formulation of the

periodic law for chemistry. Just as the periodic
table correlates the chemical elements and, less
proximately, chemical compounds, so an evolutionary
hypothesis makes possible the correlation of cell-
types, organs and organisms. It is not then a kind
of afterthought to biological investigation, as if
one might first achieve complete understanding of
various organisms and later correlate them evolut-
ionarily. It is, on the contrary, what properly
constitutes biology as an explanatory science. It
is within the context of this methodological hypothesis that the explanation of a given organism must
fall, and the hypothesis, far from being the source
of obscure generalizations, increases rather the
demand for that transition from description to explanation already repeatedly emphasized.

Let us return to the buttercup. Here observation
soon gives place to dissection and controlled experiment. In this way a description of parts and of the
role they play in the plant is reached, and the way
is prepared for more detailed and particular investigations.[18] With this stage is associated one of
the great classics of empirical inquiry - the long
series of experiments and the sequence of insights
involved in determining the role of leaves in the
plant. Such a determination is, however, only a
beginning. One must push on into physical and
chemical experiment and theory in search of an
explanatory account of the complex of energy exchanges
and chemical cycles involved, and of the interplay
of photosynthesis with various other cyclic processes
in the plant. Explanation is sought at all levels
even though it require large groups of experimenters,
a large range of experiments, and incursions into
the rarified regions of cybernetics, quantum physics,
and the thermodynamics of open systems.

In the course of such investigations one finds that
probability theory is regularly called upon to complement what we may call the classical method of empirical science, and its use gives rise to an acknowledged statistical method of investigation. Here
let us restrict ourselves to a simple example involving the three species of buttercup.

Briefly, it is found that the distribution of the
three species on ridge and furrow grassland is such
that one species betrays a clear preference for the
ridges, the second is concentrated in the furrows,

and the third occupies the intermediate zone. Now while such separation into distinct microhabitats is suggestive in many different ways, one clear suspicion that it gives rise to is that there is a correlation between species-habitat and water table. A series of experiments with potted flowers and controlled water tables serves to justify the suspicion.

Even in this simple example several general characteristics of statistical investigation can be detected.[19] In the first place, knowledge of the distribution does not immediately add to knowledge of the particular types of the plant. Rather, use is made in the definition of the distribution of the classification which was already to hand, and the knowledge which it gives is knowledge of the occurrence of these types. Again, if there had been no previous clue regarding habitat preference, the statistical enquirer would have expected a uniform distribution for all three species, but he would not have shown surprise at some departure from uniformity, for he knows that uniform distribution is an ideal from which, in the concrete, random departures are to be expected. Still, the departure in the present case is in fact significant - and such significant departure gives rise to further classical investigation concerning the species and their environment.

Presently we will touch on more complex aspects of the interplay of classical and statistical inquiry. Before doing so, however, we must turn our attention to a rather obvious question concerning the plant: "How does it grow?" More properly, we are asking about the understanding of the development of the plant, and, in an essay such as this, one cannot but raise the fundamental question, "What is development?" As Paul Weiss remarks at the beginning of his book,[20] this question seems trivial. "Does not everybody have some notion of what development implies? Undoubtedly most of us have. But when it comes to formulating these notions they usually turn out to be very vague". Weiss himself seeks to get beyond this vagueness, beyond, too, the type of explanation which "cannot survive the first rigid test on a concrete phenomenon of development",[21] by staying as close as possible in his considerations to specific phenomena. Thus, while he sees progressive differentiation as the keynote of development, detailed illustrated discussion of differentiation leaves no room for an accusation of a mere shift of obscurity. Again, the hierarchy of organizations of the organism has to be explained, first by decomposing the complex phenomenon into simple processes of biological order, then further by attempting "to trace the roots of biological process into the known realms of physical and chemical phenomena".,[22] the ultimate aim being "to describe and understand any state of the living system as conditioned by the immediately preceding states".[23]

Weiss' book represents rather the earlier stage, that of discussing processes of a biological order. Associated with the second stage, where the stress is on physics and chemistry, are the much popularized recent advances in molecular biology. We will refer to the third stage later.

The study of the development on the level described by Weiss depends to a great extent on the contrast of normal and abnormal, and this calls for experimental techniques of isolation, tissue culture, mutilation, transplantation, etc. Results vary from organism to organism; so, for example, while defect experiments in some mollusks would seem to favor a mosaic theory of development with an early specification of part function,[24] similar experiments on sea-urchin eggs betray quite startling developmental flexibility.[25] Hence the need for, and advantage of, experiments over a wide range of organisms and over the sequence of states of any given organism. Rates of development of different organs and different organisms are thus compared, the multiplicity and heterogeneity of determinative factors revealed, and the relationships of the gradients, energies and patterns of the particular fields of these factors investigated.[26] And so on. In such a way one gradually reaches verified specifications of the general principle of progressive determination.

I have referred in this fashion to Weiss' work not merely to pave the way for Lonergan's treatment of development but also because the elementary device of page references serves to draw attention to the range of phenomena and the length of investigation involved in generating some insight into development. This in turn reminds us of the nature of the task we are outlining here. It is by reproducing in ourselves the insights of the biologist that we hope to reach an understanding of his method, and we try to reproduce these insights with the stress, not on content, but on our activity. It is only in this way that we can hope to come to an understanding of how we go about understanding development, or in other words, that we can hope to reach a heuristic definition of development. One may indeed read and remember the conclusions of an author concerning development, but unless one also reproduces in oneself his insights, then one has merely replaced the common and vague notion of development by the memory of someone else's nominal definition.

In discussing the manner in which micromeres transplanted into the isolated animal half of the sea-urchin egg give rise to a practically normal individual, Weiss remarks on the possible misconception of the micromere action as deliberative, purposive.[27] As he says, even competent biologists in the past have considered regulation in this anthropomorphic way. Now while the question of purpose is no longer of serious debate, there still remains a more general question which seems by no means settled - the question of the relevance of final causes to biological investigation. Since clarity in this matter is essential to the proper understanding of development we will digress here to deal with it. This digression leads to another and more important digression concerning a general basis of explanation not unrelated to evolution theory. Only then will we have a sufficient background for a methodological analysis of development.

We concluded earlier that the type of explanation sought by the biologist was an intelligibility immanent in the data, and we related that intelligibility to the Aristotelian formal cause. In the case of the life history of the organism the data is extremely complex, but the general features of its understanding should by now be sufficiently apparent. The biologist's quest here takes the form of an investigation of development, and his basic verification is of the organism as a particular type of dynamic system, one in which movement is normally in the direction of greater specification. Now this empirically verified directed dynamism is in fact a clear instance of finality, where finality is taken in the well-defined sense of Insight.[28] But finality in this sense is clearly distinguishable from final causality. What specifies final causality is the good as cause: for

final causality to be present, not only must a
process be orientated to a term, but it must be so
orientated because the term is good.[29] On the
other hand, finality can be affirmed without reference to the term as good, even without reference
to the term as determined - for the affirmation of
finality is an affirmation of an indeterminately
directed dynamism. Final causes belong to a range
of further questions with which the empirical investigator is not concerned;[30] finality, on the contrary,
denotes an intelligibility immanent in data, which
is precisely the empirical investigator's concern,
and the causality to which it pertains is formal.

Clearly enough, however, the verified directed
dynamism of biological inquiry lends itself to
distortion. Because of the nature of his subject,
the biologist's understanding can take a proleptic
form in which his grasp of the structure of a particular stage of development is associated with a
grasp of the future stages or of the possible term
of such development.[31] But such understanding can
be unscientifically projected, and then, for example,
the foetal eye becomes a structure with an aim and
an ambition. Still, even if one adheres to verification as opposed to extroversion, one uncovers
here genuine difficulties of a related type regarding
biological processes. Thus we have the puzzle of
what Bertalanffy[32] calls static teleology, where an
arrangement seems to be useful for a certain purpose.
Again, there is the dynamic teleology of directedness
of process such as appears in the complex balanced
feedback mechanisms of the organism. Speaking of
the explanation of these, Bertalanffy remarks:
"Fitness in organic structures can probably be
explained by the causal play of random mutations and
natural selection. This explanation is, however,
much less plausible for the origin of the very com-
plicated organic mechanisms and feed-back systems".[33]
In considering these difficulties now we hope to show
the general structure of the explanation at which
Bertalanffy hints.

First, we may recall Aristotle's position on such
matters. Unlike modern biologists, he saw no hope
of an explanation through chance: for him it was
either purpose or necessity, and he opted for purpose.
His statement of the position he rejects has a modern
ring to it and may lead the reader to reflect on the
nature of the lacuna to be filled: "If a man's crop
is spoiled on the threshing-floor, the rain did not

fall for the sake of this - in order that the crop might be spoiled - but that result just followed. Why then should it not be the same with the parts in nature, e.g., that our teeth should come up of necessity - the front teeth should sharp, fitted for tearing, the molars broad and useful for grinding down the food - since they did not arise for this end, but it was merely a coincidental result; and so with all other parts in which we suppose that there is purpose? Wherever then all the parts came about just what they would have been if they had come to be for an end, such things survived, being organized spontaneously in a fitting way; whereas those which grew otherwise perished and continued to perish, as Empedocles says his 'man-faced ox-progeny' did".[34]

Now it would seem that we must indeed agree with Aristotle that chance explains nothing. But he appears here to reject a position to which we moderns find ourselves attracted. The relevant question is, "What insight did Aristotle miss?"

We have already considered the relevance of statistical method to biological inquiry. In Aristotle's time there was no theory of probability to lead him to appreciate that relevance and so he developed his own way of handling nature and chance and of accounting for the order of the universe. Nowadays the explanatory power of statistical laws is a commonplace and, taken against the general background of scientific development, it puts us in a position to go clearly beyond the Aristotelian world view. Obviously a short article is not the place in which to undertake a presentation of the resulting position; instead we shall touch on some points relevant to its understanding and, as we shall see, to an understanding of the autonomy of biology.[35]

Consider the general Newtonian equation for the path of a particle moving under a central force proportional to the inverse square of the separation distance. The equation is abstract: it represents a general conic in a Euclidean plane.[36] Furthermore, the equation is indeterminate.[37] If it is to apply to a particular orbit we must introduce initial conditions; if it is to apply to a real situation, then these initial conditions must be determined through insight into that situation.[38] Suppose that such insight yields two sets of initial conditions

for two particles whose orbits are hyperbolae.
Whether or not one is considering interaction, one
does not expect the two sets to be related.   More
precisely, they are coincidental in the sense that,
in the general case, while one can deduce either set
once one knows the details of the particles' entries
into their orbits, one does not expect to deduce them
together, from a unified set of equations, systematically.[39]   Indeed, in the concrete, far from coming
together to make possible such a systematization, the
prior conditions for these initial conditions
diverge.[40]   Somewhat similarly, in such a simple
physical system as an ideal gas there is no question
of the individual paths being beyond investigation.
Nevertheless, the whole process is non-systematic,
the events in it are a coincidental aggregate, and
the physicist does not undertake a classical account
of the motion.   Yet he does provide a statistical
account.   And here one may reach the odd insight
that lies behind statistical theory: one does not
expect the elements of a coincidental aggregate to
show systematic relations;   one is suspicious if it
is always heads and never tails.[41]

Next, let us consider the scheme of recurrence.[42]
Think of the orbits discussed above, where now they
are ellipses.   The first significant thing about
the scheme of recurrence is its power to take the
coincidental aggregate by closing the diverging series
of conditions.   Again, the scheme is a means of com-
bining various laws - one may think of the laws of
physics and chemistry which fall within the dietary
schemes of animals.   Further, the scheme of recurrence is realized in the concrete according to probabilities - a significant decrease in velocity in
a hyperbolic orbit can be excluded only by such a
proviso as "other things being equal".   Moreover,
the probability of a scheme can depend on the existence of a prior scheme, and its actual functioning
can be linked with that of another scheme.   One
may think of such examples as the dietary scheme of
herbiferous animals or the complex of schemes associated with photosynthesis.   Next must be noted that
things occur within schemes and so the probability
of emergence of things is related to the probability
of emergence of their including schemes.[43]   Already
we have noted that coincidental aggregates are not
expected to behave systematically.   Still, probability theory allows for the mere appearance of
system where in fact there is none: so, for example,
a coincidental aggregate of chemicals could go through

the process called cell-division without violating
the laws of chemistry.   Now, loosely speaking, a
thing is defined by its explained properties.   These
properties may be considered as systematizations of
coincidental aggregates of the properties of lower
things.   Since the non-systematic occurrence of
such aggregates of processes is within the bounds of
probability, one might plausibly postulate the guarantee of regular recurrence by the emergence of the
properties of higher things.

In such a manner one may come towards the notion of
a conditioned series of schemes and things which
underlies the definitions of emergent probability[44]
and the sequential postulate.[45]   At any rate our
remarks are probably sufficient to make clear the
distinction between Lonergan's view and that of
Darwin or of his successors.[46]   Darwin's objective,
indeed, would seem to have been the same: he sought
an intelligibility immanent in data, an explanation
of the distribution of species, of their emergence
and survival.   Such an explanation inevitably leans
on probability and so, while more than one biologist
has criticized the expression "natural selection of
chance variations", one has only to explicitate that
dependence on probability to reveal the significance
of the insight.   Natural selection becomes an instance of probability of survival;   chance variation
an instance of probability of emergence.[47]

The present view, however, differs from Darwinism, on
two main points.   First, it shifts the emphasis from
species to schemes of recurrence in which plant or
animal may be a component.[48]   Secondly, it regards
a species, not as an accumulated aggregate of variations, nor as defined by some microscopic complex, but
as an intelligible solution to the problem of living
in a given environment.[49]   At first sight, no doubt,
criteria involving macro- or micro-variations or
components may seem much more scientific.   But
it must be remembered that the solution in question
requires insight into a hierarchy of aggregates and
a range of previous solutions.   Furthermore, not
only does the heuristic notion of species of Insight
provide an integration of microinvestigation and
interbreeding criteria, but it also extends beyond
biology, falling as it does within a full account of
genera and species which has no rival.[50]

The foregoing discussion of development as treated by
Weiss, of finality, of emergent probability and the

associated world-view, has perhaps already led the
reader to anticipate the lines of a more basic treatment of development.[51] That basic treatment rests
on an understanding of how probability theory allows
for the emergence of the systematic from the non-
systematic. Development considered from this point
of view is seen to be a sequence of transitions in
which posterior states are systematizations of
previous states. In earlier examples, like that
of Chaos, we treated the organism and its properties
as an integration of physico-chemical cycles and
events. Such a treatment should now be viewed as
a simplification convenient for that stage of our
investigation. At this stage it can be more meaningfully pointed out that Chaos, or the buttercup,
is not one but a sequence of systematizations. This
sequence of integrations, as previous illustrations
show, is orderly but flexible. Each integration is
related to preceding ones as higher to lower, for
each integration manifests an increase in specification, in capacity for environment control. This
continuous transition is achieved because each integration, is not only an integration but also an operator, where operator connotes such a systematization
as makes way in positive fashion for its own replacement by a further integration.[52] The sequence of
integrations is dynamic, where the meaning of the
term dynamic is that associated, not with mathematical physics, but with finality.

Through such considerations one may arrive at some
appreciation of a methodological account of development. The importance of such an account lies in its
heuristic nature: for the general notion of development thus attained implies a method for studying any
particular development, a method which may conveniently be called genetic method. Just as classical
method involves the specification of an indeterminate
function, so genetic method calls for a specification of the heuristic notion of development. But
it is to be noted that, unlike the determination of
the unknown function or of the differential equation,
the specification of the notion of development is not
just a matter of precise measurement: precise measurement is necessary indeed, but its efficacy dimin-
ishes as one moves from science to higher science.[53]

In general, genetic method leads one to seek an understanding of a linked sequence of integrations through
specifying each integration as operator, as a source

of transition to further integrations.   This notion
of specifying the operator may well puzzle the reader
and lead him to ask, "What, in the particular case
of an organism, is this operator?"   But like the
much abused question, "What is life?" the question,
"What is the operator?" can be answered in only two
ways that are of scientific significance.   Either
the answer is an actual specification of the operator
through a verified understanding of the data involved,
or it is a heuristic consideration of the operator.
The latter answer is to be expected from metabiology.
The former answer can be reached only through the
collaboration of a large number of specialists in very
diverse fields of biological inquiry.[54]

One may further appreciate the nature of genetic
method by considering it as a source of sufficient
distinction of biology from physics and chemistry.[55]
Investigation of the periodic law, of gas laws, of
laws for changes of state, etc., involve classical
and statistical methods in various combinations.   But
the understanding of development calls forth this
third scientific method.   The correlations verified
in adult organisms are clearly different from those
verified at earlier stages.   But they are related:
the process leading from one set to the other is
flexible yet regular.   That regularity cannot be
explained by classical method, for classical method
does not deal with changes in classical laws.   Nor,
precisely because these changes are regular, can it
be handled by statistical method.   So the study
of the organism involves us in a type of understanding that differs from those types with which, as
physicists and chemists, we are familiar, and it
gradually distinguishes itself as a scientific method.

It is worth noting, too, that the emergence of genetic
method is itself an instance of development, the
development of human intelligence, and so its study
calls for a further application of genetic method.
Advertence to this, indeed, is relevant to a fuller
understanding of the first sentence of this essay:
for the operator in the case of intellectual development is the relevant question.   Unlike the development of the organism, however, the development of
human understanding can display an odd perversity
which can be handled scientifically only by the employment of a further, dialectic method.[56]   And awareness of this accounts, to some extent, for the structural oddities of the present chapter.

Genetic method sufficiently distinguishes biology
from physics and chemistry.   Let us now move further
to a consideration of the necessary condition of
the autonomy of biology.[57]   Briefly, this requires
the existence of a set of laws, implicitly defining
biological terms and relations, to which there is
no logical transition from the laws of physics and
chemistry.   Perhaps we might best throw light on
this by taking our start from the role of schemes of
recurrence in the genesis of science.   One may
recall such a classic instance as the investigation
of the orbit of Mars.   Now, just as the data on the
motion of Mars led Kepler to the mathematics of its
orbit and, further, led Newton to the correlation
which defined mass[58] and accounted for the scheme,
so data on the schemes of recurrence which include,
say, reproduction in protozoa, lead the biologist
first to the physics and chemistry of each scheme
and further to the correlations which define a
particular capacity for dealing with environment,
and account for the schemes.   On the one hand there
is the correlation of masses, on the other a correlation of protozoa.   Just as it was not logic but
insight that led Newton beyond Kepler's three spatio-
temporal laws to a scientific definition of mass, so
it is not logic but insight that leads the biologist
beyond cellular chemistry to an evolutionary theory
of reproduction.

Consider now the total range of schemes in which the
correlates defining reproduction occur.   Obviously
these correlates vary appreciably as we move through
the range from protozoa to primate.   In amoebae,
for instance, the same chemical aggregate is cell,
organ and animal.   On the other hand, the monkey,
as we now consider it, is an aggregate of aggregates
(organs) of aggregates (cells) of physico-chemical
events.   Each type of aggregate is, so to speak,
the locus of verification of particular correlates
relating it to the corresponding aggregates in other
primates.   These correlations lead to definitions of,
for example, the aggregate named sperm cell, the
aggregate of cells which make up the reproductive
organ, the aggregate of organs of the specific plant
or animal.[59]   Aggregates of the latter type are the
loci of verification of a unified set of physical,
chemical, biological and descriptive correlates and,
whatever the biologist's view on objectivity, he finds
the synthetic construct, the biological thing,
indispensable.[60]

This way of considering biological investigation may
seem somewhat strange. We, as it were, line up the
plants and animals, cast a chemist's eye on them, and
see in them only a coincidental sequence of four-
dimensional aggregates. Yet there is in fact a
verified systematization of these chemical aggregates
which may be given the general title of evolution
theory. The strangeness of this viewpoint resides
most, perhaps, in its contrast with the historical
development of biology which begins from a commonsense acknowledgement of living things and their reg-
ularities and moves through preliminary classification
to physical and chemical investigation, towards increasingly comprehensive biological systematization.
The stranger viewpoint, however, succeeds in clearly
opposing coincidental aggregates to their systematization through evolutionary correlations. This
opposition serves to emphasize the connection between
coincidental aggregates and the possibility of auto-
nomous sciences. Too obviously, we have not attempted
here to explain pedagogically or in detail the notion
of coincidental aggregates or the manner in which
their systematization occurs in a higher science.[61]

Indeed, as the reader familiar with Lonergan's work
will notice, the whole of the foregoing account has
some of the characteristics and failings of a popular
sketch. So, for example, while we touched on the
notions of emergent probability and development, we
came nowhere near precise definition, much less
elaborate discussion. Again, we struggled along as
best we could without introducing such notions as
empirical residue, conjugate form, etc. We have
already given reasons for attempting this type of
survey. The survey, clearly, is no more the heuristic science than popular Relativity is Relativity
Theory. Furthermore, it is a survey of a science
which is still in its infancy. The details of the
reorientation of biological knowledge[62] which it makes
possible lie in the future. To the future also
belongs its beneficial influence on text-book and
technical journal. But obviously if its development and influence are to be assured, its significance and nature as science must be seriously acknowledged, and the task of understanding which it sets
accordingly undertaken. If this article has
succeeded in drawing attention to the science, to the
general features of the task it involves, to the
foundation given it by Lonergan, to the central role
of insight throughout, then it has fulfilled its
purpose.

CHAPTER 4

MODERNITY AND THE TRANSFORMATION OF CRITICISM

Introduction

Our hope is to merge horizons of criticism, and I would
wish to make my position clear immediately. I have
no doubt that both Hermeneutic and Structuralist perspectives have enriched criticism in these recent decades, nor have I any doubt that in a basic sense they
are complementary. But neither do I doubt that something more than merging horizons is needed. There
is a dead and deadening metaphor laced through the
language of literature and criticism whose elimination[1] is becoming increasingly possible through the
dialectic pressures of modernity. Its personal
elimination can never be made easy and so, while my
paper focuses in its second part on that dead metaphor,
it does so in the manner of an invitation to a difficult personal task, a spiralling sonata of self-
discovery. I draw on the symbolism of the sonata
form. Part one of the paper represents the exposition,
with its two themes. Part two is written in the mood
of Flaubert's comment on the novel strategies of his
Agricultural Show in _Madame Bovary_: "It is a difficult section, but if I succeed, it will be truly
symphonic".[2] Following part one as the development
follows the statement of themes, it is only a bare
beginning of that development. But the seeds of the
development within the subjectivity that is each of us
should have become less inevident in the spiralling
consciousness to which attention is drawn: the vortex
of the reader's own There-being.

Part I

"From the start, we have at least four possible and
distinct types of self: the self that judges, the self
that reads, the self that writes, and the self that
reads itself. The question of finding the common
level on which all these selves meet and thus of establishing the unity of a literary consciousness stands
at the beginning of the main methodological difficulties that plague literary studies".[3]

This quotation from Paul de Man serves me well as the focus of my reflections on the future of criticism. My reflections will be programmatic: the authentic and adequate pursuit of the question of the multiple facets of self revealed to the literate self by twentieth century literature and criticism and the crisis of criticism may be hinted at in a public paper, but its initiation and realisation requires the solitary cultivation of a strange courage. The character of the strangeness, the courage and the cultivation will occupy us later.[4] Immediately, I wish to return to the book, Blindness and Insight, from which I took my initial quotation. It is not a coherent study of contemporary criticism. But it is of a mood which I consider conducive to the strange courage of which I speak. As a phenomenological critic, de Man stands within a tradition which has struggled, within the context of a fundamental over-sight, towards a solution of the hermeneutic problem: the tradition recently surveyed and conveniently represented by Gadamer.[5] So, de Man moves through a variety of critical perspectives, with the self as focus, revealing aspects of the core problem as it cripples criticism and haunts the greater authors.

The title, Blindness and Insight, relates to the basic thesis of his book: that there is a paradoxical discrepancy between the general statements about the nature of literature made by critics, and the actual results of their interpretations.[6] Moreover, "not only do they remain unaware of this discrepancy, but they seem to thrive on it and owe their best insights to the assumptions these insights disprove".[7] So, the new American criticism, focusing on the text as unit, takes us into a discontinuous world of reflective irony and ambiguity. "But from where does the contextual unity, which the study of texts reconfirms over and over again and to which American criticism owes its effectiveness, stem? Is it not rather that this unity - which is in fact a semi-circularity - resides not in the poetic text as such, but in the act of interpreting this text? The circle we find here and which is called 'form' does not stem from an analogy between the text and natural things, but con-stitutes the hermeneutic circle".[8]

Again, Levi-Strauss, to protect and cultivate the rationality of his science, finds it necessary to exclude from reality the author of myth and of structural studies: "the reflective activities involved

in the structural study of myths deals with light rays
that issue from a virtual focal point".[9]   Maurice
Blanchot considers the literary work as constituted
by the act of reading, yet the act of reading is a
passivity, adding nothing,[10] and to this is added the
paradox of the impossibility of the writer reading
his own work, an impossibility which relates to a
preparatory step for a hermeneutics of the self.[11]
Similar oddities are found in Ludwig Binswanger's
work.   Binswanger tries to establish the power of the
work of art as a sublimation leading, with difficulty,
to a balanced structurization of multiple tensions
and potentialities within the self.   The work of
art becomes an entity in which empirical experiences
and their sublimation co-exist through the mediation
of the self.   But Binswanger is led to suggest a gap
separating the artist as empirical subject from a
fictional "self".   This fictional self seems to exist
in the work, but can only be reached at the cost of
reason.   So, the assertion of a self leads to the
assertion of its disappearance.

Similar, if broader, paradoxes are noted by de Man in
regard to the works of George Poulet and to Georg
Lukacs' Theory of the Novel.   "In a case such as
Lukacs' Essay on the Novel, we come close to open
contradition.   Two explicit and irreconcilable statements face each other in pseudo-dialectic.   The
novel is first defined as an ironic mode condemned to
remain discontinuous and contingent ... Yet the tone
of the essay itself is not ironical but elegiac.   It
never seems able to escape from a concept of history
that is itself organic, tributory of an original
source - the Hellenic epic - that knew neither discontinuity nor distance and, potentially, contained
the entirety of the later development within itself".[12]
Again, the cogito, in Poulet's thought, takes the
form of a reawakened feeling of fundamental fragility.[13]
For Poulet, the intellectual history of the West from
the Middle Ages to the present reveals itself as
involving an awakening consciousness of the frailty of
our link with the world.   "The subject that speaks in
the criticism of George Poulet is a vulnerable and
fragile subject whose voice can never become estab-
lished as a presence.   This is the very voice of
literature, here incarnated in one of the major works
of our time".[14]

When we come to de Man's reading of Jacques Derrida's
reading of Rousseau, the dialectic of blindness and

insight becomes complex beyond summary. But Derrida's larger view of Rousseau gives felt hints continuous with our selective penning of modernity's frail subjectivity. For Derrida, Rousseau is not governed by his own needs and desires, but by a tradition that defines Western thought: "the conception of all negativity (non-being) as absence and hence the possibility of an appropriation or a re-appropriation of being (in the form of truth, of authenticity, of nature etc.) as presence".[15] Derrida places Rousseau at the moment in the history of Western thought when the postulate of presence is taken out of the external world and transposed within the self-reflective inwardness of consciousness.[16]

The last two essays in de Man's book, "Literary History and Modernity", "Lyric and Modernity", bring me still closer to my title and my topic, within this cumulating context.[17] The context is essential, not just for present dialogue, but for modernity in philosophy: it would require a complementary essay to relate poesis to the ongoing genesis of philosophic insight, and so to vindicate the claim to priority, not merely historical but existential, of poetry. Again, there is, in relation to history, the blindness and the insight: Nietzsche's ruthless forgetting, Rimbaud's declaration that he has no antecedents, Antonin Artaud's claim that the time for masterpieces is dead.[18] And the ambivalence of the agony of present and presence is summed up in Baudelaire's statement, a statement about an anonymous shapeless crowd: "C'est un moi insatiable de non-moi" (it is a self insatiable for non-selfhood).[19]

De Man recalls, in his final essay, the German effort to discuss the lyric as paradigm of modernity. There are profound suggestions embedded here regarding the modern self that thus might express the self: but this would carry us into a much more precise discussion. I will only note, then, that the crisis of the self in its lyric expression. De Man remarks that it can be argued that the representational moment may still be the ultimate horizon of Mallarmé's poetry.[20] Still, Yeats feels towards the need of a separation of self and soul: and "one has to move through the self, still engaged in the daylight world of reality, of representation, and of life",[21] to the soul: where representation is at a loss. We have here what Walter Benjamin draws attention to, "a tension within the language derived from experiences of perception".[22] And in an earlier essay, Benjamin has suggested that "the intensity of the interrelationship between the

perceptual and the intellectual element"[23] to be made
the main concern of the interpreter of poetry.   And
indeed it should.

But here I would like to shift, with a twisted analogy,
to my second theme, which runs to a recapitulation.[24]

Critics have pointed out that among the various
Tombeaux poems Mallarmé wrote for his predecessors,
the Sonnet on Baudelaire is oddly unsatisfying: an
oddness de Man attributes to bad conscience: the
understanding of the non-representational, allegorical
element in Baudelaire is very recent and owes little
to Mallarme.   "Baudelaire is not the father of modern
poetry but an enigmatic stranger".[25]

So I return, in enigmatic fashion, to strange courage.
Walter Benjamin focuses the issue for the modern interpreter of poetry.   But the issue - surely our random
selections conjure up that feeling - has been there as
a blossom, or briar, or bud, of history.   Still, the
surety of the feeling is not guaranteed, nor the
courage to be psychologically present[26] in the twentieth
century.   In de Man's words, there is "the deceptive
stability of everyday consciousness which, in reality,
is only a kind of stupor".[27]   And that stupor, whether
meshed with a Kantian vocabulary or not, can reach in
criticism a sophistication of post-systematic and post-
artistic meaning.   One cannot rely, then, on drawing
attention to the folly of existential amnesia or to
the failure of fantasy, or to the simple strategy of
a serious reading of a book such as Lonergan's Insight
to ensure the lifting of blindness, the redemption of
frail subjectivity.   So my theme-bridge closes: is
Insight perhaps, like Baudelaire, elusively non-representational and allegorical?

But we may try another route, meshing in with history
as teacher, with Process as Paideiad.[28]

Criticism reveals itself - one cannot rehearse here
the twists of the epiphany in history - as in more
elementary crisis.   By "elementary" here I wish to
exclude patent philosophic disputes - of the merits of
structuralism, systems theory, psycholinguistics, and
such: if you like, I am in conversation with Blackmur's
gifted amateur.

Wellek and Warren, in their Theory of Literature (1956),
indicate the various facets of the pursuit of criticism.
There are preliminary operations of establishing and
ordering texts.[29]   There is what they call the intrinsic

study of the literary work.[30]   There is the historical
dimension, and the dimension of evaluation.[31]   What
they list under "The extrinsic approach to the study
of literature"[32] might be more properly considered as
a set of mediations: "The more psychology and sociology the historian knows, the more he will increase
his interpretative powers"[33] and similarly for any
student of literature.   Again, there is the problem
of literary genres[34] and the principles implicit in
their creation and reception, and there is the need
for some coherent account of these principles.   There
is, too, the task of making the fruits of such study
accessible to concrete literary experience.   Finally,
an account of all these facets such as Wellek and
Warren attempt would appear to be another facet of
literary studies which, however, includes all the
others in some basic manner.   I have, indeed, listed
the facets of literary studies in a way that points
towards that basic ordering.   Moreover, I would suggest that the ordering provides a unique strategy "to
explore the possibility of a general critique of literary criticism (defined as any reasoned and systematic discourse about the poetic arts and their products) such as might yield objective criteria for
interpreting the diversities and oppositions among
critics and for judging the comparative merits of
rival critical schools".[35]   The subleties of the
objective criteria belong to the complex issue of
subjectivity which we touch on here only programm-
atically.   Our present concern is a specification of
an ordering of the study of literature which is
meaningfully available to naiveté.[36]

The study of literature mediates between the literary
activities of the past and the literary activities
of the future.   The evident first stage in such a
mediation is the provision of texts, both the texts
of creativity and the texts of response.   A sufficient indication of the strategies of that stage is
given in chapter six of the Wellek and Warren book.
The second task is the determination of what was
meant: and whatever the complexities associated with
the meaning of meaning, there is a naive sense in
which we can admit that we know what this task is.
Literary history is a further task which builds on
the first two.   It goes beyond the meaning of invid-
idual works to seek out the patterns of literary
advance, which patterns reveal emergent literary
doctrines.   Now the concrete achievements of these
tasks are not uniform.   The history may be Marxist,

the interpretation structuralist, and even the assess-
ment of texts can bear the mark of the fundamental
orientation of the doer of the task. But it is to
be noted that the dynamic ordering requires the tasks
to be done, whether with spontaneous or explicit
principles. Human inquiry cannot await the provision of sound critical principles: of its nature it
is an epiphany into a modern discovery of mind. And
while the set of eight tasks we are in process of
describing may be called criticism in a broad sense,
this particular task best fulfils the quest of Crane
and his school for a criticism of criticism. It is
a personal dialectic self-discovery, within the existential absorption of the conflicts of the prior tasks.
It reveals, in a dialectically ongoing manner, the
grounds, within subjectivity, of conflict and creativity, and it seeks to bring forth grounded foundations
for the set of tasks of criticism.[37] The task of
spelling out such foundations represents a shift in
the reflective mediation of literature from past to
future. One may be helped here by various images:
there is the withdrawal through four tasks towards the
fruits of a criticism of criticism; there is a parallel return. So, the historical task is paralleled
by the effort to bring forth principles of creativity
and response; a systematic task seeks for an integral
understanding of such principles; a final task
mediates the concrete transformation of creativity and
response. Again, one may be helped by the image of
a vortex, a continuous whirl of tasks, a new vorticist movement.[38]

My hurried summary of a difficult structure can be
excused in that detailed indications of it are available elsewhere.[39] Besides, without the context of
some lengthy reflections on the nature of aesthetic
meaning, comments on the special tasks of its interpretation, history and principles would ring hollow.
Before moving to a consideration of the grounds of
the structure I would like to note that the structure
is an open creative ordering of tasks that can bring
together in enriching pluralism the riches of the
spectrum of present literary studies. Moreover, part
of that enrichment is a precise locating of the task
of resolving philosophic conflicts. Too much of
contemporary literary studies is laced through with
with random asides on method which lack serious bite,
except at times the bite of vitriol: one may recall
here, for instance, "The Quarrel" between Picard
and Barthes.[40]

I turn then to the grounds of the division of tasks, to a strategy with serious bite, and indeed to the issue of subjectivity with which this paper began. One aspect of the grounds for the division has already been indicated: literary studies mediate between the past and the future. One encounters that past in four tasks, one turns to the future in four tasks. But why four tasks? Here we enter the obscurity of subjectivity, the area of strange courage. For the tasks are related to the four general levels of the subject's conscious intentionality, and the precise identification of their nature and function is one of the major achievements of the twentieth century. Here I recall a comment of Walter Benjamin: "There is no document of civilization which is not at the same time a document of barbarism".[41] The achievement has been expressed, and the expression is a possibility of the betrayal of the achievement. I recall Beckett's comment on Joyce's Work in Progress: "Here is direct expression - pages and pages of it. And if you don't understand it, Ladies and Gentlemen, it is because you are too decadent to receive it. You are not satisfied unless form is so strictly divorced from content that you can comprehend the one almost without bothering to read the other. This rapid skimming and absorption of the scant cream of sense is made possible by what I may call a continuous process of copious intellectual salivation. The form that is an arbitrary and independent phenomenon can fulfil no higher function than that of a stimulus for a tertiary or quartary conditioned reflex of dribbling comprehension".[42] We have come round full circle - or perhaps one might say through a turn of the vortex - to the focal issue of our initial quotation. The issue is the self that reads itself: the self that may only read Insight. "To say it all with the greatest brevity: one has not only to read Insight but also to discover oneself in oneself".[43] To face that task adequately is to go beyond the troubled subjectivity to which we referred at length at the beginning. It is to go beyond both the untroubled subjectivity of naiveté, and the mistaken Kantian thematic that clouds all modern criticism that is not naive.[44] Nor is that "going beyond" concretely probable without the subject including modern science as part of the empiricality of the subject's own subjectivity. Without that existential inclusion of scientific modernity there may indeed be "copious intellectual salivation" but there will be no adequate epiphany. Moreover, the existential inclusion is not

a centrally anxious inclusion: it requires rather the
quiet admission into consciousness of such elements
of the world of theory of the natural sciences as
would gain for one a differentiated[45] grasp of the
structure of one's consciousness, and a sophisticated
break-through from the problem which, as both Poulet
and Derrida intimate, clouds Western thought with
increasing poignancy, since the the Middle Ages.
However, this modernity must be meshed with a poetic
modernity such as de Man touches on in his two concluding essays, if the range of problems and potentials
of subjectivity with which we began is to be transformed into human progress. The lived understanding
of these problems and these potentials and their
dramatic transformation in history requires the constitution[46] of present and future subjects in the solitude of authentic subjectivity. That adequate
constitution requires a creative memory and an ongoing
re-membering, embodying, of "startling strangeness"[47]
which will occupy us in part two. Without it one just
cannot resonate with, and sublate, the mood of Blanchot
or the paradoxes in Binswanger, the problem of the
unrepresentable self in Baudelaire or of the hidden
soul in Yeats, the intense relationship that Walter
Benjamin speaks of, between the perceptual elements
and the intellectual element.

Finally, the symbiosis in strange courage of both
modernities towards a total existential heuristic will
be progressively necessary for adequate participation
in the eight tasks of criticism.[48] The philosopher
or critic can less and less dodge the mediation of
a personal activity of science, of a personal passivity of psyche. So, for instance, one cannot take
seriously such advice as F. W. Bateson gives regarding
the discomforting complexity of linguistics: "Because
of its latent premise of discontinuity, linguistics,
whether historical or descriptive, can contribute
little to critical study of literature. Some recent
attempts to provide linguistic interpretations of
poems by Donne, Hopkins and Larkin have been dismal
examples of ingenious irrelevance. Let us follow
Socrates' example with the poets, crowning these
linguistic invaders of literature with garlands of
wool and anointing them with myrrh - and sending them
away to another city".[49]

I have no doubt that contemporary linguistics, like
systems theory and structuralism and German hermeneutics, suffers from a deficient perspective both

on objectivity and on the aggreformic[50] hierarchic
structure of subject and object.   But neither do I
doubt that our symbols, our language, our words, are
objectifications of the complexly hierarchic incarnate
subject.   I would recall the work of Betcherev and
Durand relating symbolism to our physics, chemistry
and reflexology.[51]   I would recall Langer's remark:
"The rhythm of language is a mysterious trait that
probably bespeaks biological unities of thought and
feeling which are entirely unexplored as yet".[52]
Finally, I would recall Bachelard: "If we were to
look upon the wealth of our own vocabulary for verbs
that express the dynamics of retreat, we should find
images based on animal movements of withdrawal,
movements that are engraved in our muscles".[53]   I
would suspect, indeed, that there is "never a twisted
thought without a twisted molecule".[54]

The vortex of method will turn, not with the relent-
lessness of the wheels of time, but with sufficient
schedules of probability, to guarantee the ongoing
symbiotic epiphany of the descriptive, the explanatory, the aesthetic, the concretely dramatic, the
ongoing epiphany of human subjectivity.

Part II

I once wrote, vortex-wise: "It is only in the Eye
of the Storm that one can Name the Mystery",[55] bringing together Patrick White's Stendahl-reading stran-
gers[56] and Langdon Gilkey's students of the Whirlwind,
[57] Spirans.   La Spirale was the title of a novel
sketched by Flaubert, of which it has been said, "if
La Spirale had been written it might have prevented
the stupid label of 'realist' from ever being attached
to Flaubert".[58]   It was to have been a transfigur-
ation of reality through dream and fantasy.[59]   To
this cumulating context I would add Gerhard Adler's
remark in The Living Symbol, A Case Study of the
Process of Individuation: "The movement of the
spiral - here reinforced by the dynamic action of the
vortex - is characteristic of the 'indirect approach
by means of the circumambulatio'.   It is as if an
unknown centre, which we can define only as the
psychological self, produces a constant centripetal
movement, or in Jung's words 'acts like a magnet on
the disparate materials and processes of the unconscious... Often one has the impression that the
personal psyche is running round like a shy animal, at
once fascinated and frightened, always in flight, and
yet steadily drawing nearer'".[60]

Our problem, only a problem if it dis-ease us as an almost schizoid problem 'till resolved, is a personal vortex, a tortuous dialectic symmorphosis[61] to core consciousness. Not core consciousness as defined in the mouths of men, "coffined thoughts around me, in mummycases, embalmed in the spice of words. Thoth, God of libraries, a birdgod, mooneycrowned. And I heard the voice of that Egyptian highpriest. In painted chambers loaded with tilebooks. They are still. Once quick in the brains of men",[62] Once, slow, I tried to draw attention to that core conscious- ness out of defilement: I mean, I leaned on dialogue about dialogue in Hegel's Phenomenology of Spirit as a possibility of epiphany:[63] but talk of Hegel turns too quickly and deadly to tilebooks: no longer you and I but two professors role-ing in their separate tiles. Plato's cave too is a moribund myth: it is illuminating only to those who come to its mouth another way. More generally we are caught in that thematic of reasoning which Voegelin describes as part of "the murderous grotesque of our times".[64]

So I am led to consider Falubert's Madame Bovary as more relevant, or Proust's Swann's Way, or some per- sonal modern way of science and therapy towards insight out of blindness. What may help is some twisted image or little phrase turning within consciousness, as does in Swann's Way the little phrase from Vinteuil's sonata: "The little phrase, as soon as it struck his ear, had the power to liberate in him the room that was needed to contain it: the proportions of Swann's soul were altered".[65] But the Way of which I speak here is a deeper remembering, boning up, embodying, than Proust's, and the basic relevant little phrase is symbolic of a core task, a profound expectation, an epiphanous escape: "...one escapes only through the discovery (and one has not made it yet if one has no clear memory of its start- ling strangeness) that there are two quite different realisms, that there is an incoherent realism, half animal and half human, that poses as a half-way house between materialism and idealism and, on the other hand, that there is an intelligent and reasonable realism between which and materialism the half-way house is idealism".[66]

It is on the central task associated with that phrase that this section focuses. That central task consists in a coming to grips with one's own understanding, the core of There-being, as Gadamer notes: "understanding is not just one of the various possible behaviours of the subject, but the mode of being of There-being itself".[67]

But surely - and Gadamer's massive Truth and Method
itself stands as witness - I am talking here of an
ancient struggle, with victories great and small
over the centuries? Coming closer to our present
specialty, is not the task I name the central concern
of the Geneva school of criticism? Sarah Lawall, in
her study entitled Critics of Consciousness remarks
that "all these men, including Blanchot, analyze the
human consciousness in literature at its very focal
point or genesis".[68] Elsewhere she remarks: "The
critics of consciousness want to observe the writer's
perceiving mind, to discover the patterns embodied in
his work, and to understand how these patterns of
perception coordinate with the formal patterns of
the text".[69] Fredric Jameson, in the concluding
chapter of his Marxism and Form seems to home in
precisely on that task I have in mind. He writes:
"Faced with the operative procedures of the nonref-
lective thinking mind (whether grappling with philosophic or artistic, political or scientific problems
and objects), dialectic thought tries not so much to
complete and perfect the application as to widen its
own attention to include them in its awareness as
well: it aims, in other words, not so much at solving
the particular dilemmas in question, as at converting
those problems into their own solution on a higher
level, and making the fact and the existence of the
problem itself the starting point for new research.
This is indeed the most sensitive moment in the
dialectic process: that in which an entire complex
of thought is hoisted through a kind of inner leverage
one floor higher, in which the mind, in a kind of
shifting of gears, now finds itself willing to take
what had been a question for an answer, standing
outside its previous exertions in such a way that it
reckons itself into the problem..."[70]

I have quoted at some length, and might have quoted
thus from other sources, to show an apparent community
of intent. But my quotations would also serve, as
the above does, to manifest the presence of what I
call a dead and actively rotting metaphor. It is
a presence which renders opaque the entire critical
enterprize. So, for instance, I would claim that
two recent substantial works on metaphor, that of
Ricoeur, La metaphore vive[71] and that of Hester, The
Meaning of Poetic Metaphor,[72] are rendered sickly by
the hidden presence of the deadly metaphor. That
deadly metaphor is associated with the question,

"What is knowing?", easily slipped into another
version "What is knowing like?". It is a question
whose first version could qualify for Maurice
Blanchot's "most profound question"[73] and to the
second version, which automatically calls forth
the deadly metaphor, one might apply his comment
in that article: with the answer "we lose the
straightforward, immediate datum, and we lose the
opening, the richness of possibility. The answer
is the misfortune of the question".[74]

I have mentioned here an automatic calling forth of
dead metaphor, and I will recall a further point from
Blanchot (whose work is illuminating in its negativity)
when he remarks on an automatism embodied in language
which the writer in anguish must strive to overcome.[75]
That automatism makes inevitable the presence of dead
metaphor in these early millenia of the discovery of
mind.[76] I wish to draw attention to the focus of
necessary anguish, or better perhaps of necessary and
prolonged concern. But first let us review the dead
metaphor's haunting of the philosophic tradition.

In a short suggestive essay entitled "On being Present
to the Mind: A Sketch for the History of an Idea",
John W. Yalton remarks: "Locke's essay was 'concerning human understanding', but he does not tell us
much about the nature of the act of understanding, of
comprehension. His contribution was to outline a
genetic theory of the emergence and acquisition of
ideas, to identify a number of mental activities
unsolved in this genesis of ideas. He frankly
admitted that he did not understand the connection
between the physical activity of objects and nervous
system and the cognitive acquisition of idea-signs.
He appreciated that taking ideas as entities which are
present to the mind, does not help in our understanding
of this relation either: it only borrows an analogy
from spatial presence without illuminating understanding or significance".[77] In a series of articles in
the thirties Peter Hoenan points to similar weaknesses
in the scholastic tradition after Aquinas.[78] Again,
Professor Frederic Lawrence has detailed in the past
decade the handicap of what I would call dead metaphor
in the massive struggle of the hermeneutic tradition
running through Dilthey, Husserl, Heidegger and
Gadamer.[79] Finally, I would note Bernard Lonergan's
pinpointing of a more remote source of modern disorientation: "Scotus posits concepts first, then the
apprehension of nexus between concepts ... The Scotist

rejection of insight into phantasm necessarily reduced the act of understanding to seeing a nexus between concepts; hence, while for Aquinas, understanding precedes conceptualization which is rational, for Scotus, understanding is preceded by conceptualization which is a matter of metaphysical mechanics. It is the latter position that gave Kant the analytic judgments which he criticized; and it is the real insufficiency of that position which led Kant to assert his synthetic apriori judgments..."[80]

So, contemporary scholarship is revealing the history of dead metaphor. And the sketch, as Yalton would hold, needs filling. One must, for instance, add Saurez, and the Jesuits and Descartes. One might, indeed, track back, right back to Plato's Cave: where, as I have noted, we do not want to be. There is something deadly about pure philosophy.[81]

Roger Poole, in his short but significant study Towards Deep Subjectivity remarks: "The greatest difficulty for subjective method is to get going after, and in spite of, Husserl".[82] The present essay gives one part of my answer to that difficulty: one may step aside from the philosophic tradition into a modernity of science and literature with which, at all events, that tradition does not seem to have been comfortable.[83]

The fundamental issue, indeed, is adequate empiricism,[84] and I take a vortex clue from a question which Peter Hoenan raised regarding the possibility of a one-sided surface in our accepted three-dimensional space: a surface on which a fly could walk around in its entirety without having to take wing to walk on 'another side'. It is a discomforting question for a scholastic tradition which has lost track of the nature of understanding. I would raise a further deeper question, of the possibility that consciousness is one-sided. It is a possibility that eludes in varying degrees the philosophic traditions we have touched on. It is a possibility that eludes the thematic efforts of contemporary critics. The one-sided surface can be discovered empirically. That consciousness is one-sided can also be discovered empirically. But only if one takes Yeats' seriously: "Why should we honor those that die upon the field of battle; a man may show as reckless a courage in entering into the abyss of himself".[85]

The reckless courage may ironically require a focusing on the apparently pedantic. I recall now Flaubert's courage in taking up, in Madame Bovary, the "bourgeois" subject of the Delamares almost as a penance in agreement with his friends' criticism of his first Temptation of St. Anthony. I recall too George Lukac's view of irony as a strategy of freeing the novel from its reception as imitation of reality: "Irony steadily undermines this claim at imitation and substitutes for it a conscious, interpreted awareness of the distance that separates an actual experience from the understanding of this experience".[86] Our personal problem is the liberation from an imitation of reality: my present task is an intimation of the distance that may separate your actual experience of knowledge from your understanding of this experience. And would it not be ironic to find one's Way, alone at last along the riverun past Kant and Descartes, from metaphor that leads astray, through Bovary and rounds and ovals by a commodius vicus of recirculation back to an intimate epiphany of oneself and Environs?

So we turn to the so-called father of realism to see if we can twist into our own consciousness towards a new critical realism. And while I focus our attention comfortably on the consciousness of Madame Bovary, I must remind you that I am inviting you to share uncomfortably Flaubert's exclamation: "La Bovary, c'est moi".

Eric Auerback selects our starting point with his concentration on a key paragraph: "But it was above all at mealtimes that she could bear it no longer, in that little room on the ground floor, with the smoking stove, the creaking door, the oozing walls, the damp floor-tiles; all the bitterness of life seemed to be served to her on her plate, and, with the steam from the boiled beef, there rose from the depths of her soul other exhalations as it were of disgust. Charles was a slow-eater; she would nibble on a few hazel-nuts or else, leaning on her elbow, would amust herself making marks on the oilcloth with the point of her table-knife".[87]

Of the phrase "all the bitterness of life seemed to be served to her on her plate", Auerback remarks: "Flaubert does nothing but bestow the power of mature expression upon the material which she affords, in its complete subjectivity. If Emma could do this she would no longer be what she is, she would have outgrown herself..."[88] Here I am intent on spiralling

further into the material of her complete subjectivity.[89] Within that complete subjectivity, that
consciousness, there is a deep power, genetic source
of such bestowed expressions as "seemed to be". To
this we must twirl our reluctant minds.

Georges Poulet tackles the same paragraph, with a
subtlety that is marred by dead Metaphor. He finds
Auerback's discussion "enlightening, yet not completely
satisfying",[90] and moves in from his own perspective
of Metamorphoses of the Circle: "Here the concept
of the circle and its emanating center represent man
as a perceiving, active figure who reacts to his
environment. The pattern of human experience, says
Poulet, is a central emanating thought which proceeds
in increasing concentric circles to vivify and unite
the immense 'interior distance' existing for man
between himself and the ultimate range (the 'circle')
of his perceptions".[91]

Poulet is clear: as clear and confused as his intellectual ancestor Descartes. He takes Auerbach's
point: that Emma does not simply see, but is herself
seen as one seeing, but then he is carried off by
dead metaphor. "If Flaubert had simply decided to
paint her from the outside, she would be merely an
object among objects. With the room, the stove, the
walls, the plate and the husband, she would be part
and parcel of the plurality of things. If, on the
other hand, Flaubert had wanted to make of her somebody like Bloom in Ulysses, or Clarissa Dalloway in
Mrs. Dalloway, i.e., a purely subjective being, then
there would have been no husband, plate, walls, stove
or room. Nothing would have been left, except the
sensations and emotions caused in Emma by these objects;
and there would have been no Emma, or at least in us
no consciousness of her as a person standing against
the background of things, since she would have been
reduced to the status of a stream of thoughts and feelings. In both cases something essential in Flaubert's
novel would have been lost, in one case the objective
world, in the other the subjective mind, and in both,
the extremely delicate relationship between objective
and subjective, which is the very substance of the
novel".[92]

Later, Poulet remarks: "It is the business of the
critic to examine, with the text, by what action Flaubert accomplished his purpose, i.e., to show vividly
the interrelation of a consciousness and its environment".[93]

It is, indeed, the vivid business of the critic: but
what chance of vivid business when a fundamental
perverse opaqueness dogs every turn of mind and pen?
I respect the range of valid insights in Poulet's
observations regarding psychic motion and space crossed
over by bitterness:[94] but the sublety is sickened
at its core.   At core, this is just not what goes on
in Emma's consciousness.   If I may press a counter-
metaphor, the pattern of Emma's experience is not a
centre proceeding, or oscillating, in increasing
circles: it is a dynamically expansive Möbius strip,
a one-sided spiral surface.

My counter-metaphor is grounded in non-metaphor:
human consciousness is a structured enterprize which
achieves transcendence not by going beyond a known
or unknown knower, but by reaching object and subject
alike on the single immanent surface in affirmation.[95]
Emma's consciousness, unrevealed to her, but spontaneously operative, was an immanent structured reach for
"her dreams dropping in the mud",[96] for the fragrance
of the eau-de-Cologne that Bovary Senior used up at
the christening,[97] for the "I understand"[98] however
mistaken, in relation to Rodolphe, for the twisted
truth reached when "she knew now the littleness of
those passions that art exaggerates",[99] for the clouded
value imprinted in those late words to Charles "You are
a good man".[100]

And here lies a possibility of "a clarification of subjectivity" that goes beyond "the ambiguities underlying naive realism, naive idealism, empiricism,
critical idealism, absolute idealism".[101]   But not
by philosophic dialogue: rather by entering into the
abyss of our modern selves in the bourgeois details
of our literary and scientific consciousness.

Let us return to Emma's plate, to Emma's greyhound
running round and round in the field,[102] but more
accurately to the inner vortex of our own consciousness.   Have we not all seen circular plates, caut-
iously circled dogs?   But have we seen a circular
plate?   Or was it perhaps an oval sight?   Or was
the oval or circle seen?   And consciousness may
stir, beyond visibility, questioning that beyondness.[103]

Then what of dogs?   The greyhound's lost, and Emma's
tears are called to halt by the draper "with various
instances of long-lost dogs recognizing their
masters".[104]

But the deeper inner issue here is masters recognizing
dogs: "As this threatens to engulf us in the epis-
temological bog, a brief orientation now may save
endless confusion later. A useful preliminary is to
note that animals know, not mere phenomena, but things:
dogs know their masters, bones, other dogs, and not
merely the appearances of these things. Now this
sensitive integration of sensible data also exists
in the human animal and even in the human philosopher.
Take it as knowledge of reality, and there results the
secular contrast between the solid sense of reality
and the bloodless categories of the mind. Accept
the sense of reality as criterion of reality, and you
are a materialist, sensist, positivist, pragmatist,
sentimentalist, and so on, as you please. Accept
reason as a criterion but retain the sense of reality
as what gives meaning to the term "real", and you are
an idealist; for, like the sense of reality, the
reality defined by it is non-rational".[105]

The issue I am raising for you is contained in the
question, what is the structured inner striving of
consciousness that moves us - or Emma - to say in
certain circumstances, "Yes the dog is lost".[106]
It is the basic issue of criticism. It is, to quote
Lonergan, "a momentous issue with repercussions
throughout the whole of one's philosophic attitude",[107]
and, I would add, one's attitude in criticism.
Furthermore, I would agree with Lonergan that "attention to the consequences can obscure the stark simplic-
ity of the issue itself".[108]

My metaphor is a live discomforting metaphor: that
consciousness is one-sided; that objectivity has to
be complexly[109] conceived as coming inside, coinciding
with, that one-sidedness. And the metaphor can give
place to the precise question: "Is it a fact that
our intellectual knowledge includes an apprehension,
inspection, intuition, of concrete, actual existence?
Or is it a fact that our intellectual knowledge does
not include an apprehension, inspection, intuition,
of concrete, actual existence?"[110]

In so far as that issue is not personally resolved by
spiralling uncomfortably into the vortex of our
modern[111] consciousness, a dead metaphor will remain
curled round our thoughts and tongues and treatises;
criticism will remain opaque.

In so far as the issue is met adequately and communally

it will ground a focus of lucidity which can spread to
an axial transformation not only of criticism but of
art.[112] Richard Cross, in his study Flaubert and
Joyce remarks that "few critics would deny that the
most significant development in the novel during the
past century has been the discovery of new techniques
for the sustained and intensive probing of mental
life".[113] Progoff, in an introduction to a new
edition of his book, Depth Psychology and Modern Man[114]
speaks of a next step in the evolution of our species.
Flaubert once remarked, "no human mind can now fore-
see upon what dazzling psychic suns the works of the
future may unfold".[115] I would speak of a new species
of meaning, with profoundly novel techniques of
critically-appropriated subject-referent language, in
which we would twist in and round and out of the babel
and the birth of Joyce's "Oxen in the Sun" towards a
wombless caveless Platoless prose, a new expression of
meaning going round and beyond Finnegans Wake, a
knowingsome prose of our meaning and Emma's meaning
when each of us says "Yes", and of Bloom's Molly's
meaning too when she says "yes and his heart was
going like mad and I said yes I will yes".[116]

But the twisting round and in and out, I know, are in
dialectic solitude, like Pound's cage or Cage's piano.
Interest in those cousins, the little words "is" and
"Yes", will remain peripheral, not only in this conference, but in this thousand years. And that peripheral
interest, I am convinced, will leave us with peripheral
vision. So there will be people talking past each
other in a dangling conversation fogged by dead metaphor cloaking the absence of common ground. "Empiricism, idealism, and realism name three totally different horizons with no common identical objects. An
idealist never means what an empiricist means, and a
realist never means what either of them means".[117]

Still, like Frederick Crowe, I take heart in the presence, in criticism and literature, of this fifth
column, the little word is: "They cannot stop using
the word 'is'. Using it, they cannot forever refrain
from asking what it means, not for more than five or
ten thousand years anyway, much less if they are willing to learn with and from tradition".[118]

I recall, in conclusion, Arnold Toynbee's remark about
man's achievement so far: "the most ironical of all
the unintended consequences of Man's achievements

during the first million years of his existence is
that his struggle to become master of his situation
has resulted in the exchange of one servitude for
another".[119]

In the past three thousand years a sophistication of
the central cancerous metaphor has contributed not
inconsiderably to that servitude.   But the second
million years are on our side.   So I twist to
conclude in the roundabout of Finnegans Wake with a
note of hope: "And your last words todate in cam-
parative accoustomology are going to tell stretch of
a fancy through strength towards joyance..."[120]

CHAPTER FIVE

MODERNITY AND THE EMERGENCE OF ADEQUATE EMPIRICISM

> "Why should we honor those that
> die upon the field of battle; a
> man may show as reckless a courage
> in entering into the abyss of
> himself".[1]

My title includes a suitably apocalyptic number of
words, seven: which might lead those so inclined to
suspect an eschatological dimension to the chapter.
The occurrence of the words "emergence" and "adequate"
in that title could ground that light suspicion more
firmly in meaning.   And indeed the dimension is
present, and to it we will return in the conclusion
of the paper.

My immediate concern, however, to borrow some of
Lonergan's terminology,[2] is not with inner religious
but with outer-socio-cultural factors, and I would
like to think that I am enlarging on a possibility
that he noted at the beginning of his paper on
"Prolegomena to the Study of the Emerging Religious
Consciousness of our Time":   "It may be that inner
religious and outer socio-cultural factors come
together to constitute a new religious consciousness
inasmuch as (1) the inner religious factor resembles
an infra-structure which (2) the outer socio-cultural
factor makes possible, or begins to countenance, or
expresses, or interprets the religious experience".
My concern, indeed, through this book is with the
modern socio-cultural factors in their possibilities
and probabilities of transformation through the procedural reflection which is central to the third stage
of meaning.

Now, my brief comments on this chapter in the introduction, and the quotation there from Lonergan[3] give
reason to suspect a triple psychological absence of
churchmen and students of religion.   Like truncated
subjectivity, that absence is not easily noticed or
acknowledged in its seriousness, and whatever the
goodwill of individuals, only a vast revamping of the
education of such people into modernity can overcome
that absence in the longterm.   Above all, without a

thorough entry of religious people into the modern
horizon of science, the full challenge of a methodical
procedural analysis will be mimed rather than met.
This applies most discomfortingly to students of
religion or "pure philosophy" who find Lonergan attrac-
tive.   The point has been made regularly by Lonergan,
and I have returned to it repeatedly, but it is
essential to draw attention clearly to this need in
the present context.   There is a growing volume of
thesis work being done at present on Lonergan where
the student focuses on generalities of particular
elements in Lonergan's view.   Such a focus on generalities can generate illusions.   Knowing the sonata
form is not producing the sonata.   What Heinrich
Schenker wrote, in an article on "Organic Structure
in Sonata Form", can be applied tellingly here: "To
effect an agreement between general concepts and
specific details is one of the most difficult tasks
of human understanding.   In order to reduce the world
of appearances to only a few concepts, knowledge must
seek general truths.   At the same time, one must
examine the particulars to the last details, in all
their secrets, if one wishes to grasp correctly these
general concepts, which are, after all, supported by
particulars.   The task is difficult because generalities, however arrived at, easily mislead men into
a premature satisfaction which spares any further
effort concerning specifics.   Through continuous
disregard for detail, knowledge of general truth is
impaired;   it does not ripen into truth, but remains
limited to a scheme".[4]   So, if one wishes to grasp
Lonergan's view on reductionism, one must look to long
days and months in such a field as biochemistry before
one has even the personal data necessary for the inquiry;   a search for insight into the heuristics of
development is a commitment to first accumulate in
oneself the webs and sequences of insights involved
in understanding a growing plant;   and if one seeks a
seriously contemporary understanding of God, one or
three, one surely is ill-advised to neglect what has
emerged in the cosmos during the past four hundred
years of insights;   and so on.   Such are the requis-
ites for the procedural analysis of generalized
empirical method, generative of a detailed transformation of outer socio-cultural factors.   And how can
inner religious experience come together with such
factors, and reach expression in them, if those who
take a stand on religious experience choose, either
clearly or subtly, to live apart from modernity?
There is little subtlety about the remoteness of many

recent religious groupings from modern concerns, but
the remoteness of Christian thinkers may be less
apparent. So, students of religion can formulate
types of commitment for a post-Newtonian age, yet be
lost in front of a second order differential equation,
advocates of novel political theologies will turn out
new titles in the absence of any serious economic
knowledge, good or bad, and Roman pontiffs can get
clerics of another age to write encyclicals. The
learned theologian can stand in Manhatten in a mesh
of the velocities and accelerations of money, engines
and people, a stranger, absent, but, in truncation
alas, not bewildered. Like Mr. Sammler, Saul Bellow's
hero, he may witness, near Lincoln Center, brutal
conflict and a detached audience and note with Mr.
Sammler a modern beatitude: "Wouldn't anyone help?...
Though there was nothing to hear, Sammler had the
sense that something was barking away. Then it
struck him that what united everybody was a beatitude
of presence. As if it were - yes - blessed are the
present. They are here and not here. They are
present while absent. So they are waiting in that
ecstatic state. What a supreme privilege!...."[5]
And the learned absent one, lesser indeed than Sammler who had risen from a tomb, might go on to echo
in diminished fashion Sammler's concluding conviction,
"the terms which, in his inmost heart, each man knows.
As I know mine. As all know. For that is the truth
of it - that we all know, God, that we know, we know,
we know".[6]

But do we know? The serious appreciation of the
interrelation of realities, be they electrons or
adrenalin or aggression or The Neurotic Personality of
our Time[7], is a modern venture: or, I should say, it
has its beginnings in these our modern times. Not to
seriously share in that venture, particularly in the
most elementary science, physics, is to leave onself
sadly psychologically absent as an academic of the
twenty-first century, and to deprive oneself of a
bridge[8] to clarity of subjectivity and authentic
nescience, two central components of integral academic
adult growth, but most especially academic religious
adulthood.

My views, of course, are not generally welcome, and
excuses can be offered. Contemporary religious studies is a welter of scholarship, and keeping up with
one's field or one's colleagues is, by common consent,

on the edge of possibility.   But there remains the
challenge: "the use of the general categories occurs
in any of the eight functional specialties",[9] and
the categories in question constitute an integral
perspective inclusive of modernity.   So perhaps it
is a matter of just not keeping up with your field or
your colleagues?   Indeed, keeping up with your field
as an exclusive preoccupation leads easily to the loss
of sight of the landscape: the particular war may be
over, with some eager units holding down an island.

But, apart from the use of the categories, there is
the immediate personal value: which of course is not
apart at all.   I recall now the months I spent grappling hopelessly with the twisted insights at the end
of Gödel's original work, or the less hopeless but
still exhausting months trying to understand the self-
energy of the electron.   Such efforts are a revelation of the puniness of our search for insight.   I
find it odd that theologians can accept a notion of
history as revelation, yet not admit that a contemporary effort to understand the electron can lead ad
amorem invisibilium.[10]

There are others of course who learn to read the
universe through the tortuous ways of Zen, or the
dark mansions of Avila, or the kind contemplations of
Julian of Norwich.   But I write here of academic
religious adulthood.   I write of the need of being
truly in the modern world, psychologically present,
though not of it.   I write of the enormous challenge
of fostering outer socio-cultural factors adequate to
make possible, countenance, express, interpret,
modern religious experience.

Throughout this book I have been detailing that challenge to academics, and in this chapter I have noted,
with some realism, the particular difficulties faced
by those involved in religious studies.   But the
difficulties, as any academic reading this knows in
his or her bones, are an all-pervading presence of
politics and power, of paranoia and paper, of committ-
ees and non-conversations, and, at its deepest, of
intellectual necrophilia.[11]   I am not here writing
about clear instances of corruption:[12] I am writing
about the daily flow of talk and tests and memos and
meetings in its continual contribution to alienation.[13]
What Rousseau remarked about 18th century government
is uncomfortably true of the 20th century university
government: "Ancient politicians incessantly talked

about morals and virtue, those of our time only talk
of business and money".[14]

The roots of the rot go deep.   "Isn't it a shock",
writes Professor F. Lawrence, following Leo Strauss,[15]
"to discover that the trajectory of political thought
stretching in one way from Machiavelli through Hobbes,
Locke, Smith, and in a second wave from Rousseau
through Kant, Hegel and Marx is rooted in the Machia-
vellian option to, in Lonergan's formulation, 'develop
"realist" views in which theory is adjusted to practice and practice means whatever happens to be done'"?[16]
And prior to the disorientation of the thematic of
value by Machiavelli one may discern the disorientation
of the thematic of mind by Scotus.   "The Scotist
rejection of insight into phantasm necessarily reduced
the act of understanding to seeing a nexus between
concepts; hence, while for Aquinas, understanding
precedes conceptualization which is rational, for
Scotus, understanding is preceded by conceptualization
which is a matter of metaphysical mechanics.   It is
the latter position that gave Kant the analytic judgments which he criticized; and it is the real insufficiency of that position which led Kant to assert his
synthetic _apriori_ judgments..."[17]

We live in the life-blood of these two major disorient-
ations.   So, a priority of concepts and a rejection
of insight into phantasm legitimates ever more detailed
planning to be followed by unthinking application;[18]
again, if expediency is what counts than a rhetoric of
responsibility must develop to disguise the reality of
self-interested short-sightedness.   Management and
bureaucratic centralization replace creativity and
subsidiarity, and government plays God.   A recent
book by Cornuelle entitled _De-Managing America_ makes
the point with wit and vigour: we badly need someone
to tackle the title _De-Managing the Academy_.

The transformation of this socio-cultural monster,[19]
which both privatizes and negatively conditions
religious experience, is the major challenge of these
coming centuries and beyond.   The transformation,
however, is not to occur by just another set of planning and management operations, but by the mildly
miraculous slow shift of patterns of education on all
levels that we noted at the beginning of chapter one.
That shift has been our topic all along, but particularly, the shift as it must needs occur in the

institutions of higher learning. Who is to educate the educators of educators - and of managers, lawyers, politicians, doctors, presidents, party-secretaries?

It is not fundamentally a question of a new plan or a new committee, but a question for solitary reflection. It is the question raised by the massive effort of Lonergan sketched in the final chapter here; it is the question raised by this book. The challenge of Lonergan to academy and economy is not initially a challenge to a community: one can only hope that some few might be as eccentric as that odd Irishman Stephen McKenna, who confided to his private journal on his thirty-sixth birthday, with Plotinus' challenge before him, that it was "really worth a life". There were two decades of interpretation, translation and poverty before him.[20]

Thus arriving at the fine point of Lonergan's challenge I must re-emphasize that it is to be heard through a slum conventionality[21] that is massive, systematic and subtle, and that it can be heard only through leaps and plunges into a transformed sense of biography, history and mystery.

Present disorientation's massiveness has already been sufficiently indicated. But it is also subtle, literally beyond our dreams and expectations, shrinking discretely the roots of enlargement at both the lower level of consciousness of the dream and the higher consciousness of discourse regarding self. So, on the relation of conventionalization to dreams Schachtel notes: "The distortion of a dream thought which resistance wants to keep from awareness has to be distinguished from the process of conventionalization, which more or less all dream elements undergo because the medium of dream language is incompatible with the medium of the conventional world of waking life. In the degree of this incompatibility there are, of course, considerable variations between different people and, even more so, between different cultures. But modern Western civilization with its streamlined efficiency, uniform mass culture, and emphasis on usefulness in terms of profitable, material production is particularly and strikingly at the opposite pole from the world of dreams....It is the trans-schematic quality of early childhood experience as well as of dreams which makes it difficult or impossible for the memory schemata to preserve and recall voluntarily such experience. Yet it is also this quality in which potentialities of progress, of going beyond the conventional pattern, and of widening the scope of human life are forever present and waiting to be released".22 And a like, and related, subtlety of conventionalization can direct consciousness in discourse even when we are speaking of the self. So it is that self-knowledge can become a central topic at a conventionalized convention: one can "revisit Hume on self-knowledge", discuss "the conditions of knowing knowing", even write books about human understanding, and remain in truncation.23 So too, perhaps, one may grow learned in Lonergan studies and subtly dodge the warning, "one has not only to read Insight but also to discover oneself in oneself".24

To the massive subtleties of modern truncation and alienation the academy adds system. The systematic exclusion of subjectivity in Skinner is evident; systematic nominalism of subjectivity is an unfortunate and deplorable aspect of economics, management, medical, legal, and political studies; but the systematic misdirection of concerned psychology and sociology is far from evident and so more deplorable.

Eric Fromm finds Horney's category of "competition", superficial,25 Heidegger and Sartre on the essence of man unhelpful,26 and seeks his own view, "by empirical analysis of the anatomical and neurophysiological structure and its psychical correlations which characterize the species homo. We thus shift the principle of explanation of human passions from Freud's physiological to a sociobiological and historical principle".27 Fromm does include the psychic, and he does present a sound thesis against Lorenz. But what I wish to draw attention to is the manner in which his strategy does not push for explanatory correlations on the higher levels of consciousness. I have selected Fromm for this criticism, not because he is an exception, but because he is a highly regarded rule.28 I draw attention to a lacuna in methodology which undoubtedly requires much lengthier treatment to make clear: that the road to adequate explanatory terms and relations in the sciences of man is through what Lonergan calls intentionality analysis. So, for example, human aggression includes components of understanding and misunderstanding, judgments and concerns, anxieties and alliances. These components are data to be understood. Because they are unavoidably data and yet data of consciousness they are necessarily included by a subtle nominalism but trenchantly avoided in their full seriousness as data. It follows that a great deal of the modern systematics of man stands for its own brand of necrophilia.

I am not arguing for a restricted focus in human sciences on higher consciousness: I share indeed Fromm's view of the insufficiency of Sartre, Heidegger and Horney. I am arguing for a strategy that pushes for complete explanation, a strategy that clearheadedly appreciates the linkages of anatomy, neurology, physiology, biochemistry, with the upper levels of human consciousness, a strategy that does not mistake the necessary shift[29] from description to explanation on lower levels for a sufficient understanding of the upper level.

The situation in the human sciences is multiply complex due to a parallel failure in the lower sciences, and the failure needs correction from below upward. This, indeed, I find a useful general strategy of dialogue: so, for example, difficulties with regard to the objectivity of God or of insightful man may well be an obscurity about the objectivity of dogs.[30]

At all events, such is the cultural context in which one may be invited to seek an understanding of one's own understanding, and I have suggested that it is of some help to turn expectantly to one's own sense of biography, of history as towards the future, of mystery.

The thematic issue of biography is, indeed, a basic underlying issue of this work, but the sense of biography may be revealed, for example, in the personal resonances the attitude of people like Stephen McKenna or Edmund Husserl or Carl Jung evoke in one. Certainly, without some biographic resonances Lonergan's insistence on Augustine's long years of struggle towards a glimpse of realism[31] takes no hold on the reader, and questions such as I raised earlier[32] pass that reader by. But perhaps at this stage they have more bite. "Will my view at 60 years be essentially the same as my view at 40, at 30?"

Or perhaps man's view in this life is never more than a heuristic, layered with thin meaning, "all straw" yet "most fruitful",[33] potentially accelerating through the years into the transitional sensibilities of old age?

Such a sensibility, in our times, needs a cultivation of fantasy,[34] as does the correlative sense of history: are we, each or all, an acorn or an oak? Am I now, and is history, a theme for a sonata to be written, or a chorus to be repeated?

But let us leave deeper fantasy behind and take a brief glance at the present possibilities of the sciences and the arts. Herbert Butterfield remarks, in The Origins of Modern Science, that "since the rise of Christianity, there is no landmark in history that is worthy to be compared with" the seventeenth century revolution in science.[35]

Immediately after that remark, Butterfield begins a chapter entitled: "The Postponed Scientific Revolution in Chemistry".

From an adequate heuristic perspective it is not surprising that chemistry emerges as scientific in the late eighteenth century: for chemical reality is more difficult to understand than physics. The shift of the biological sciences into explanatory perspective was a nineteenth century achievement, but it is noteworthy - and I am not entirely jesting - that Konrad Lorenz got a Nobel Prize in the present decade for discovering that zoology was about animals.[36]

My point, then, is that the scientific revolution did not happen: it is happening, and it is only beginning. Moreover, it stumbles, or is cornered, into strategies adequate to physics, chemistry, botany, zoology and human studies, with a statistics that relates to that list, written as it is in the order of increasing complexity, difficulty, intelligibility.

Zoology, then, calls out for contemporary discovery, for maturity. Might it not be that human studies could come to maturity, in later centuries, so that it would acknowledge the core of human rights[37] as worthy of study?

The appreciation of the core of human rights, of human intentionality, could indeed, as we have noted, transform human science. But what of the arts?[38] I recall here a curious and suggestive remark of Pierre Boulez regarding James Joyce, particularly regarding Finnegans Wake: "It is not only the way the story is told that has been upset, but also that the novel, if one dares to put it this way, observes itself as a novel; and this results in a logic and cohesion of this prodigious technique that is constantly on the alert, creating new universes. It is in this way that music, as I see it, is not destined solely to 'express' but must become aware of itself, become an object of its own reflection":[39] Brian Moore concludes, in lighter but literate fashion, towards a helpful shadow of this point at the end of his novel An Answer from Limbo. "Finnerty raised his hand, and as a cat cleans its eyes, wiped his knuckles across his face. I noticed the small, brown liver spots of age on the back of his old man's hand, and as I stared, unashamed and fascinated by the fact of his tears, a stranger's tears, the stranger within me said: remember this.

They were filling in the grave. I remembered that yellow face, the jaw bruised, eyes slitted: that face which stared up from the pit as clods of earth fell noisily on the coffin lid. Above the pit, their shovels moving as one, the grave-diggers dug, filled; dug, filled. Earth fell on earth. The wood was silent. The priest shut his prayer-book. Remember this.

And then, as though he had come up beside me, that drunken, revengeful Brendan (was he alive only four months ago?) repeated in my ear his angry words at Dortmunder's party: 'Standing by his wife's bedside watching her face contort, the better to record her death agony. He can't help doing it. He's a writer. He can't feel: he can only record'". And the novel shortly concludes with the words, "I have altered beyond all self-recognition. I have lost and sacrificed myself".[40]

"Remember this", "Memento ergo sum",[41] echoes through here, miming Proust, transmembering Descartes. And might it not be that there is a recording that mediates rich and remote feeling? And might it not be that there is a deeper recognition beyond all self-recognition that is seminal in our artistic time? Might we not make Boulez more precise by noting that not the novel but the writer must become aware of self, an object of the self's reflection: moreover, that the novel does remain "solely to 'express'", but an immanent axial shift in the meaning of self will call forth a parallel shift in self-meaning, in expression?[42] "I have lost and sacrificed myself", says Moore's hero: might not the fuller loss be the paradoxical loss of the muddled modernity of subjectivity, of the blindness within the insight of literature,[43] and might not the fuller sacrifice be the elemental sacrifice of self-attention, to the stranger within? So that, indeed, biography is discovered and, too, "history is discovered as the process in which reality becomes luminous for the movement beyond its own structure; the structure

of history as eschatological"[44] - as is the structure
of biography.

The elemental sacrifice is deep and lonely; for the
elemental sacrifice to the stranger within is ultimately to the echo of ultimate mystery.   So our vortex
searching pivots round an elemental ground.   "Prior
to the neatly formulated questions of systematizing
intelligence, there is the deep-set wonder in which
all questions have their source and ground.   As an
expression of the subject, art would show forth that
wonder in its elemental sweep",[45] and the elemental
sweep radars round "an orientation to transcendent
mystery".[46]

So, one might envisage, in an emergent luminosity of
expression, brought into being by the experiment of
history far beyond the point of Lonergan's linguistic
feedback[47] or the pointers of Joyce's "Oxen in the Sun",
a redemption and transformation of the epiphany of
human understanding which is expression.   One might
envisage the twisted title of Herman Hesse's novel,
Narziss und Goldmund, coming true and through, so that
a reflection of the self would speak goldenly: "'I
believe', he (Goldmund) said to him (Narziss) once,
'that the cup of a flower, or a little slithering
worm on a garden path, says more, and has more to hide,
than all the thousand books in a library.   Often, as
I write some Greek letter, Theta or Omega, I have only
to give my pen a twist, and the letter spreads out, to
become a fish, and I, in an instant, am set thinking
of all the streams and rivers in the world, of all
that is wet and cold; of Homer's sea, and the waters
on which Peter walked to Christ.   Or else the letter
becomes a bird, grows a tail, ruffles out his feathers,
and flies off.   Well, Narziss, I suppose you think
nothing of such letters.   But I tell you this: God
writes this world with them'".[48]

So, I twist back vortexwise to the beginning of this
chapter.   Of course there is an apocalyptic echo in
my early words, in all my words.   But neither you nor
I can hear it more than faintly.

We may move slowly, darkly, daringly, to hear it better
and speak it better, in a meta-transformation of our
sensibility: if we take courage and enter into the
abyss of ourselves, our concrete modern total man and
woman selves.

So, I conclude, recalling Lonergan's point regarding the constitution of a new religious consciousness. Modernity's challenge, briefly, is to replace blindness and naiveté by a modern symbiosis of mystery and method in the genesis of insight and human progress.

CHAPTER 6

AN IMPROBABLE CHRISTIAN VISION AND THE ECONOMIC
RHYTHMS OF THE SECOND MILLION YEARS.

Introduction

"The term, alienation, is used in many different
senses. But on the present analysis the basic form
of alienation is man's disregard of the transcendental
precepts, Be attentive, Be intelligent, Be reasonable,
Be responsible. Again, the basic form of ideology
is a doctrine that justifies such alienation. From
these basic forms, all others can be derived. For
the basic forms corrupt the social good. As self-
transcendence promotes progress, so the refusal of
self-transcendence turns progress into cumulative
decline.

Finally, we may note that a religion that promotes
self-transcendence to the point, not merely of justice,
but of self-sacrificing love will have a redemptive
role in human society inasmuch as such love can undo
the mischief of decline and restore the cumulative
process of progress".[1]

These two paragraphs conclude the chapter on the human
good in Lonergan's Method in Theology. The present
essay, in its five parts, is located in the Beethoven
pause between these paragraphs. One must, however,
consider those early chapters of Method in Theology as
they recur,[2] sublated, within the general categories.
These five parts are:

1.   The Vision: Praxisweltanschuung;

2.   Its improbability and the unity of
        proportionate Being;

3.   A component of the vision: economic praxis;

4.   Economic heresies and accumulating
        alienation;

5.   The deeper challenge of the improbable
        vision.

The first two sections name densely the challenge that
Lonergan's work presents and the concrete probabilities

of its being met in our time. Within that perspective we raise the issue of the fundamental disorientation of economic theory. Section three and
four are only a pale shadow of the larger strategy
of assembly, completion, comparison, etc.[3] which the
functional specialty dialectic involves: that spec-
ialized effort calls for something of the dimensions
of Schumpeter's History of Economic Analysis.[4]
Section five draws attention to the fact that the
required effort coincides with one feature of the
crisis of theological modernity.

Section 1: The Vision: Praxisweltanschauung.

The vision, Praxisweltanschauung, is a controlling
construction of the constructions and aspirations of
the human spirit.[5] It is an ongoing context[6] which
is a psychological present, reaching and reaching for
a harmonious[7] genesis of subject and world. It is
all-inclusive and self-inclusive. It is "an overall
view of the stages and variations of human meanings,
values, structures"[8] laced together by "a phylogenetic
set of schemata"[9] which concretely conjugates sets
and sequences of differentiations of consciousness[10]
within the general form[11] of emergent probability.

In being all-inclusive it is self-inclusive, but in
a manner proper only to the third stage of meaning.[12]
This proper meaning may be indicated by relating the
vision to recognizable theology and to traditional
philosophy.

Recognizable theology may insist that it is a reflection on the significance and role of religion in a
cultural matrix: but the vision locates that theological reflection as deeply culture-bound and of another
age,[13] whatever its praise of modern science or its
appropriation of the strategies of nineteenth century
history. And it is only by an effort of third-stage
self-inclusion, a shift from praise to practice and
from appropriation to self-appropriation, that such
theological reflection can recognize itself as a
product of limited culture.

Traditional philosophy is a span of effort from Parmen-
ides to Hegel and beyond.[14] It is not open-eyedly
methodological, historical, empirical, and passionate
in its terms and relations. Regularly it arrives at
general terms and relations: the Aristotelians had

theirs, in our times the analysts and the Whiteheadians
have theirs, and even Heidegger cannot regress to the
compact consciousness of the early Greeks. But like
Butterfield with the Renaissance and Reformation,[15]
the vision would recognize that tradition as episodic
between the first and the third stages of meaning.[16]
When terms and relations have meaning in that vision,
"their meaning is to be known not by a definition but
by a history of questions asked and answers given".[17]
The self-inclusion shows itself in the presence within
that history, that construct, of present questions,
questioners, answers and aspirations.

Normatively,[18] the visionary is any academic of the
second million years. The vision involves specializations:[19] otherwise the "overall view tends to be
either a tentative summary ... or a popular simplification of issues that are really not simple at
all".[20]   The vision, a psychological present inclusive
of the general categories[21] includes also the praxi-
heuristics of functional specialization. And the
functional specialist needs that vision, since "the
use of the general categories occurs in any of the
eight functional specialties".[22]

The notion of survival[23] which the thinker-doer is,
may thus self-digest into these operative categories
of the fuller genesis of the third stage of meaning.
An image of this genesis and of this self-digestion is
the vortex.[24]

The vision is Christian in origin[25] and in content:
at its centre is the visionary's ever-growing practical
heuristic word of the Word.[26]   But there is the content, identifiable as general categories, generated
by listening to the Cosmic Word, which makes the
vision universalist. And it is this universalist
heuristic word of our communal structured quest,
within the passionate finality of being, that is now
most necessary if we are to restructure theology and
life beyond recognition.

There emerges, then, the existential question about
one's degree of sympathy[27] with the project and one's
commitment to cultivating the achievement in later
generations, and in oneself in later years, so that
one might eventually borrow Bachelard's words:
"Late in life, with indomitable courage, we continue
to say that we are going to do what we have not yet
done: we are going to build a house".[28]

And there remains Mystery.[29]

Section 2:   The Improbability of the Vision and
             the Unity of Propertionate Being.

One needs a diagram if one is to think, to construct
praxi-heuristically, the unity, the unification, of
proportionate being.[30]   "In quaestione longiori atque
difficiliori phantasma conveniens haberi non potest
nisi per diagramma quoddam adiuvatur ipsa imaginatio;
et ideo qui omnia per modum unius apprehendere velit,
diagramma quoddam faciat in quo et elementa quaestionis
omnia omnesque inter elementa nexus symbolica repres-
ententur".[31]   And the question of the unity of proportionate being is surely long and difficult.   In
the psychological present of the foundational visionary that question has the form of generalised emergent
probability[32] which, with diagrammatic underpinning,
makes possible and probable the strategic fragmentation
of questions and quest.   So, for instance, one wishes
to think correlatively of the dinosaurs of the bio-
sphere that disappeared 65,000,000 years ago, and of
the multinational corporations of the noosphere that
appeared at the beginning of the first million years
A.D.   An imaginative synthesis may generate enthusiasm
but it does not carry the thinking subject to a
construct of praxis.   One is correlating sets of
entities $g_x(p_i, c_j, b_k, z_1,)$[33] with global distributions
within shcemes of emergence and survival over a period
of years, with sets of structures, whose focal reality
are n men: $\sum_n f(p_i, c_j, b_k, z_1, u_m, r_n)$, with similar
distributions.   The former distributions of schemes
are a history of emergence, survival and breakdown
which is still only partly understood;   the latter
distributions are a contemporary making of man and a
communal responsibility.[34]

The diagrammatic underpinning must be such as to
pressure one towards explanatory praxi-thinking.[35]
Such thinking is a normative concern for the actual
in its emergence within the vision of emergent probability.   I recall key elements in that vision: the
notions of actual, probable and possible seriations.
One should recall too that the heuristic form of
emergent probability is filled out by science in its
broadest meaning.   Illustrations related to our particular topic, economics, may help.   "The actual
seriation is unique".[36]   Parts of that actual

seriation are the "economic rhythms of production and exchange"[37] ranging from the daily rhythms of muscle and machine to the rhythms of booms and slumps assoc- iated with the dates ... 1831. 1837, 1847, 1854, 1857, 1866, 1873, 1883, 1890, 1900, ...[38] Parts also of that actual seriation are the sets of schemes within the academy and the economy that made probable the recurrent thought patterns - to be touched on later - of Marx and Mitchell, Keynes and Hansen.

"The probable seriation has to exhibit the ramificat- ions of probable alternatives".[39] The visionary, seeking to think towards the unification of proportion- ate being, thinks explanatorily of "all that would occur without systematic divergence from the probab- ilities".[40] Nor is what might have occured without consequence to the thinker: reviewing the past in this sense is not nostalgia but relates to the imple- mentation of dialectic associated with selecting and developing positions and leading "to an idealised version of the past".[41] But one is not here seeking an ideal associated with the possible seriation: one is seeking from the Cosmic Word the education assoc- iated with such questions as "what precisely went wrong?" "What might have happened if Hansen had stayed with Mitchell's thinking and sensed the burden of statics in Keynes?" "Would Samuelson, who followed Hansen, have not produced two million hand- fuls[42] seeding other schemes of thought and policy?" More explanatorily, one asks for "the flexible circle of ranges of schemes of recurrence"[43] that contribute to the making or maiming of man. One seeks out the defensive cycles[44] and the manner in which probabil- ities shift from product to sum.[45] One searches out, thus, thinking within the statistics and schemes of probable seriation, how it was that "from physics to Semitic literature, from Semitic literature to biology, from biology to economics, or from economics to depth psychology, the defenders were left in the unenviable position of always arriving on the scene a little breathlessly and a little late".[46] Such thinking leads to enlarged foundations.

Finally, there is the possibile seriation, "still more remote from actuality. It includes all the schemes of recurrence that could be devised from the classical laws of our universe. It orders them in a conditioned series that ramifies not only along the lines of prob- able alternatives but also along lines of mere possib- ility or negligible probability".[47] That contemplation

is essential to enriched foundations for man's future.
It is not a fourteenth century preoccupation with the
principle of contradiction. It is, rather, an extra-
polation from the forms of our universe, leaping
probabilities to envisage elements either of cosmopolis
or of further alienating shifts in "the monster
that has stood forth in our time."[48]   Such praxi-
thinking of the possible seriation is not only relevant
but reverent: it can both touch on the Impossible
Dream and mediate a more generous conception and
implementation of the probable and actual seriations
of the second million years.

It is within this Praxisweltanschuung of the unification
of proportionate being that one can conceive most
adequately of the improbability of the vision. The
vision within the third stage of meaning may be novel,
but the species has recurred throughout history with
low probabilities of survival. Praxis would seek out
the ranges of schemes of recurrence associated with
such low probabilities. It would envisage the relevant shifting of schemes, the conditions for jumps in
probability, the strategies that would realise those
shifts and those conditions. It would do so with a
clear-headed admission of present statistics of growth
and adult-growth, and of the present radical deficiencies of the academy.[49]   It would do so also with hope
in the new dynamism of the Metaxy[50] offered by the
crisis and emergence of the third stage of meaning.

Yet it is not "It" but you and I that possibly,
probably, actually, will hope and admit, not in any
extrinsicist sense, but, in the tension of limitation
and transcendence,[51] hope into consciousness and admit
into consciousness.[52]

Section 3: A Component of the Vision:
            Economic Praxis.

By economic praxis I mean that component[53] of the vision
which seeks to mediate the transformation of "the tot-
ality of activities bridging the gap between the pote-
entialities of nature, whether physical, chemical,
vegetable, animal, or human nature, and, on the other
hand, the actuality of a standard of living".[54]   That
seeking is attentive to the actual and probable seriations of schemes of recurrence in all their complexity:
here there is an epiphany of the Cosmic Word's refusal
to be intuited. Indeed, the schemes of recurrence

relevant for economic praxis were long in emerging.
As Toynbee notes, part of the new species of society
created by the Sumerians involved an economic surplus
and surplus production.[55]   The Romans had their
economy and the medievals theirs.   But regular rhythmic crises became a fact of economic life only at
the beginning of the eighteenth century, and it was
only in the twentieth century that a clear conviction
regarding the central significance of economic rhythms
emerged and that a fullsome analytic effort was made:
"...another indictment stands against the vast majority
of the economists of that period (1870 on) if it be
indeed proper, considering the analytic situation in
which they worked, to call it an indictment: with
few exceptions, of which Marx was a most influential
one, they treated cycles as a phenomenon that is
superimposed upon the normal course of capitalist
life and mostly as a pathological one; it never
occurred to the majority to look to business cycles
for material with which to build the fundamental
theory of capitalist reality".[56]   Such was Schumpeter's conviction, and his two volume work on Business
Cycles[57] represents his own effort towards an integral
view.   The basic analytic achievement is Lonergan's
Circulation Analysis.[58]   But first, let us note some
earlier efforts.

Schumpeter mentions Marx as exceptional.   With Schumpeter I distinguish here Marx the economist from Marx
the philosopher, the prophet, or whatever.[59]   One can
draw out from Capital the set of elements "from which
follows all the events that we connect with the trade
cycle.   Neither the labour theory of value nor the
ponderous mechanism of the theory of surplus value is
necessary to deduce this result".[60]   Indeed, the real
trouble is, as Schumpeter pointed out, that the labour
theory of value as a tool of analysis worked very
badly and leaves it exceedingly difficult to piece
together a coherent view, more than Marx indeed had,
of cycles.   Nonetheless, he stands out from previous
economists of prosperities and crises: "it must not
be forgotten that the mere perception of the existence
of cyclical movements was a great achievement at the
time.   Many economists who went before him had an
inkling of it.   In the main, however, they focused
their attention on the spectacular breakdowns that
came to be referred to as 'crises'.   And those
crises they failed to see in their true light, that
is to say, in the light of the cyclical process of
which they are mere incidents.   They considered them,

without looking beyond or below, as isolated misfor-
tunes that will happen in consequence of errors,
excesses, misconduct, or of the faulty working of
the credit mechanism. Marx was, I believe, the
first economist to rise above that tradition and to
anticipate - barring the statistical complement - the
work of Clement Juglar".[61] But Marx stands out also
as representing what I might call the mood of praxis:
"Reaching the goal would have been ineffectual,
analyzing the social process would have interested
only a few hundred specialists. But preaching in the
garb of analysis and analyzing with a view to heart-
felt needs, this is what conquered passionate alleg-
iance and gave to the Marxist that supreme boon which
consists in the conviction that what one is and stands
for can never be defeated but must conquer victoriously
in the end".[62]

It was Clement Juglar, however, who brought into focus
by his "great book of facts"[63] the need for a theory
of business cycles rather than a theory of crises.
He gave his attention mainly to that cycle of, roughly,
ten years' duration with which his name is associated,[64]
distinguishing phases in it: 'upgrade', 'explosion',
'liquidation'. He amassed an extraordinary amount of
time-series material (prices, interest rates, central
bank balances) relating to business oscillations in
England, France and the United States, from 1696 to
his own day. He concluded that one can get behind
the various accidents of war etc., to establish that
depressions were adaptations of the economic system
to situations created by preceding prosperities.
Therefore, the basic problem of cycles' analysis
centred on the question of the causes of prosperity.
To this question he failed to provide a satisfactory
answer.

Let us return to Schumpeter's contribution, a contribution which bears comparison with that of Lonergan.
Indeed, Lonergan has already made that comparison, and
it is worth quoting at this stage even though its
comprehension requires familiarity with Lonergan's
analysis and terminology:

"Schumpeter and Lonergan:
My real and my circulation phases involve no distinction between growth (mere increase in size) and
development (new productive combinations). For
Schumpeter these two are specifically distinct - the
new production functions create new situations that

increase enormously the average of error and bring
about the cycle(s).

However, the ideas of capital, credit, interest, etc.,
that Schumpeter advances appear more clearly and more
generally and in more detailed a fashion. The relevance of Schumpeter's insistence on development as
opposed to growth is in the concatenation of the
phases, e.g., Schumpeter's development can take place
in my static phase if $DQ''_n > O$ and if the new combinations are continuously offset by equal liquidations
of former enterprises".[65]

Schumpeter focuses his attention on innovation, on
new ideas, new men, new techniques. The quotation
from Lonergan mentions error as significant in Schumpeter's analysis, and this significance helps to bring
out the normative nature of Lonergan's own analysis.
"Most people will link up recessions with errors of
judgment, excesses (overdoing), and misconduct. This
is no explanation at all; for it is not error, etc.,
as such but only a cluster of errors which could
possibly account for widespread depressive effects.
Any 'theory' that rests content with this must assume
that people err periodically in the way most convenient to the economist. Our model, by showing the
emergence of situations in which it is understandable
that mistakes of all sorts should be more frequent than
usual (i.e., when untried things are being put into
practice and adaptation to a state of things becomes
necessary, the contours of which have not yet appeared)
does away with this and shows the place of the element
of error in the various phases of the process, without
having to introduce it as an independent, still less
as a necessary, element".[66] In a footnote, Schumpeter
adds "It is believed that our arrangement assigns its
proper place, not only to errors of various types, but
also to other kinds of aberration of economic action,
and makes them analytically workable. The actual
quantitative importance of the element of error is,
however, a different question. The writer has not
been able to answer it to his own satisfaction".

Lonergan centres his attention on the rhythms of the
productive process and derives a theory of cycles which
does not call for the inclusion of error. Lonergan
does, in fact, treat of error in relation to human
inadaptation to the rhythms of economic process.

The comments in the second paragraph of the quotation

from Lonergan need the exposition of Lonergan's coherent analysis. Schumpeter's discussion of the "New Economic Space"[67] created by innovation is a meshing of all that happens in terms of costs, wages, interest, prices, credit. Lonergan's analysis involves a clear separation of elements regularly confused or brought together by economic accountancy. What Lonergan says of interest rates may perhaps be taken as characteristic of his entire analysis: "Traditional theory looked to shifting interest rates to provide the automatic adjustment between the productive process and the rate of saving ... The difficulty with this theory is that it lumps together a number of quite different things and overlooks the order of magnitude of the fundamental problem".[68]

Lonergan's analysis reveals the productive process as inherently cyclic in a manner "not to be confused with the familiar trade cycle. The latter is a succession of booms and slumps, of positive and then negative accelerations of the process. But the cycle with which we are here concerned is a pure cycle. It includes no slump, no negative acceleration. It is entirely a forward movement which, however, involves a cycle inasmuch as in successive periods of time the surplus stage of the process is accelerating more rapidly and, again later, less rapidly than the basic stage. When suitable classes and rates of payment have been defined, it will be possible to show that under certain conditions of human inadaptation this pure cycle results in a trade cycle. However, that implication is not absolute but conditioned, not something inevitable in any case but only something that follows when human adaptation is lacking".[69]

An analogy drawn from an earlier typescript throws light on Lonergan's strategy: "A study of the mechanics of motor-cars yields premises for a criticism of drivers, precisely because the motor-cars, as distinct from the drivers, have laws of their own which drivers must respect. But if the mechanics of motors included, in a single piece, the anthropology of drivers, criticism could be no more than haphazard".[70]

Lonergan moves neither in the manner of the descriptive economist who proceeds to a nuanced general view through descriptive language, nor in the manner of the

statistical economist whose terminology is dominated
by the proximate possibility of measurement. His
analytic approach differs from both these: "Out
of endless classificatory possibilities it selects
not the one sanctioned by ordinary speech nor again
the one sanctioned by facility of measurement but the
one that most rapidly yields terms which can be defined
by the functional interrelations in which they stand.
To discover such terms is a lengthy and painful process
of trial and error. Experto crede. To justify them,
one cannot reproduce the tedious blind efforts that
led to them; one can appeal only to the success, be
it great or small, with which they serve to account
systematically for the phenomena under investigation.
Hence it is only fair to issue at once a warning that
the reader will have to work through pages, in which
parts gradually are assembled, before he will be able
to see a whole and pass an equitable judgment upon
it".[71]

Before concluding this section, I would note that study
of business cycles has been pursued by others but with
little of the analytic perspective of Schumpeter or
Lonergan. Indeed, the study is regularly influenced
by the viewpoint to be described in the next section.
So, for example, Arthur Burns, commenting on Hick's
book, A Contribution to the Theory of the Trade Cycle,
[72] remarks: "It is a sophisticated book, not to be
confused with vulgar Keynesianism. It shares, however, the aggregative, mechanical, 'real' slant of
much of the recent literature on economic theory".[73]
Burns himself represents a tradition of interest in
business cycles which derives from the influence of
Wesley Clair Mitchell (1874-1948). Mitchell, as
Schumpeter puts it, wanted to explore rather than to
turn round and round on a small piece of land. So he
moved with complete commitment to the concrete reality
of economic process from his thesis on the Greenback
episode to a life-long study of the business cycle
"which made Mitchell the foremost world authority on
the subject".[74] While he was averse to theory, he
gave the National Bureau of Statistics an orientation
towards empirical research of business cycles during
the twenty-five years (1920-45) of his chairmanship,
an orientation which survived under Arthur Burns. The
orientation grounds a healthy respect for economic
reality and a source of criticism of the ongoing
theorizing and practice of the new economics which
emerged in the thirties.[75] The present situation is
well summed up by Burns: "The only things we can be

reasonably certain of in the proximate future are, first, that our economic system will continue to generate cyclical tendencies, and second, that the government will at some stage intervene to check their course".[76] One is led to recall a remark of Lonergan's regarding cyclical tendencies, in particular the pure cycle: "One may say that it is solidly grounded in a dynamic structure of the productive processes; and one has only to think of the practical impossibility of calculating the acceleration ratios... to smile at the suggestion that one should try to 'smooth out the pure cycle'".[77]

Section 4:   Economic Heresies and Accumulating
             Alienation.

"The business cycle was par excellence the problem of the nineteenth century.   But the main problem of our times, and particularly in the United States, is the problem of full employment".[78]

This remark was made by Alvin Hansen, "The American Keynes"[79] in the presidential address to the American Economic Association at their annual meeting, December 1938.   As in the previous section I picked out a handful of heroes, so here I name some of the villains who made probable and actual the schemes of recurrence within which emerged the textbook tradition associated with the name of Paul Samuelson and the concomitant inert and alienating schemes of recurrence of contemporary economic thought and practice.   I will, however, be brief in this section, for several reasons.   In the first place, Joan Robinson has provided a substantial amount of critical comment on the last hundred years of economics and it could not be briefly reproduced.[80]   In the second place, the tradition in question here is the current climate of opinion.   Any undergraduate economist will recognize the names and the theses that I briefly mention.   Those who have not had such undergraduate studies would find even lengthier description obscure.   But all may recognize in the reports and policies of governments and banks, in the criticisms and suggestions of journals and editorials, the prevalence of that inert climate.[81]

I will begin by noting three points of criticism of the present tradition.   In the first place, the tradition includes no serious effort at analysis of the productive process.   Secondly, even when it takes on the

trappings of a theory of growth, it remains economic
macrostatics. Thirdly, inbuilt into it and into
its political application, there is a fundamental
ideology of alienation.

Joan Robinson regularly returns to the absence of
serious analysis in her writings. She characterises
the neo-classical theory of production as follows:
"There is a mysterious substance, let us call it leets,
measured in tons, which is used in conjunction with
labour to produce output. There is a well-behaved
production function in leets and labour for every
kind of output, including leets. There is no distinction between the past and the future. An investment of leets, once made, can be squeezed up or spread
out into a new form, instantaneously and without cost,
if it becomes profitable to do so.

What is still more remarkable, leets can absorb technical progress without changing its identity, again
instantaneously and without cost, so that new invent-
ions raise the output from a ton of leets, without
any investment being required.

All of this has been very candidly spelt out by Professor Meade. (In the first edition of A Neoclassical
Theory of Economic Growth he refers to what I have
called leets as 'steel'). It is the essence of
Professor Ferguson's concept of 'capital'".82

The difficulty of conceiving adequately of capital and
of production is not superficial. It is a difficulty
of heuristic conception. "The intending that is
conception puts together both the content of the
insight and as much of the image as is essential to
the occurrence of the insight; the result is the
intending of any concrete being selected by an incom-
pletely determinate (and, in that sense, abstract)
context".83 As opposed to the impoverished abstract-
ion84 "leets" there is an enriching abstraction which
holds together,85 within a general heuristics of
process, the aggregate of rates at which goods and
services move, directly or indirectly, into a standard
of living, without excluding wheat and cotton, bread
and dresses, ships and machine tools, management and
innovation.

Wedded to the difficulty of conceiving capital, as
Robinson notes in the quotation above, is the difficulty

of conceiving change.[86]   Nor can this be surprizing
if the accusation of macrostatic thinking is valid.

An early villan was Leon Walras (1834-1910), a hero
of Samuelson[87] but also paradoxically a hero of Schumpeter's history.   Schumpeter's admiration was based
on his recognition of the masterly analysis of economic
equilibrium which Walras achieved, by methods cousin
to nineteenth century statics, but Schumpeter did not
consider this the peak or ideal of economic achievement.   "Now, an observer fresh from Mars might excus-
ably think that the human mind, inspired by experience,
would start analysis with the relatively concrete and
then, as more subtle relations reveal themselves, proceed to the relatively abstract, that is to say, to
start from dynamic relations and then proceed to working out static ones.   But this has not been so in any
field of scientific endeavor whatsoever".[88]   Later,
he speaks of Marshall, despite his extra-static
considerations, failing to cross the Rubicon.   He
notes pointers by Pantaleoni, Pareto, Samuelson: but
"they left the main body of economic theory on the
'static' bank of the river";[89]   "no attack on the whole
front of Walrasian theory has as yet developed".[90]

Just as one can solve the equilibrium problem of a
set of rods and other elements, through the principle
of virtual work, so one may solve the equilibrium
problem of prices, of demand and supply, through the
application of marginal analysis.   However, while a
set of rods can settle in equilibrium with one rod at
10o angle to the vertical, it is disconcerting to find
the set of economic elements in equilibrium, with the
factor of employment at 10% off full employment.
Keynes arrives on the scene to set that right and "the
old theology closed in again.   Keynes himself began
the reconstruction of the orthodox scheme that he had
shattered.   'But if our central controls succeed in
establishing an aggregate volume of output corresponding to full employment as nearly as is practicable,
the classical theory comes into its own again from
this point onwards ... It is in determining the volume,
not the direction of actual employment that the existing system has broken down'".[91]   As Schumpeter notes,
"the exact skeleton of Keynes' system belongs, to use
the terms proposed by Ragnar Frisch, to macrostatics,
not macrodynamics".[92]   But Keynes' reconstruction
bears little resemblance to the theory and practice
associated with Sir John Hicks' IS and LM curves,[93]
which found its way particularly into the American
tradition.

Hansen, whom we quoted at the beginning of this section, is the central figure of that tradition. He
began his career closer to the interests of Wesley
Mitchell,[94] but became the leading figure in the
evolution of American Keynesianism. I do not need
to document that tradition here.[95] After Hansen,
comes Samuelson. Abba P. Lerner, whose functional
finance specifies strategies of government operation,
provides another strand. Then there is Milton
Friedman of whom Robinson remarks: "There is an
unearthly, mystical element in Friedman's thought.
The mere existence of a stock of money somehow promotes
expenditure".[96]

Hansen's characterization of the shift of interest in
the twentieth century takes on a different hue from
the perspective of Praxisweltanschuung and of the
third stage of meaning. Then one sees it as an aband-
onment of the search both for a dynamic economic theory
and for democracy. An image I find suggestive of
modern economic theory and government practice is that
of a hydrostatic control of a whirlpool.[97] A certain
aggregate of elements in the whirlpool "ought" to have
a property called employment. Employment is a matter
of adjusting valves. It is very remote from the
notion of employment as pivoting on communal and
individual attention, intelligence, reasonableness
and responsibility; on the praxis of micro-autonomy,
on coherent economic theory, and on a profoundly
different notion of control.[98] So we come to the
third point of criticism: the embedded ideology of
alienation.

One must be careful how one conceives of alienation.
There is no question, within the vision, of talking in
popular terms of Alienated Man. I recall here my
comments and suggestions of sections one and two. One
thinks, then, of alienation in terms of the history of
aggregates of persons $H \gtrless f(p_i, c_j, b_k, z_l, u_m, r_n)$, pivoting in one's searching of past and future on some imaginative device. The alienation of the modern politico-
economic structure reaches like leukemia into every
vein of modernity. You can hear it's molecular
echoes in radio-new's vocal muscles; you can see it
in the stagnation of the five o'clock subway people's
attention, intelligence, reasonableness and responsibility; you can sense it in the corridors of academe:
but only if you are labouring towards the vision.
"What I want to communicate in this talk on art is the

notion that art is relevant to concrete living, that
it is an exploration of the potentialities of concrete
living, that it is extremely important in our age when
philosophers for at least two centuries, through doctrines on economics, politics and education, have been
trying to remake man and have done not a little to
make human life unlivable".[99]   But how many of us
smell, taste, feel, the unlivability? And even if
wo do, ever so slightly, how many of us build the
discomfort into our academic vortex which is - if we
are of third stage meaning - a praxis vortex, a personal vortex of generalized empirical method.   And
I recall that the present paper is bracketed between
a paragraph on alienation and a paragraph on redemptive progress.[100]

Section 5:   The Deeper Challenge of the
              Improbable Vision.

"I have urged that so great a transformation needs a
renewed foundation, and that the needed renewal is
the introduction of a new type of foundation.   It is
to consist not in objective statement, but in subjective reality".

The transformation, then, is of subjects, and I would
recall that "this transformation of sensitivity penetrates to the physiological level".[102]   I find indeed
that there are too many things, everything, to recall,
to "remember"[103] in a novel fashion in this new context,
and in order to keep this final section brief I will
restrict myself to some few related points.

The transformation in question is the genesis of foundations persons who would mediate the presence of users
of the general categories in all functional specialties.   In particular, I note here the need for that
presence in the genesis of doctrines. My concern in
the two previous sections has been with the transformation of economic policy or doctrines. My broader
concern is with the transformation of theological
doctrines.   Moreover, the two transformations mesh:
the moral theology of the economic process is not based
on a doctrine of the family wage.[104]

Fr. Frederick Crowe has drawn attention, in this matter
of the transformation of doctrines, to the notion of
transposition in Lonergan's Method in Theology. I

share his concern, repeat his "plea to Lonergan students for more concentrated attention on the topic
of dialectic",[105] and add a plea for a hard look at
the general categories that sublate both Insight and
Method in Theology.[106]   So, doctrines will be trans-
positions of dogmas, reached through the use of "the
functional specialty, foundations to select doctrines
from among the multiple choices presented by the
functional specialty, dialectic".[107]   But all this
involves the "transposition that theological thought
has to develop if religion is to retain its identity
and yet at the same time find access into the minds
and hearts of men in all cultures and classes".[108]
The new subjective realities, incarnate foundations,
"provide the basic orientation",[109] an orientation
including "the transposition of systematic meaning
from a static to an ongoing dynamic context",[110] so
that "the intelligibility proper to developing doctrines is the intelligibility immanent in historical
process".[111]   Such an intelligibility can emerge in
the theologian only through "a long-delayed response
to the development of modern science, modern scholarship, modern philosophy",[112] only through three basic
differentiations of consciousness, all three "quite
beyond the horizon of ancient Greece and medieval
Europe"[113] and, I would add, beyond the horizon of
most of contemporary theology.

The message would seem loud and clear.   Present foundations, doctrines and systematics belong to another
age: they just do not ground a reaching into the
minds and hearts of present and future people.   While
the issue calls for detailed discussion and exemplif-
ication, I must restrict myself to one general point
of precision.

The notion of transposition is explicitly introduced
in Insight.[114]   "True propositions may be merely
descriptive; to assign their metaphysical equivalent,
they must be transposed into an explanatory form".[115]
Moreover, there is also required a structural transposition to move from logic to metaphysics.[116]   Failure
to observe such a strategy "results in the substitution
of a pseudo-metaphysical myth-making for scientific
inquiry".[117]   The communal effort to observe that
strategy, in the use of, and ongoing genesis of, general categories, is what will eventually lift forward
dogma and history to doctrinal adequacy.

Let us return, parenthetically, to the issue of economic doctrines.   When we seek light here we are
eventually moved, transposed, to a dialectico-genetic
grasp of economic policy.   Emerging economic doctrines are such only within that grasp, and the relevant
grasp is within the vision, Praxisweltanschauung:
"the appropriate theoretical framework for creativity
is open system and so basically transcendental method".
118   Within that view one finds redefined, with third
stage meaning integrality,119 the sequence of economic
dogmas terminating with transcendental openness and
doctrinal specificity in the present aspirations of
men.   The old dogmas, thus contextualised, present in
their roots and in their fruits, are transposed beyond
popular recognition.120   So, for example, through the
foundational grasp of ongoing process - through the
use of the general categories - one transposes dogmatic
movements in history such as the nineteenth century
"imperialist dogma",121 or doctrinal drifts in authors
like Adam Smith.   The imperialist dogma can be identified as a descriptive advertence to the disruption
of the phase of basic expansion in the pure cycle,
probable within a statistics of emergence of global
economic maturity.   The movement in Smith can be
identified as a heretical enthusiasm for the priora
quod nos of price, leading to a reliance for salvation
through price analysis which fathered Walras.122   One
locates too, not with the vagueness of popular discontent,123 but with praxis precision, the history
and future of nationhood,124 government,125 monopoly,
126 and the significance of upper and lower leisured
rentier classes.127   One locates proleptically: one
is seeking the expansion of micro-autonomy through a
poetics128 and ethics129 of Economic Space.   One
envisages, within emergent probability, the possible
and probable schemes of recurrence of intermediate
technologies and micro-technologies130 which would
shift in future centuries the global statistics of
alienation.   In particular, such innovative movements
towards micro-autonomy, within a global economic
maturity, would mesh with the eventual epiphany of an
economy of aggregate, if not synchronic, pure cycles.

We are still in a Beethoven pause between two paragraphs on page 55 of Method in Theology, and our problem and privilege is to be drawn out of alienation
into chemical, psychic, mindful harmony with the compositional energy of history.   Henry Simons was not
optimistic about the outcome of the struggle between

labour and capital, but he still could write: "It
is easy to argue that the whole problem is so hard
and ominous politically that no effort should be made
to solve or even to see it - that the real choice lies
between a certain, gradual death of economic democracy and an operation ... which would cure if successful but is almost certain to kill. I am no fore-
caster and am not in direct communication with the
Almight. Consequently, I can only maintain that it
is immoral to take such absolute dilemmas seriously.
Democracy would have been dead a thousand times if
it paid much attention to historical extrapolations".131

The love of God, the third stage of meaning, and the
second million years are on our side.

The foregoing parenthetic consideration of issues of
economic policy is evidently not without relevance
to the set of necessary developments of doctrines
in theology. "It is not in some vacuum of pure spirit
but under concrete historical conditions and circumstances that such developments occur, and a knowledge
of such conditions and circumstances is not irrelevant
in the evaluational history that decides on the legit-
imacy of developments".132 So we are led again to
focus on the present crisis of theology by focusing on
what is relevant to evaluational history, to dialectic.
Moreover, the crisis in dialectic is necessarily personal, and, in conclusion, I would like to symbolise
it in the turning of a page, the turning over of a new
leaf.

In Insight the crisis page is page 388: a strategic
position is offered which is "startlingly strange"133
and the beginning of a new way of life. In Method in
Theology the crisis page is page 250: a larger strategy is offered inclusive of the strategy of Insight.
Turning over that page the theologian is faced134 with
a task of assembly which includes events and movements
of the past four centuries to which recognizable
theology has been external.135 Such are the present
schemes of recurrence of contemporary theological
education and discourse that probabilities of theologians psychologically present in the fruits of those
four centuries are low. The transposition of theology
into the end of the twentieth century is comparably
remote. The turning of that page, that leaf, is
discomforting, can be dreadful. "Classical culture
cannot be jettisoned without being replaced; and
what replaces it, cannot but run counter to classical

expectations.   There is bound to be formed a solid right that is determined to live in a world that no longer exists.   There is bound to be formed a scattered left, captivated by now this, now that new development, exploring now this and now that new possibility.   But what will count is a perhaps not numerous centre, big enough to be at home in both the old and the new, painstaking enough to work out one by one the transitions to be made, strong enough to refuse half-measures and insist on complete solutions even though it has to wait".[136]

CHAPTER 7

THE REVOLUTION IN ECONOMIC DYNAMICS: POINTS OF
COMPARISON.

> "There can be little doubt of the difficulty
> of changing any ingrained habit of thought or
> thinking. Keynes spoke of his 'long struggle
> to escape' from the conventional approach to
> the analysis of unemployment. Given that
> the neoclassical approach dominates the
> teaching of economics in the Western world,
> it would be surprizing if a non-neoclassical
> growth theory attained any large measure of
> acceptance independently of a transformation
> in economic theory in general".[1]

Lonergan's macroeconomics does not easily bear comparison with other contemporary authors. His analysis
resembles most clearly, perhaps, that of Adolf Lowe in
his recent book, The Path of Economic Growth, produced
at the age of 83. In the introduction Lowe remarks:
"Fifty years ago, in 1925, I published an essay outlining the stages and patterns characteristic for the
process of industrialization. This investigation was
my first contact with the problems of economic growth.
.... The search for a verifiable model of 'cyclical
growth' has remained at the centre of my writings".[2]
Later he remarks: "if so many astute minds have failed
to come up with answers satisfactory at least to themselves we cannot suppress a suspicion that they may
not have asked the right questions".[3]

Clearly then, Lowe would sympathize with the direction
of inquiry considered in section three of the previous chapter, and his suspicion is one that I have
expressed there in detail in section four. Still,
a comparative study of Lowe and Lonergan would not, I
think, help overcome the problem of communicating
Lonergan's view. For one thing, Lowe's view is
unfamiliar to the student of standard economics. Also,
Lowe's analysis has deficiencies which would cloud the
issue further: his basic analysis is of a stationary
dynamic system to which changes of rates of change have
later to be added; the generality of his analysis is
further limited by an early introduction of prices,
the priora quoad nos of economics, using a clue from

Piero Sraffa;[4] he shares too with neoclassicism a problem mentioned earlier,[5] in that the "determination of (certain) coefficients presupposes that the 'value of capital stock' is a meaningful concept".[6]

For purposes of comparison I have selected the recent textbook of Robinson and Eatwell. In the first place, it is an introductory book, so it is not inaccessible to the non-economist. Secondly, it is written, in collaboration, by a respected economist of the tradition of Keynes who spells out her criticisms of the predominant North American trends, so that an economist of the accepted viewpoint might be expected to give it a sympathetic reading. Lonergan himself remarked, at the Boston College Conference of June 1977, that he showed his typescript to various economists in the forties without success, and the situation has not changed greatly in thirty-five years. In the majority still are the "equilibrium" economists, some of them in heavy dynamic disguise.[7] There are theoreticians of the business cycle, like Hicks, on whose work Arthur Burns comments: "the result is a closely reasoned and attractively written essay about a possible cycle, but - as far as I can see - a dubious aid to students seriously concerned with the actual alterations of good and bad trade to which the Western world has been subject in modern times".[8] There is the tradition of empirical studies of business fluctuations associated with Burns himself and with his predecessor at the National Bureau of Statistics, Wesley Mitchell. T. C. Koopmans remarks on the difficulties of inquiry without preconceptions and notes that "the authors' insistence on seeing, counting and measuring cycles before anything else reminds one of Kepler's preference for circular motion".[9] There are other traditions more closely historical, such as that associated with Rostow[10] or the "New Economic History" the consideration of which, however, would take us beyond this brief sketch.[11]

There have, of course, been others in the neoclassical period, like Frish and Kalecki, who conceived of the problem of dynamic economics more adequately. Kalecki's work is now becoming better known,[12] indeed it underlies a good deal of the Robinson and Eatwell analysis, but I would like to draw attention here to the work of Ragnar Frish in the early thirties. He poses the problem clearly and undertakes an analysis that can be fruitfully compared and contrasted with Lonergan's

work.   His posing of the problem focuses the criticism of macrostatics: "the propagation problem is
the problem of explaining by the structural properties
of the swinging system what the character of the
swings would be in case the system was started in some
initial situation.   This must be done by an essentially dynamic theory, that is to say, by a theory that
explains how one situation grows out of the foregoing.
In this type of analysis we consider not only a set of
magnitudes in a given point of time and study the
interrelations between them, but we consider the magnitudes of certain variables in different points of
time, and we introduce certain equations which embrace
at the same time several of these magnitudes belonging
to different instances.   This is the essential characteristic of a dynamic theory.   Only by a theory of
this type can we explain how one type of situation
grows out of the foregoing.   The type of analysis
is basically different from the kind of analysis that
is represented by a system of Walrasian equations;
indeed in such a system all the variables belong to
the same point of time".[13]   I add on the following
page some diagrams associated with Frish's effort
towards a dynamic theory which may be usefully compared
to Lonergan's fundamental diagram as it is explained
later in the essay.   Frish's failure to develop a
significant theory typifies the failure of economists
who search for a dynamic heuristic.   As well as a
fundamental disorientation of approach there is also
a tendency to shift to an inadequate level of abstraction with a premature introduction of boundary conditions in a determinate set of differential and diff-
erence equations.   We will gradually focus on these
deficiencies.

Schumpeter speaks of the basic difficulty in economics
in terms of crossing the Rubicon: "By the phrase
'crossing the Rubicon', I mean this: however important those occasional excursions into sequence analysis
may have been, they left the main body of economic
theory on the 'static' bank of the river; the thing
to do is not to supplement static theory by the booty
brought back from these excursions but to replace it
by a system of general economic dynamics into which
statics would enter as a special case...an increasing
number of workers see the new goal; but for the time
being this is practically all..."[14]   Seeing the new
goal with such perspective as to abandon the static
bank entirely and relocate and redefine the classical

Diagrams from Frish, 1933: 157, 161.

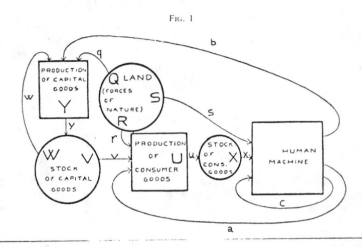

Fig. 1

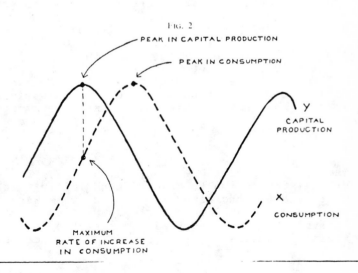

Fig. 2

and neoclassical baggage is an achievement beyond
the evidence of presently published literature.
Robinson would identify Keynes as one who sought "to
supplement static theory by the booty brought back
from excursions" into dynamics: "But if our central
controls succeed in establishing an aggregate volume
of output corresponding to full employment as nearly
as is practicable, the classical theory comes into its
own again".[15]

Robinson and Eatwell's historical survey in part one
of their book adds further dimensions to these introductory points. They conclude that survey with the
remark: "It is time to go back to the beginning and
start again".[16] We focus here on some of the characteristics of that fresh start.

Robinson and Eatwell clearheadedly settle on the
dynamic bank but, as we shall see, their classical
baggage of social relations, expectations, profits,
wages, prices etc., hamper their analysis considerably.
It is as if, to use a point already noted from an
early manuscript of Lonergan, one attempted to study
the performance of the motor car in a manner that
included the psychology of drivers, good and bad.
Lonergan's strategy, on the other hand, is to focus on
the car, to look under the bonnet, to seek out the
rhythms of the engine, to study the mechanics of motor
cars in order to find premises for a criticism of
drivers, "precisely because the motor cars, as distinct
from the drivers, have laws of their own which drivers
must respect". Robinson and Eatwell's analysis proceeds by way of simplified models, beginning with a
Richardian-type model of agricultural production, and
moving to a model for industrial production, "a simple
economy in which men work with machines to produce a
single consumption good and to produce new machines".[17]
One could draw out in detail parallels between the
treatment by Robinson and Eatwell of this simple model,
fit their various numerical illustrations into Lonergan's diagram of flows[18] and correlate the variables
in the two approaches. But what is important here is
to contrast the two methodologies.

The viewpoint of those chapters (Book 2, chapters 1-4)
of An Introduction to Modern Economics in which we are
particularly interested is succinctly expressed by the
opening paragraph of chapter two: "The foregoing
analysis was designed to illustrate the importance of
social relations in the process of production. Even

in the simple agrarian economy, social relations were
seen to dominate the way in which production was
carried on and the product distributed.   For the next
few chapters we will be concentrating on a simplified
version of an advanced capitalist economy, an economy
in which the means of production are owned by one
particular group - the capitalists - each of whom
attempts to earn profits with the stock of means of
production that he owns".   Attention here is clearly
distracted from the structure of the productive process by an equivalent to the psychology of drivers, so
that when the structure of the process shows through,
it does so without analytic bite.

Lonergan's analysis is concrete but heuristic.   It
focuses on functional relations intrinsic to the
productive process to reach eventually a general theory
of dynamic equilibria and disequilibria.   I will make
an attempt here to summarily indicate that part of
his analysis which deals with a closed economy, as a
context for reflection on Robinson and Eatwell's work.
There is a foolishness about such an attempt that I
deeply appreciate: what Lonergan's analysis needs is
elaboration, not summary.   However, there is the possibility and hope that the brief indications here,
within the context of the previous chapter, would
raise the suspicion in the bones and minds of economists that there is something there, thus getting beyond
the first stage of the fate of creative theory described by William James: "First...it is attacked as
absurd; then it is admitted to be true but obvious
and insignificant; finally it is seen to be so important that its adversaries claim that they themselves
discovered it".[19]

Indeed, one might hope to hear a claim of obviousness,
and then the issue becomes whether the theory is significant.   For it is obvious that the productive process
includes both producer and consumer goods.   Moreover,
it has been obvious to some for over a hundred years
that fluctuations are intimately associated with this
division.[20]   The question may then be, whether an
analysis based on such a division can be significant
in modern economics, where the process may involve a
spatio-temporally random aggregate of innovative
activities often indescriminately directed to producer
and consumer goods, even within planned socialism.

That question of significance cannot be seriously
tackled without some strategic elaboration of the

obvious aspect.   Let me touch then, illustratively,
on the obvious dynamic features of an elementary
exchange economy.   The illustration will help, also,
to contrast abstract model thinking with concrete
heuristic thinking.

I envisage an isolated island community, with a non-
horsepower technology.[21]   I envisage some sub-group
grasping the innovative idea of the plough, with horse,
oxen, whatever.   In so far as the sub-group carries
the community towards the realization of a plough
culture, there occur definite fluctuations in the
exchange economy (inclusive of banking etc.) of the
island.   The fluctuations are associated with the
fact that for a period energy and money are being
devoted to the carpentry, tannery, horse-training,
etc., which is to make concretely possible the
plough culture.   What is evident is that the community is building towards a period of higher consumption, greater leisure.   Less evident are the
fluctuations in the flow of finance on the island
required to make the innovation possible and eventually
to make increased consumption a reality.   But clearly
one may note an initial period of reorientation of
present resources preparatory to the emergence of a
new aggregate of capital ventures associated with
horse-ploughing; there is a following period when
production of horse-ploughs is underway, accelerating,
gradually levelling to the demands of maintenance
and replacement; there is the later period when the
benefits emerge in consumption goods and better times.

There is the obviousness, then, about the rhythms
efficient for the island economy, even if they involve
problems of monetary circulation.   But, as was noted
above, the modern economy cloaks that obviousness in
its spread of innovations and its indiscriminate
distribution of resources and talents to surplus and
basic activities.   Let me then have recourse to
parallels in astronomy and hydrodynamics to make a plea
for the significance of such an analysis as is hinted
at by the island illustration.

There is no doubt that the solar system, even macro-
dynamically speaking, involves an aggregate of bodies.
Was, then, the solution of the two-body problem
irrelevant?   Again, there is no doubt that tidal waves
are not sinusoidal.   Should we then drop the dynamic
question and settle for some equivalent of photography
and comparative statics?   Or should we not make sense

of elementary rhythms, momenta, etc., acknowledging that we are only paving the way for such developments as Fourier analysis?

Let me now return to the challenge of giving a summary impression of Lonergan's analysis of the closed economy.

The productive process must be conceived, concretely and heuristically, as an aggregate of activities proceeding from the potentialities of nature and terminating in a standard of living. One is understanding here such diverse activities as mining and managing, welding and weaving, acting and advertising. The dynamic reality of the productive process evidently does not include what has passed into the standard of living as consumer goods, but it does include the use of producer goods. An aeroplane in production is part of the process: only the commercial use of a completed aeroplane is part of the process. Immediately, here we have a central functional distinction: the productive process terminates directly in the standard of living with consumer goods (purchased); producer goods complement the potentialities of nature. The distinction can be refined to deal with higher levels of complementation: one may think of levels of machine-tools, and the levels can be related indeterminately but adequately in point-to-line, point-to-surface etc., correspondence: one last is sufficient for a line or flow of shoes, the last-making business results in a flow of flows.

The emergent standard of living is an aggregate of rates at which goods and services pass from the productive process into the standard of living. That emergence is from what may conveniently be called the basic stage of the productive process, besides which there are the series of stages which we may title "the surplus stage" characterized by the fact that their products do not enter the standard of living.

One may note immediately that the division is not a matter of social relations or of property or of the properties of things: it is a functional analysis. The distractions introduced at the beginning of the Robinson-Eatwell analysis are avoided. The aim of the analysis is to reveal the possibilities of the productive process as a dynamic system. One moves forward to that revelation in so far as one appreciates the different ways in which basic and surplus stages

may relate. Recall our island illustration: spades
and hoes may be just maintained and replaced; but
there is also the possibility of more, or more efficient, capital equipment. And with the realization
of that possibility is linked an inevitable cycle.

In dealing with the island community as illustration
we raised the question of monetary correlatives to
the productive flow. The question may bring to mind
J.-B. Say, or the Malthus-Ricardo debate, or Major
Douglas' "A + B Theorem", but consideration of such
parallels would distract from our present indications.

To reach the relevant set of correlations one must
move through a classification of payments to a specification of rates of payment.

We are dealing with a complex closed exchange economy,
and we seek out exchanges related to the divisions of
the productive process. Immediately there emerges a
remainder class of exchanges: exchanges such as
certain aspects of banking, insurance, the second-hand
trade, which are extrinsic to the productive process.
They may be called re-distributive exchanges. Exchanges intrinsic to the productive process may be called
operative, and such exchanges take on the divisions of
the productive process. Just as the productive process is an aggregate of rates of proceeding from the
potentialities of nature to the standard of living in
different ways, so there is a corresponding aggregate
of payments with their rates. There are initial
payments to factors of production; there are transitional payments between entrepreneurial units within
the process; there are final payments taking the
product out of that level of the process. The
details of precise classification can be tedious, but
the classifications are perhaps sufficiently evident
to make plausible an eight-fold division of rates of
payments, fE' (flow of basic expenditure), fE''
(surplus), fR', fR'', fO', fO'', fI', fI'': divisions
of expenditure, receipts, outlay and income. Expenditure and receipts are the familiar two aspects of
final payments, to which outlay can be related only
by allowance for lags. The flow of income in a functional analysis, however, requires somewhat more
attention: it is the corner of the analysis which
holds the key to the sublation both of Keynes' problems
of consumption, savings and investments, and of
Kalecki's dictum that the workers spend what they get
and the capitalists get what they spend.

The analysis is functional and leads us to define
five monetary functions which reveal a set of circul-
ations of money. The diagram on the following page
helps to shorten our already sketchy account. Money
held in reserve for a defined purpose is in one of
the monetary functions of supply, demand, or redistribution. The redistribution function corresponds to
the class of payments noted earlier to be extrinsic to
the productive process, and its precise isolation is
a feature of the clarity of Lonergan's analysis. It
leads later to a precise handling both of international
trade and of government operations. But more immediately interesting is the functional relating of outlay and income.

Obviously outlay and income are related:

$$fO'+fO'' = fI'+fI''.$$

But the functional division of income is determined by
recipients of income, so that basic and surplus income
can be related to basic and surplus outlay only by
cross-over ratios:

$$fI' = (I - G')fO' + G''fO'',$$
$$fI' = (I - G'')fO'' + G'fO',$$

where G' is the fraction of fO' that moves to surplus
demand, and G'' is the fraction of fO'' that moves to
basic demand.

Now whatever the difficulties of measurement, the
functional distinction is undeniably valid. Moreover,
coupled with the difficulty of measurement is the
evident difficulty of control,[22] a difficulty central
both to economic theory and to economic practice in
these past centuries. It is a difficulty associated
not just with ineffective demand, but with oscillations of two distinguishable effective demands: effective basic demand and effective surplus demand. The
monetary equivalent of these oscillations is embedded
in the immediately preceeding equations, in so far as
the cross-over ratios are envisaged as adjusting what
may be called the rate of savings to the demands of
the productive process.

One may note that little is being said about the
redistributive function. Undoubtedly the redistributive function has a role to play: the diagram
indicates possible flows which can be identified with
a variety of monetary expansions and contractions
effecting either the basic or the surplus circuit,
and indeed the diagram as shown simplifies the relations

Diagram of Transfers between Monetary Functions

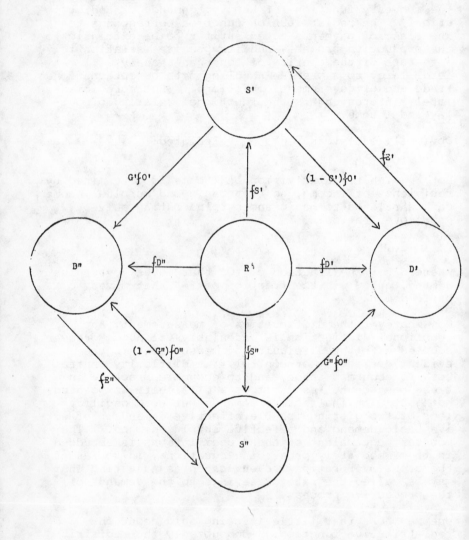

of the cross-overs to the redistributive function.
Again, later parts of Lonergan's analysis reveal that
apart from an essential role in the oscillations of
economic expansion, there is a role of redistribution
in catering for maladjustment of the rate of savings
to the rhythms of the process.

However, I focus attention away from the redistributive
function in order to bring out a more elementary but
fundamental point. That fundamental point is that,
in the absence of an adequate heuristic, an absence
to which we will shortly return, the redistributive
function - which we associate not only with banking,
stock-marketing, etc., but also with government operations and international economics - can become what
I might call an escape hatch of apparent efficiency.
The 19th century version of that escape hatch was a
target of leftist criticism: the strategy of a favour-
able balance of payments easily realized in colonial
structures. Twentieth century leftist criticism is
partly in continuity with that tradition, but fits
also to the Keynesian escape-hatch tradition of deficit
spending, taxation and monetary policy. In all these
criticized cases what is regularly present is, not an
adjustment of the rate of savings to the efficient
cyclic functioning of the productive process, but an
adjustment of the productive process to the rate of
savings leading to a variety of trade cycles and, in
particular, to an exclusion of the full benefits of
the basic expansion. Speaking historically one may
recall that although Britain experienced a series of
significant take-offs from the late 18th century
on, wage rates did not increase until 1870; speaking
in terms of our illustrative island, one may find the
community exporting ploughing equipment and dodging,
by accident or design, the issue of the egalitarian
shift in income called for by the shift of economic
phase from surplus expansion to basic expansion.

These comments, I hope, make evident the need for a
prior attention to the productive process of the closed
economy in the rhythmic demands of its two fundamental
circuits. Our island illustration could bear the
burden of detailed analytic development, an analytic
development which would parallel but leave methodologically behind the detailed analysis Robinson and
Eatwell give of their model of a simple industrial
economy. Lonergan's detailed analysis remains
unpublished, and so here I can only give indications

and ask for an admission of plausibility. I have
already grounded the plausibility: one may envisage,
in an innovative take-off of some significance, an
initial period of all-round expansion leading to a
surplus expansion; the surplus expansion involves
the emergence of the aggregate of equipment required
for basic expansion, at a rate which increases to a
maximum and levels off, without necessary decline, to
cater for replacement and maintenance; the consequent
basic expansion is characterized by the egalitarian
income shift already noted, coupled with the decrease
of that part of surplus income available, not for
replacement and maintenance, but for new expansions.
Let me then turn to some further specification of our
divergence from Robinson and Eatwell.

I have already noted that suppositions regarding social
relations are out of place in the early stages of the
analysis. But meshed with such suppositions in
Robinson and Eatwell are suppositions regarding profits, expectations, etc., which cripple the analysis:
indeed these suppositions have been long since recog-
nized by Robinson as problematic for economic
analysis.[23] For an analysis to be capable of accounting generally for dynamic equilibria and disequilibria
it must take its start from some such supposition as
"suppose we have an efficiently equilibrated dynamic
economy". The Robinson and Eatwell analysis, on the
contrary, is laced with such suppositions as "suppose
that in the corn sector the wage is $3/4$ of a unit per
year, and 1 man produces 1 unit of corn per year. Then
in the corn sector, the ratio of profits to wages is:

$$1/_4 : 3/_4 \quad \text{or} \quad 1:3 \ldots \text{"}[24]$$

One might be reminded here of a parallel in hydrodynamics: if what is at issue is a general specification of the dynamics of free water waves, a premature
introduction of general boundry conditions or worse,
specific channel conditions, botches the analytic
possibilities. But the issue, as we shall see, is
more complex in economics. Technically, one may say
that the Robinson and Eatwell analysis is hampered,
not only by an absence of paradigmatic heuristic
thinking in a field whose principles involve ends,
but also by their building the economic priora quoad
nos of profits, wages, prices etc., into the explanation, when in fact the priora quoad nos are last in
analysis: they require explanation.

As Robinson herself points out, in the conclusion of
her Economic Heresies: "It is easy enough to make
models on stated assumptions. The difficulty is to
find the assumptions that are relevant to reality. The
art is to set up a scheme that simplifies the problem
so as to make it manageable without eliminating the
essential character of the actual situation on which
it is intended to throw light. Keynes found out that
the doctrines still orthodox in the inter-war period
were drawn from models which require the assumption
that the wage bargain is made in terms of the employ-
er's product and that the decisions of households to
save govern the rate of investment that firms undertake. These assumptions have been smuggled back
into neoclassical models".25

The models in A Modern Introduction to Economics escape
the static bank symbolised by Leon Walras; they escape
the confusions regarding "capital" and "leets" and
other "substances" of much modern theory,26 but they
represent only a half-way house to the methodological
model of circulation analysis. That model and that
analysis involves an enlargement of perspective and a
proper ordering of assumptions. In chapters one and
six I have already discussed the enlarged perspective
of Praxisweltanschauung: what we are more closely
dealing with in the present context is the ordering
of assumptions in that perspective. But I must note
immediately how intimately the ordering is within the
perspective: "as the hypothesis is the principle in
mathematics so the end is the principle in praxis".27
The movement of Lonergan's analysis might be described
as a paradigmatic descent from a concrete heuristic of
the productive process determined by the end of that
process. The monetary order is conditioned by, and
correlated to, the rhythms of production adequate to
the end. Only later in the analysis can one arrive
at an adequate account of the monetary distributions
commonly called wages and profits. That account
springs from a characterization of possible types of
productive rhythms which lead to the specification of
adequate human adaptation to the demands of the process,
and also to a determination of inadequate strategies
of adaptation such as variations of interest rates,
varieties of taxation and monetary policy, and unbal-
anced international trade. Thus, for example, one
determines the oscillations of basic income which
may be briefly described as anti-egalitarian during
surplus expansions but egalitarian during basic

expansions. Again, distinctions are required within
surplus income: what requires attention during expansion is that fraction of it, which we may call pure
surplus income, that goes to new fixed investment. It
is evidently subject to cyclic variation. Of it
Lonergan wrote in the early forties: "At the root of
the depression lies a misinterpretation of the significance of pure surplus income. In fact, it is the
monetary equivalent of the new fixed investment of an
expansion: just as the production of new fixed investment is over-and-above all current consumption and
replacement products, so pure surplus income is over-
and-above all current consumption and replacement
income; just as the products of new fixed investment
emerge in cyclic fashion, so also does pure surplus
income emerge in cyclic fashion. It is mounting
from zero at a moderate pace in the proportionate
expansion; it is mounting at an enormous pace in the
surplus expansion; but in the basic expansion first,
average, and then, aggregate pure surplus begin to
decline and eventually they have reverted to zero.
Now it is true that our culture cannot be accused of
mistaken ideas on pure surplus income as it has been
defined in this essay; for on that precise topic it
has no ideas whatever".[28] A lengthier analysis could
make evident how we have institutionalized that absence
of ideas ever more firmly in the corporate and finan-
cial structures of the past thirty years.

Against this background one may return to the weakness
of the structuring of assumptions in the best of modern
economcs. Robinson and Eatwell discussed Sraffa's
work "in order to understand the central problem of
economic philosophy - the nature of profits".[29] What
Sraffa's work shows, indeed, is that the nature of
profits is not the central problem of economics:
without an analysis such as Lonergan's, the nature of
profits cannot be determined.

Finally, the analysis of the closed economy comes to
the issue of prices, the most manifest priora quoad
nos of economic activity. But before indicating
the direction of that analysis I would like to add some
comments on the shift across the Rubicon.

I recall, somewhat fully, Schumpeter's considerations
of economic statics and dynamics, considerations
influenced by Ragnar Frish: "By static analysis we
mean a method of dealing with economic phenomena that
tries to establish relations between elements of the

economic system - prices and quantities of commodities - all of which have the same time subscript,
that is to say, refer to the same point of time. The
ordinary theory of demand and supply in the market of
an individual commodity as taught in every textbook
will illustrate this case: it related demand, supply,
and price as they are supposed to be at any moment of
observation - nothing else is taken into consideration.

But the elements of the economic system that interact
at a given point of time are evidently the result of
preceeding configurations; and the way itself in
which they interact is not less evidently influenced
by what people expect future configurations to be.
Thus, to keep to our example, we may conceive of the
situation in our market as determined, or at least
influenced by previous decisions of producers which
cannot be understood from the conditions of the point
of time chosen for observation but only from the conditions that prevailed at the time when those decisions
were taken.   Hence we are led to take into account
past and (expected) future values of our variables,
lags, sequences, rates of change, cumulative magnitudes, expectations, and so on.   The methods that aim
at doing this constitute economic dynamics".30

Now, what I wish to draw attention to is a possible
oversight in reading these paragraphs.   "Hence we
are led to take into account past and (expected) future
values..."   But such a taking into account does not
constitute the creative key transition to dynamics.
Those familiar with elementary statics and dynamics
will appreciate the shift in thinking involved in
passing from equilibrium analysis - even if one is
discussing virtual displacements - to an analysis
where attention is focused on second-order differential
equations, on $\ddot{\theta}$, $\ddot{x}$, $\ddot{y}$, on a range of related forces,
central, friction, whatever.   Particular boundry
conditions, "past and future values", are relatively
insignificant for the analysis.   What is significant
is the Leibnitz-Newtonian shift of context.   As
second-order differential equations are the upper blade
in large areas of physics, as the heuristics of genetic
development are the upper blade for an integral study
of plants, so a Praxisweltanschauung on efficient world
productivity provides the upper blade for dynamic
economics.

The question of prices, then, last in Lonergan's analysis of the closed economy, is faced within the

developed dynamic perspective. (I - G')fO' and
G"fO" are conveniently named costs. A basic price-
spread ratio, J, being a selling-price index, $\bar{P}'$,
over a cost-price index, p', can be defined as:

$$J = \frac{\bar{P}'}{p'} = a'+a''R,$$ where a' is a basic acceleration factor (related to the usual lag: today's costs
buy products of an earlier date), a" is a surplus
acceleration factor, and R is a measure of surplus
to basic activity. A heuristic analysis of $\partial J/\partial t$
over the phases of an economic expansion reveals
cyclic fluctuations of the basic price spread which
are reminiscent of cycles noted by Kitchin, Crum, and
Juglar.

These last summary statements are inadequate to generating comprehension. They are, rather, impressionistic of the results of a unique strategy, the creative
possibilities, I am sadly sure, will not reach the
streets during this century. The present issue is,
will they reach the academy?[31]

CHAPTER 8

LONERGAN'S QUEST AND THE TRANSFORMATION OF THE
MEANING OF LIFE.

I am very pleased to be with you this evening at the
beginning of the College's courageous project of
enormous promise.[1]   In 1970 an international gather-
ing in Florida honoured Fr. Bernard Lonergan and the
slogan "ongoing collaboration" was in the air, but in
the seventies there were few signs of serious collaboration. More recently, in a series of lectures to
be delivered this year in Australia in honour of
Lonergan's 75th year, Fr. Frederick Crowe speaks of
the giant challenge to theology of Lonergan's organum
novissimum and discomfortingly indicates the 50 or 100
years required to get some main ideas on the move.
Fr. Crowe talks too of the need for institutions where
the conditions of collaboration would be present.
Such an institution is present in embryo in Lonergan
College: indeed Lonergan College goes beyond the
scope of Fr. Crowe's considerations, for he is considering a renewal of theology, while the reach of Lonergan College is to the wider task of a renewal of cult-
uré and a transformation of modernity. Moreover, I
would see a danger in an institution not explicitly
concerned with that wider task, a danger of which, I
have no doubt, Fr. Crowe is aware. For Fr. Crowe and
I share the view expressed in Lonergan's Introduction
to his Method in Theology, "A theology mediates between
a cultural matrix and the significance and role of a
religion in that matrix". There can be no adequate
theological mediation if the cultural matrix is not
atttended to, understood, put in perspective, criticized and transformed, in symbiosis with the best of
modern science and scholarship. Such a symbiosis is
a key feature of Lonergan College.

As my title indicates, however, I wish to discuss the
challenge and the promise of Lonergan's perspective
not as it will effect the College in, say, the next
fifty years, but as that promise emerged in the last
fifty years of Lonergan's efforts, efforts so well

characterized by his own description in Insight of the intellectual pattern of experience: "To learn thoroughly is a vast undertaking that calls for relentless perseverence. To strike out on a new line and become more than a week-end celebrity calls for years in which one's living is more or less constantly absorbed in the effort to understand, in which one's understanding gradually works round and up a spiral of viewpoints with each complementing its predecessor and only the last embracing the whole field to be mastered".[2] My title further indicates that I wish to specify that quest, that relentless effort to understand, in its concrete concern for the transformation of the meaning of life. In doing so I am first of all dissociating Lonergan from Eric Voegelin's criticism of a long history of reasoning subtly contributing to what Voegelin calls "The murderous grotesque of our time".[3] More proximately, I am dealing with a popular misconception of Lonergan's work as highly and remotely intellectual and detached. I will do so both by drawing attention to aspects of Lonergan's life and work which are little known, and by slanting the achievement of his better known works towards concrete living the transformation of which is the goal of that serious type of reflection which Lonergan has recently been calling Praxis. Such a slanting will undoubtedly involve popularization and shortcutting, and here I ask for the patience of the experts. After twenty years of grappling with Lonergan's meaning I have no doubt about the proximate relevance of his thought for the men and women in streets, subways, offices and churches, for those who govern, for those who teach, for those who enter kindergarden. It is this proximate relevance that I wish to intimate in the short time at our disposal.

There are two areas in particular in which Lonergan's concern for daily living has been expressed vigorously, although his work in these fields remains largely unpublished. These are the areas of art and of economics, and I will say something about his perspective in each of these areas, for that perspective leads eloquently to a rounded view of the man, his life, his quest. I have already noted the absence of such a rounded view, and the adverse effect of such an absence will become clearer as we proceed. I recall now one questioner at the Florida conference - surely he was some type of rationalist - who asked Fr. Lonergan whether it was through reading Scheler that he, Lonergan, discovered feelings. Lonergan looked at him through a Beethoven pause and then remarked: "I've got feelings too"!

I come directly to my first topic, art and concrete
living, by quoting Lonergan's own feelingful words,
spoken at the beginning of a lecture on art during a
summer school which he gave on education in 1959.
He remarked: "What I want to communicate in this talk
on art is the notion that art is relevant to concrete
living, that it is an exploration of the potentialities
of concrete living, that it is extremely important in
our age when philosophers for at least two centuries,
through doctrines on economics, politics and education,
have been trying to remake man and have done not a
little to make human life unlivable".

Over the years I have heard Lonergan, in private and
in public, speak of the dimensions of that unlivability, and of the centuries-old disorientation at its
root which, as he noted in the preface of Insight,
"springs from a communal flight from understanding and
is supported by the whole texture of civilization".[4]

The unlivability of which he speaks is the fabric of
our uncreative workdays and our shrunken fun.   It is
the mindlessness, at the lower level, of the deceitful
jingles of the ads., and at the higher level of the
plannings of boards of higher education and government bureaucracies.   Lonergan spoke of the importance
of art, in all its forms, in countering that unlife.
For art is a vital liberation of sensibility, a lifting of the person out of the ready-made world, a
translation from the pressures of home and office,
economics and politics, from the time of daily doing
to the time of the music, from the print and prose of
news and science to language no longer instrument of
literal meaning but pool of psychic possibilities.
It is a withdrawal from practicality to an exploration of the possibilities of living in a richer world.

There is the painting, which draws men out of the
weary space of common life into a virtual.space, a
space which is not real, which is not measured by the
steps of the fly walking on the canvas.   There is
music and song which may open man to his history and
his potentialities, revealing to him through layers of
resonances the meaning of his life, his people, his
world.   There is the dance, calling forth virtual
powers and dynamic tensions.   There is sculpture,
the objectification of self and environment for the
sense of sight.   There is the statue and there is

architecture, related to each other as the lyric and
the drama. While the statue is a visual presentation
of the space that feels which is man, architecture is
expressive of the orientation of a people. So one
may come to consider the broader objectification of
human meaning, the manscaped landscape of country and
city. It is the product of meaning and meaningless-
ness, with street names and land structures echoing
the rich or thinned existential memory and orientation
of the people. That dialectic of meaning and meaning-
lessness may, in our time, have left the city soulless
in unfelt fields, its heart the haunt of admen, pulsing
with hasty movement, encompassed by beige suburban
dullness. So there stands the challenge of man's sensibility and creativity, a challenge of ultimate significance, for, to quote from the conclusion of Lonergan's lecture on art, "man is nature's priest and
nature is God's silent communing with man". Such
is Lonergan's view on the significance of art, on the
importance of what he calls, with Vico, the priority
of poetry in human life. Such too is his view, a
perspective enabling the survival of the unsurvivable,
of the cosmos as Word, a view so brilliantly enlarged
on by Fr. Crowe when he writes of the Cosmic Word of
God.5

At this stage, however, I find it convenient to locate
Lonergan's quest, in particular his searchings into
economics, more concretely in the events of his life.

Born in Buckingham, Quebec, in 1904, Lonergan's first
venture into formal philosophy was in the Jesuit Schol-
asticate of Heythrop College in Oxfordshire in the
late twenties. Suarezianism was the main diet there,
so Lonergan turned to Newman's Grammer of Assent
and to illustrations of insight relating to mathematics.
It was at this early stage that he became interested
in economics. Fr. Lewis Watt, the professor of ethics,
was writing a book on Capitalism and Democracy and
posed the problem bluntly: you starve the workers to
keep capitalism going, or you feed the workers and
ruin capitalism. A further stimulus to his interest,
on his return to Canada in 1930, was the depression
and the emergence of William Aberhart's Social Credit
Movement in Alberta. The movement was based on the
views of a Scottish engineer, Major Clifford Douglas
(1878-1952). As assistant director of the Royal
Aircraft Works in England during the first world war,
Douglas made comprehensive studies of cost accounting
which led him to the view that, in over 100 industrial

establishments, the weekly sum-total of wages and
salaries was continuously less than the weekly
collective price of the goods produced. This led him
to his famous A + B theorem: according to Douglas,
there is a permenent discrepancy between A (the pur-
chasing power of consumers) and A + B (the total cost
of production). The view leads to a requirement of
consumer credit, a requirement manifest in the Social
Credit Movement launched by Aberhart in the autumn of
1932. Lonergan has remarked to me about his continued
interest in economics in the thirties: "I wanted to
find out what was wrong with social credit". So,
while he taught classics until 1933, when he returned
to Rome to study theology, his files of handwritten
notes and of incomplete typescripts bear witness to
the breadth of his reading and the depth of his thinking about economic process over a period of about
fourteen years. In 1944 he had a complete and coherent typescript of about 130 pages entitled <u>Circulation
Analysis</u>. He made that manuscript available to a
number of economists at the time, but the reaction was
one of incomprehenşion. Why that was so has already
been discussed in the two previous chapters. Lonergan
returned the analysis to his file, and as we shall see,
moved into deeper areas of inquiry. I myself knew
nothing of this solitary search and achievement until
the summer of 1968 when I received a postcard from
Lonergan asking whether I knew of any economist who
would read his manuscript and assist in revising its
terminology. The next day I received a second postcard from him indicating that the first card had been
stimulated by his reading of Metz' political theology,
and added the comment that the basis of economic
morality was to be found, not in some view of the family
wage, but in an adequate economic analysis. In the
years since, neither Lonergan nor I have succeeded in
finding the economist. A few years ago I settled
down to the uncomfortable task of trying to understand
Lonergan's 130 page typescript. Slowly and sweatily
the incredible achievement dawned on me: Lonergan had
done for economics what Kepler, Newton, Laplace, had
done for astronomy. Furthermore, a serious reconsid-
eration of the history of economic theory and practice
in the past two hundred years leaves the classic instance of scientific obtuseness, the philogiston debate,
quite in the shade. Nicholas Kaldor locates, with
remarkable precision, where economic theory went wrong.
In the Cambridge Economic Journal of 1972 he remarks:
"The difficulty with a new start is to pinpoint the

critical area where economic theory went astray ... I
would put it in the middle of the fourth chapter of
Vol.I of The Wealth of Nations ... in (that) chapter,
after discussing the need for money in a social economy,
Smith suddenly gets fascinated by the distinction between money price, real price, and exchange value and
from then on, hey presto, his interest gets bogged
down in the question of how values and prices for products and factors are determined.   One can trace a
more or less continuous development of price theory
from the subsequent chapters of Smith through Ricardo,
Walras, Marshall, right up to Debreu and the most
sophisticated present-day Americans".[6]   Leon Walras'
economic statics of the 1870's,[7] influenced by a notion
of general equilibrium, derived from an engineer,[8]
dominates economic thinking in this past century.
Whatever was of value in Marshall and Keynes evaporated
in the simplification, the IS/LM analysis, proposed by
John Hicks in 1937.[9]   Hicks' view is the backbone of
modern textbooks in economics especially in Canada and
in the United States.[10]

There is, however, another tradition of economic
thinkers interested in economic dynamics: one may
recall Clément Juglar,[11] Karl Marx,[12] Wesley Mitchell,
[13] Joseph Schumpeter,[14] Adolf Lowe.[15]   But for a complex variety of theoretical, historical, personal, and
political reasons they have had little impact on standard economic thinking.   Besides, their positions may
be considered as lacking what Lonergan calls, in an
early unpublished economic manuscript, "the imperious
pressure of really significant ideas".   And I do not
think that I could conclude better my comment on
Lonergan's dedicated work on economics than by quoting
rather fully, indeed a page or so, from that incomplete
and unavailable typescript:

"...as makeshift follows makeshift, it becomes increasingly difficult to distinguish between a democratic
and a totalitarian economy.

But economists can be champions of democracy as well
as advisers to dictators or planning boards.   The
proof of the possibility is an historical fact: the
old political economists were champions of democracy;
and if the content of their thought has been found
inadequate, its democratic form is as valid today as
ever.   That form consisted in the discovery of an
economic mechanism and in the deduction of rules to
guide men in the use of the economic machine, a rule
of laisser faire for governments and a rule of thrift

and enterprise for individuals. It is now fully
apparent that these rules serve their purpose only in
particular cases, but it is still insufficiently grasped that new and more satisfactory rules have to be
devised. Without them human liberty will perish.
For either men learn rules to guide them individually
in the use of the economic machine, or else they surr-
ender their liberty to be ruled along with the machine
by a central planning board.

The reality of that dilemma measures the significance
of an effort, however tenuous and incomplete, to formulate the laws of an economic mechanism more remote
and, in a sense, more fundamental than the pricing
system. Now there is little dispute that the dilemma
is real, for the liberal dream of an automatic economy
has, like all dreams, at long last broken. The necessity of rational control has ceased to be a question,
and the one issue is the locus of that control. Is it
to be absolutist, from above downwards? Is it to be
democratic from below upwards? Plainly it can be
democratic only in the measure in which economic
science succeeds in uttering not counsel to rulers but
precepts to mankind, not specific remedies and plans
to increase the power of bureaucracies, but universal
laws which men themselves administrate in the personal
conduct of their lives. Thus the breaking of the
liberal dream of automatic progress provokes a revision of judgment on the old political economists. Their
greatness lay not in fostering an amoral devotion to
automatism but in developing an economic science and
from it issuing universal precepts of proper economic
conduct. The automatism is a husk that has withered
and fallen, and to cling to it is to fall into the
totalitarian abyss. The old science and the old
precepts have gone the way of Ptolemy and Newton. But
to deny the possibility of a new science and new
precepts is, I am convinced, to deny the possibility
of the survival of democracy".

In his recent book, entitled, The Path of Economic
Growth, Adolf Lowe, at the age of 83, indicates that
the problem of economic dynamics has preoccupied him -
I would say without total success - for 50 years.
What I have been touching on just now is Lonergan's
solitary and successful preoccupation with the same
problem during fourteen years, a preoccupation which,
in the light of his other work at the time, would seem
to merit the name of a distraction. For, by 1940 he
had completed his first major study of Aquinas, his

doctorate thesis on Grace and Freedom substantially published in the early forties in Theological Studies and more recently in a book.[16]   It was a monumental achievement, rescuing Aquinas from a long history of Jesuit/Dominican debates regarding grace, time, eternity, predestination.   But, if one takes that work in the personalist existential perspective that is our present interest, it is a central liberation of the thinking man, towards adult growth - in the sense harmonious with that intimated by Maslow, Aresteh, Progoff - in his collaboration with God in the making of man and the ongoing transformation of the meaning of life.

Lonergan left Italy at the edge of war in 1940 and began his teaching in the Jesuit seminary in Montreal. To his concern about economic life, and about the life of understanding and truth revealed by Aquinas, were added various theological concerns, one only of which I will note.

Professor Doms of Breslau had opened up, in the thirties, some thorny issues on the nature and end of marriage.   The Holy Office cut off discussion in March 1944, ruling as inadmissable the opinion of certain writers who either denied that the generation and education of children was the primary end of marriage or taught that secondary ends were not essentially subordinated to the primary.   Meantime, however, Lonergan had thought the matter through: his views appeared in Theological Studies of 1943 under the title "Finality, Love, Marriage".   It is a brilliant elucidation of the dynamics of love and marriage within a comprehensive view of world process, but like Joseph Schumpeter's study of Business Cycles, published in 1939, its appearance was untimely: if Hicks, Hansen and the war killed interest in economic dynamics, the Holy Office and the war on heresy killed interest in sexual dynamics.   Yet in Lonergan's article was the kernel of the solution to a problem which has troubled the Catholic Church publicly since the emergence of that unfortunate encyclical Humanae Vitae.   Lonergan found the encyclical a depressing expression of an unthinking establishment but did not enter into controversy on the subject.   His perspective, however, may be gleaned from the quip, picked up by him, if I recall correctly, from Fr. Lewis Watt in Heythrop: "Contraception is no more immoral than shaving".   More technically, however, Lonergan's view can be put as follows. An activity's intrinsic finality cannot include as essential end an effect which is related to that activity only statistically.   Aristotle in his work on

The Generation of Animals gave a view of the process
of conception somewhat akin to sculpting which would
support a view of conception as an essential end: but
Aristotle could not have been expected to anticipate
the results of 19th century biology. One might,
however, have expected someone in Rome to have noted
the passing of Aristotle's view.

In the mid-forties Lonergan began his second major
study of Aquinas, published in 1967 as a book entitled
Word and Idea in Aquinas but at that stage (1946-49),
it appeared as a series of articles in Theological
Studies. There are many ways of characterizing what
Lonergan achieved in that period, but I would here
characterize it in continuity with my title as the
core specification of the necessary contemporary transformation of the meaning of life. Let me try and
indicate that core specification in somewhat popular
fashion. David Riesman, in his book The Lonely Crowd[17]
presents a study of the transition of American culture
from the inner-directedness of the Founding Fathers
to the present other-directedness of people whose conversation has decayed into patterns of convenient
expected and expedient response. One may think here
of an upper-management cocktail party, with its
"looking-over-the-shoulder" minute talks calculated to
make sure that one meets the right people and that one
says the right things to them. One may think here,
too, of the lyrics of many of Paul Simon's songs summed
up in these words from "The Sounds of Silence": "people
talking without speaking, people hearing without listening". Our times are times of abundant non-conver-
sation, and so it is vital to raise the issue "what
constitutes a real conversation"? Moreover, as I
wish now to indicate, that issue is identical with the
quest for some grasp of the nature of the Christian
Divinity.

So, if one asks who is God and what is the Trinity the
answers may come in the form of four questions.[18]
There is the basic question, "When did I last have a
real conversation"?, and its threefold specification,
"When was I last understanding, understood"?, "When
did I last speak"?, "When did I last listen"? That
there is a theological dimension to these questions
emerges when one recalls, and I quote Lonergan, "God
is the unrestricted act of understanding, the eternal
rapture glimpsed in every Archimedian cry of Eureka".[19]
The four questions broaden the strategy towards a
glimpse of the Christian God. Thus, in so far as one

has tried to understand one's own real conversations, one has tried to understand the unique image of the Triune God. So, for example, in so far as one has really spoken, really flowed forth in word and gesture, one has data through which, by dedicated contemplative reflection, one may glimpse what occurs in God. There is speech in God, in an ambience of Unrestricted Understanding. That speech is not about God: it is God, a single rapturous Word. Again, in so far as one has listened, not merely with ear but with understanding eye and heart and toe muscle, then one may reflectively move to some glimpse of that absorbent Joyous Ear of God which is the Spirit. Such is the profound coincidence of the core of human meaning and of our grasp of the Christian Trinity. I must add that the real conversations of which I speak need not be linguistically revelatory of the deep joys and sorrows of those who converse. They may also be of the type of conversation which Georg Simmel discusses in his "Sociology of Sociability" where friends flow forth in purposeless speech, or such conversation as is intimated by Rainer Maria Rilke's words: "love consists in this, that two solitudes guard and bind and greet one another". Finally, I must note that the nature of all such conversation and of God is plumbed centrally through solitary self-attention and self-discovery. Towards the end of his book Riesman remarks: "If the other-directed people should discover how much needless work they do, discover that their own thoughts and their own lives are quite as interesting as other people's, that, indeed, they no more assuage their loneliness in crowds of peers than one can assuage one's thirst by drinking sea water, then we might expect them to become more attentive to their own feelings and aspirations".[20]   Lonergan, in profounder but parallel fashion, speaks of the neglected subject that does not know himself and, worse still, of the truncated subject who not only does not know himself but has no knowledge of this lack of knowledge.[21]

The book Insight was seriously undertaken by Lonergan in 1949, though its structure is already visible in unpublished notes from a Thomas More Institute course of 1945, and its seeds are already present in short articles written by Lonergan when he was studying philosophy in England in the late twenties. Apart from consultations with the mathematician Eric O'Connor, now of the Thomas More Institute in Montreal, regarding some early chapters, Lonergan seems to have worked

ahead in solitary fashion.   Fr. Crowe of Regis
College, Toronto, recalled to me the day in 1953
when Lonergan came into his room with a surprizing
1,500 page typescript for Crowe's perusal.   Later
Fr. Crowe took four months to produce an outstanding
index and the 785 page book appeared in 1957.

In this context I would like to recall an evening I
spent with Lonergan in Halifax in October 1974.   We
were listening, after dinner, to some music - Brahms'
D Minor piano concerto and Beethoven's Kreuzer Sonata
for piano and violin among other things - and I became aware of his enormous perceptiveness.   My curiosity about his background in music drew him out.   I
recall his remarking; "well, it got me through Insight",
and I recall, too, the delight with which he told me
of first hearing the Kreuzer, his eyes bright with
recollection of the small boy that he was pausing in
a garden when he overheard his mother playing a piano
version of the sonata.

The book Insight can be characterized in a large
number of ways.   Much later, in Method in Theology,
Lonergan speaks of the challenge of modernity and
the need for an adequate apprenticeship in order to
deal clearly and accurately and explanatorily with
that modernity.   He concludes a paragraph specifying
that modernity in a manner which echos the table of
contents of the first part of Insight with the statement: "To say it all with the greatest brevity: one
has not only to read Insight but also to discover
oneself in oneself".22   Insight is a strategically
structured invitation to come to grips, through a
generalized empirical method, with the data which is
generically the inner dynamism of our human consciousness in its reach towards beauty, understanding, truth
and value.   That reaching is what fundamentally gives
meaning to life, and one might popularly describe the
reaching in each of us as minding.   Here I recall again
Paul Simon's lyric: "people talking without speaking,
people hearing without listening" and I add a third
phrase, "people living without minding", so, echoing
Fr. Lonergan's statement quoted earlier about the
unlivability of life in our times.   One can note immediately that we are close to our title "Lonergan's Quest
and the Transformation of the Meaning of Life", when
we note that the basic quest of Insight is a minding
of minding which would mediate a new level of livability.
Lonergan speaks in Insight of "a transforming reorientation of ... scientific opinions and ... commonsense".23

Here I draw attention to an obvious point, that transformed commonsense means transformed patterns of daily
perceptions, understandings, truthfulness, and the
dynamics of goodness; it means a larger public epiphany
of what man is, in a modern world which is a mess and
mesh of systems relentlessly persuading man that he is
much less than what he is.   I recall now Narziss'
introduction of the single word as epiphany, in Herman
Hesse's novel.[24]   I recall Stephen Hero's view of art
as epiphany, and I quote here Harry Levin's Introduction to The Essential James Joyce, "...a sudden illum-
ination, if not a divine revelation, a slight but
definite insight into other lives, a fragmentary clue
to the meaning of life as a whole.   Even the stroke
of the Ballast Office clock can have this effect, says
Stephen, and we may regard Ulysses as an extended
commentary on his remark.   God is manifest, Stephen
now believes, as 'a noise in the street'".   If art
contributes to that epiphany much more so does the
minding of minding to which Insight invites us.

I cannot delay here to speak of the transformation of
science, itself a mediation of concrete living, to
which Insight invites the modern scientist and philosopher.   I can only briefly note in passing the enormous potentiality in the work for a renewal of foundational work in mathematics, for a clarification of
the obscurities of present physics and chemistry, and
for the rescuing of botany and zoology from the pressures of reductionism.[25]   Moreover, such renewal and
clarification and rescuing ultimately ground a technology of liberation and an unimaginable renewal of
our oneness with nature.

In 1953 Lonergan began teaching at the Gregorian
University in Rome.   He taught courses in Trinitarian
theology and in Christology, and the massive Latin
texts which he produced during those years show the
same capacity for cutting through controversy and
generating profound theological insights.   But the
fundamental drive of the eleven years he was in Rome
was towards a solution to the problems of modernity,
and of specialization, and of understanding in
theology.

I do not wish to describe here that well-known set of
problems, nor the strategy that sublates them.   I
wish rather to specify the achievement of Lonergan's
Method in Theology in a way that relates to my title,
that dovetails with my description of Insight, and
that brings out the role of Method in Theology in

specifying academic life of the 21st century.

I recall now Ezra Pound's figure of "words as elec-
trified cones, charged with the power of tradition,
of centuries of race continuousness, of agreement,
of association", expressive of Vorticist aspiration[26]
to digest and bring forth the past. The book Method
in Theology goes profoundly beyond Vorticist aspirations in its precise specification of Simmel's Wendung zue Idee, of the present minding of past minding
which is required to transform the future minding
of men, women and children.

I have occasionally, not entirely frivolously, drawn
a parallel between Joyce's Ulysses and Finegans Wake
and, on the other hand, Lonergan's Insight and Method
in Theology. Stuart Gilbert remarked once, regarding
Joyce's Work in Progress, as it was called, in the
twenties, "The subject of Work in Progress may easiest
be grasped by a reference to Vico's Scienza Nuova.[27]
In 1959, during the "work in progress" towards Method,
Lonergan remarked in a book review, "I am led to
believe that the issue, which goes by the name of a
Christian philosophy, is basically a question on the
deepest level of methodology, the one that investigates
the operative ideals not only of scientists and philosophers but also, since Catholic truth is involved,
theologians. It is, I fear, in Vico's phrase a
'scienza nuova'".[28] What had been embryonically in
the tail of Ulysses came forth in the Wake, an enormous novel circularity, "a gigantic epiphany of mankind".[29] So too, what, in a sense, was embryonic in
the tail of Insight came forth, a novel vortex strategy,
and it is the heuristic of an ongoing gigantic epiphany
of mankind, a methodology which transforms the meaning
of academic life.

That transformation has been our topic throughout the
present volume, but here I will recall two illustrations, previously fully discussed[30] of the need for the
functional specializations detailed in Method in Theology. There is the field of musicology, and here the
American journal, Perspectives of New Music may be
taken as symbolic of the crises, conflicts and fragmentation. David Lewin remarks, in an article in
that journal entitled "Behind the Beyond": "what is
needed to clear the air is first an exposition of the
nature of and relations among theory, analysis and
criticism, then secondly, an examination of the pertin-
ence of all this to compositional procedure".[31] What

is needed, indeed, as one finds when one investigates
the literature on ethnomusicology, history of music,
musical traditions and innovation, music criticism and
composition, is seen to be a deep heuristics of musical
meaning, structuring not only the enterprizes of music-
ologists, but mediating a transformation of musical
experience through the transformation of human subjects.

We have already considered in detail the parallel
aggregate of problems in literary studies, where Paul
de Man's book, Blindness and Insight may be taken, in
title and content, as symbolic of the problematic.
The confusion regarding "the self that judges, the
self that writes, the self that reads, the self that
reads itself"[32] is a confusion which characterizes not
just contemporary literary studies but all of contemporary aesthetics.

Since the completion of Method in Theology in 1970,
Lonergan has written and lectured on a wide range of
topics relating to theology, adding subtle refinements
to his already complex world-view. At times I think
of him in these years in relation to Beethoven of the
last quartets and I recall the comment of George Marek,
a recent biographer of Beethoven: "The works which
occupied him almost exclusively in the last years were
the final five string quartets. These late-harvest
products are unique, unique for Beethoven, unique in
all music. The quartets carry music to a summit of
exaltation and to the deepest depth of feeling".[33]
More regularly I think of Lonergan in these years in
terms of an image that emerges in the final page of
Marcel Proust's great novel, Remembrance of Time Past.
It is the image of the elder towering in meaning, as
it were on giant stilts.

The man "on giant stilts" is at present giving a sem-
inar in Boston College on economics, labouring beyond
his present energy to enlarge on, and communicate a
view of, economics that seems to be little more acceptable now than it was in 1944. It is a view potent to
transform the meaning of daily living, but as he has
remarked to me, one may not expect that transformation
for a century or more.

I would like to conclude this intimation of Lonergan's
quest by turning to the question of liberal education
as it is discussed by Leo Strauss. Writing on the
place of great books in education he remarks: "the
facile delusions which conceal from us our true

situation all amount to this: that we are, or can be, wiser than the wisest men of our past. We are thus induced to play the part, not of attentive and docile listeners, but of impressarios or lion-tamers".[34] He goes on to speak of the role of great men and great books: "Just as the soil needs cultivators of the soil, the mind needs teachers. But teachers are not so easy to come by as farmers. The teachers themselves are pupils and must be pupils, but there cannot be an infinite regress: ultimately there must be teachers who are not in turn pupils. These teachers who are not in turn pupils are the great minds or, in order to avoid any ambiguity in a matter of such importance, the greatest minds. Such men are extremely rare. We are not likely to meet any of them in any classroom. We are not likely to meet any of them anywhere. It is a piece of good luck if there is a single one alive in one's time".

In Canada, in Quebec, we have had a piece of good luck.

Notes: Introduction

1.   Thomas Pynchon, Gravity's Rainbow, Picador,
     London, 1975, 105.

2.   His remarks were made during a conference on
     Structuralism and Hermeneutics: Merging
     Horizons, held in York University, Toronto,
     November 1978.

3.   The Hogart Press, London, 1976, 268 ff.

4.   Victorino Tejera, Modes of Greek Thought,
     Appleton-Century-Crofts, New York, 1971, 2.

5.   A Maslow, Towards a Psychology of Being, 1968,
     204, speaks of less than 1% of adults growing.
     A. R. Aresteh comments on the absence of ref-
     lection on adulthood; "Unless the psychologist
     has himself experienced the state of quest of
     final integration in the succession of identit-
     ies he will hardly acquire an understanding or
     incentive for doing research on it", Final
     Integration in Adult Personality, Leiden, 1965,
     18.

6.   The slim possibility is precised in section two
     of chapter six, 95-7.   Chapter five discusses
     a related negative modernity, 83 ff. which has a
     positive aspect in its sharpening of the
     challenge.

7.   On the three relevant types of conversion see
     Lonergan, Method in Theology, 238.   The stress
     in the present work is on intellectual conver-
     sion in the context of praxis (see 21 ff.)

8.   L. van der Post quotes Jung's remark and comm-
     ents on the event, op.cit., 156.

9.   Quoted in H. Spiegelberg, The Phenomenological
     Movement, Vol. I, The Hague, 1965, 89.

10. Samuel Beckett, Proust and Three Dialogues with
     Georges Duthuit, John Calder, London, 1965, 19.

11. Gaston Bachelard, The Poetics of Space, Beacon
     Press, Boston, 1969, 61.

12.   On the five-fold differentiation see Lonergan,
      Method in Theology, 273-75; on intellectual,
      moral and religious conversion see ibid., 238.
      Differentiations and conversions have a complex
      intertwined history of ongoing discovery of
      mind and heart and soul.   But it is our present
      personal history that concerns us here.

13.   A spectrum of feelings are associated with such
      unacceptability, e.g., "a rejection of the other
      may be passionate, and then the suggestion that
      openness is desirable will make one furious";
      "less differentiated consciousness finds more
      differentiated consciousness beyond its horizon
      and in self-defence, may tend to regard the more
      differentiated with that pervasive, belittling
      hostility that Max Scheler named ressentiment".
      (Lonergan, Method in Theology, 237, 273).

14.   What is symbolically expressed in this sentence
      is treated more elaborately and technically in
      "Authentic Subjectivity and International Growth:
      Foundations", the epilogue of The Shaping of the
      Foundations (see following footnote).

15.   Principally my Wealth of Self and Wealth of Nat-
      ions, Exposition Press, N.Y., 1975; Randomness,
      Statistics and Emergence, Gill Macmillan and
      Notre Dame, 1971; The Shaping of the Foundat-
      ions, University Press of America, 1977; Music
      That Is Soundless, University Press of America,
      1977.   These are strategic pointers towards
      self-realization through Lonergan's achievement.
      They aim at countering the ever-present threat
      of a shrinkage of that achievement and that
      realization.

16.   P. McShane, "The Foundations of Mathematics",
      Modern Schoolman, 40, 1963, 373-87.

17.   Collection, ed. F. E. Crowe, Herder and Herder,
      19, 74-88.

18.   See note 2, above.

19.   "Metamusic and Self-Meaning", The Shaping of the
      Foundations, chapter 2.

Notes: Introduction

20.   B. Lonergan, Method in Theology, Darton,
      Longman and Todd, London, 1972, 317.

21.   A refinement emerges when one moves to gener-
      alized empirical method, 18 ff.

22.   The truncated subject not only does not know
      himself or herself but has no knowledge of this
      lack of knowledge.   See Lonergan, "The Subject",
      A Second Collection, eds. W. Ryan and B. Tyrrell,
      Darton, Longman and Todd, London, 1974, 73.

23.   A concluding remark of George Smiley, the
      fictional academic involved in some of the real
      business of peace: John le Carré, The Honour-
      able Schoolboy, Pan Books, London, 1978, 543.

Notes: Chapter 1

1.   Originally this essay was three-part.   The
      third part, "The Core Psychological Present
      of the Contemporary Theologian", appeared in
      Trinification of the World, a Festschrift in
      honour of F. E. Crowe, edited by T. A. Dunne
      and J.-M. Laporte, Regis College Press, 1978,
      84-96.

2.   B. Lonergan, Insight, 429.

3.   Ibid., 401.

4.   B. Lonergan, Method in Theology, 318.

5.   Gaston Bachelard, The Poetics of Space, Beacon
      Press, Boston, 1969, 14, 21, 47, 83.

6.   On Jaspers' notion of encompassing, see Gerhard
      Knauss, "The Concept of the 'Encompassing' in
      Jaspers' Philosophy", The Philosophy of Karl
      Jaspers, edited by P. A. Schlipp, New York,
      1957, 141-175.

7.   Fichte's Sun-Clear Statement was printed, in the
      English translation of A. E. Kroger, in The
      Journal of Speculative Philosophy, Vol.II, 1868.

8. This is the main thesis of the work The Shaping of the Foundations: Being at Home in Transcendental Method.

9. Marcel Proust, Remembrance of Things Past, Random House, New York, Vol.II, 1123.

10. My emphasis here is more on attitude than achievement. For the same point in a complementary context see the Epilogue, "Being and Loneliness", to my Wealth of Self and Wealth of Nations: Self-Axis of the Great Ascent, Exposition Press, New York, 1975.

11. Edmund Husserl, The Crisis of European Sciences and Transcendental Phenomenology, North Western University Press, 1970, 168-69.

12. Karl Jaspers, The Origin and Goal of History, London, 1953, chapter 1.

13. B. Lonergan, De Deo Trini II, Pars Systematica, Gregorian Press, Rome, 1964, 199.

14. The precise meaning here may be gleaned from the discussion of possible, probable and actual seriations of schemes of recurrence in B. Lonergan, Insight, 119-120.

15. B. Lonergan, Collection, Herder and Herder, New York, 1967, "Dimensions of Meaning", 255-256.

16. Gerhard Knauss, op. cit., 167.

17. See Alfred Tarski, "The Semantic Conception of Truth", Readings in Philosophical Analysis, edited by Herbert Feigl and Wilfrid Sellars, New York, 1949, 53, where he indicates his primary interest in the notion of truth for sentences.

18. B. Lonergan, "The Dehellenization of Dogma", A Second Collection, Darton, Longman and Todd, London, 1974, 15.

19. The issue is technical. See Insight, 388.

20. Margaret Masterman, "The Nature of a Paradigm", Criticism and the Growth of Knowledge, edited

by Lakatos and Musgrave, Cambridge U. Press, 1970, 61.   This volume will be referred to later as Criticism.

21.   Ibid., 60.

22.   Ibid., 59

23.   Ibid., 60

24.   For the meaning of "radical", one must draw on Insight, 356-59;   see also Method in Theology, index under Notions.

25.   Thomas Kuhn, "Logic of Discovery or Psychology of Research?", Criticism, 1.

26.   Stephen Toulmin, Human Understanding, Vol.1, Oxford, 1972, 8.

27.   The issue is complex; see the lengthy footnote 122, pp.25-26 of B. Lonergan, Verbum: Word and Idea in Aquinas, University of Notre Dame Press, 1967.

28.   Intellectual process has been the focus of Lonergan's attention in at least four of his major works: those cited already in footnotes 13, 24 and 27.

29.   Recall footnote 14.   There is an underlying theory of history involved here which is a filling out, through the inclusion of concrete details of actual, probable and possible significant shifts of meaning-schemes within the basic viewpoint of generalized emergent probability.   See Insight, index under Emergent Probability; Method in Theology, 286-88.   We will return to the topic in chapter six.

30.   Imre Lakatos, "Methodology of Scientific Research Programmes", Criticism, 183-84.

31.   Ibid., 132.

32.   J. W. N. Sullivan, Beethoven: His Spiritual Development, Vintage, New York, 1960, 85.

33. <u>Insight</u>, 647.

34. <u>Ibid</u>., 646-47. See also 515-20.

35. Obviously the basic pointers are to the works of
    Lonergan themselves. Helpful points of entry
    are the articles reprinted in the two collections
    cited above in footnotes 15 and 18. I would
    refer forward here, however, to my comments, in
    the text at footnote 41, on background, fore-
    ground, and the parts of <u>Insight</u>. <u>Method in</u>
    <u>Theology</u>, the two collections, and other works
    are too easily erroneously grafted into contem-
    porary theological and philosophical debate if
    the challenge of part one of <u>Insight</u> is not met.
    See <u>Method in Theology</u>, 260.

36. "... as though his mind had become full, or his
    brain exhausted, or his judgment had lapsed
    into the error of those that forgot man to be
    potency in the realm of intelligence", <u>Insight</u>,
    748.

37. I recall here Friedrich Schlegel's remark, quoted
    in H. G. Gadamer, <u>Wahrheit und Methode</u>, Tübingen,
    1960, 274, footnote 2: "A classic is a writing
    that is never fully understood. But those that
    are educated and educate themselves must always
    want to learn more from it".

38. Sullivan, <u>op</u>. <u>cit</u>., 150. I would like to quote
    at length here from a more recent biography of
    Beethoven. It serves to bring out rather con-
    cretely some of the points I have been trying to
    make regarding growth and the relative inacess-
    ibility of classics: "The works which occupied
    him almost exclusively in the last years were
    the final five string quartets. These late-
    harvest products are unique, unique for Beethoven,
    unique in all music. The quartets carry music
    to a summit of exaltation and to the deepest
    depth of feeling. There is no 'message' in
    these works, no 'philosophy'. They are beyond
    definition in words. To probe their variety
    of mood, sweetness, power, intensity, humor, com-
    passion, assertion of life, a book by itself is
    needed, one which it would be beyond my ability
    to write. Yet we may let the music speak -

without a preliminary word. Each of the five
quartets is an experience which makes one break
out in perspiring superlatives. (I think that
the slow movement of Opus 135 is the most
beautiful piece of music ever written). Each
is peerless. They have a reputation for being
difficult, and some listeners shy away from them.
Difficult they may be, as The Tempest or Faust
or The Idiot is difficult; but not abstract,
not severe, not inacessible, save possibly the
Great Fugue (Op. 133).

All great artists travel the road upward. For
some the climb is not a steep one, and the level
they reach lies near the level at which they
started. Others ascend continuously from youth
to age, and reach so high a plateau that they
leave their early works far in the valley.
Raphael and Mendelssohn were accomplished artists
almost from the start, and while their work shows
development, it is not a startling development.
(Both died young, however). Beethoven is like
Rembrandt: a world separates "The Anatomy Less-
on", painted when Rembrandt was twenty-six, from
the "Self Portrait" in the Frick museum, painted
at the age of fifty-two. When Beethoven was
twenty-six, he worked on the Piano Sonata, Op.7,
a charming piece known in his lifetime as "The
Maiden in Love"; when he was fifty-two he was
thinking of the first of the last quartets. It
was an immense journey". George R. Marek,
Beethoven, Biography of a Genius, Kimber, London,
1970, 602.

39.   B. Lonergan, Insight, 278.

40.   A. Walton Litz, The Art of James Joyce: Method
       and Design in Ulysses and Finegans Wake, London,
       1961, 92-93.

41.   Heinrich Schenker, "Organic Structure in Sonata
       Form", Journal of Musical Theory, 12, 1968, 180.

42.   F. E. Crowe, "The Origin and Scope of Bernard
       Lonergan's 'Insight'". Sciences Ecclesiastiques
       9, 1957.

43. _Method in Theology_, 177.

44. _Insight_, 517.

45. The next section deals with actual context. The "position on being" is that to which the first XXX + 388 pages of _Insight_ invites the reader. We are discussing here something more remote, more refined, more incarnate than that preliminary achievement, but the dimensions of the preliminary achievement should not be minimized: "Unfortunately, some people have the impression that while Tertullian and others of his time may have made such a mistake, no one repeats it today. Nothing could be further from the truth. For until a person has made the personal discovery that he is making Tertullian's mistake all along the line, until he has gone through the crisis involved in overcoming one's spontaneous estimate of the real, and the fear of idealism involved in it, he is still thinking just as Tertullian did. It is not a sign that one is dumb or backward. St. Augustine was one of the most intelligent men in the whole Western tradition and one of the best proofs of his intelligence is in the fact that he himself discovered that for years he was unable to distinguish between what is a body and what is real". B. Lonergan, in a talk on "Consciousness and the Trinity", 1964 (unpublished).

46. "To strike out on a new line and become more than a weekend celebrity calls for years in which one's living is more or less constantly absorbed in the effort to understand, in which one's understanding gradually works round and up a spiral of viewpoints with each complementing its predecessor and only the last embracing the whole field to be mastered", B. Lonergan, _Insight_, 186.

47. I recall here the aspirations of the Vorticist movement, to digest and bring forth the past. See Hugh Kenner, _The Pound Era_, University of California Press, 1971, 238-39.

48. _Method in Theology_, 258-62, 273-76, 303-05.

49. _Ibid._, chapter 5 and Part Two.

Notes: Chapter 1

50.   Recall the text on p.4, at footnote 15, and
      the reference there.

51.   Method in Theology, 163.

52.   For the meaning of "perspective" see Method in
      Theology, index under perspectivism.   For light
      on the meaning of dynamic see B. Lonergan,
      Philosophy of God and Theology, Darton, Longman
      and Todd, 1973, index under Viewpoint.

53.   Insight, xxv-vi.

54.   Ibid., 72, 243.   See pp.18 ff. below.

55.   Method in Theology, 95.

56.   See R. Doran, Jung, Ricoeur and the Problem of
      Foundations, University Press of America, 1978.
      Recall also the comments at the conclusion of
      the Introduction.   See also below, 117, n.19.

57.   See Randomness, Statistics and Emergence, also
      chapter 1 of The Shaping of the Foundations.

58.   Insight, xxviii.

59.   See footnote 45.

60.   Criticism, 265-66.   See also the text above, 4,
      at footnotes 17 and 18.

61.   See, for example, Hierarchy Theory: The Chall-
      enge of Complex Systems, edited by Howard H.
      Pattee, George Braziller, New York, 1973.

62.   Albert Wilson, "Systems Epistemology", in The
      World System, edited by Ervin Laszlo, Braziller,
      New York, 1973, 125-26.

63.   B. Lonergan, Collection, 20.

64.   I have treated this in some detail in Randomness,
      Statistics and Emergence, chapter 9.

65.   On Schemes of Recurrence see Randomness, Statis-
      tics and Emergence, chapter 10.

66. <u>Method in Theology</u>, 97-99.

67. Peter Berger, <u>Pyramids of Sacrifice</u>, Basic
     Books, New York, 1974, xii.

68. The title of its final chapter.

69. <u>Ibid</u>., 213.

70. <u>Insight</u>, 226-42.

71. See <u>Method in Theology</u>, 363. There Lonergan
     is speaking of the church as a process of
     self-constitution.

72. M. Lamb, <u>History, Method and Theology. A
     Dialectical Comparison of Wilhelm Dilthey's
     Critique of Historical Reason and Bernard
     Lonergan's Meta-methodology</u>, Doctorate Thesis,
     University of Munster, 1974, 42: to be
     published.

73. On literary criticism R. P. Blackmur remarks:
     "Every critic like every theologian and every
     philosopher is a casuist in spite of himself":
     "A Critic's Job of Work", <u>Five Approaches of
     Literary Criticism</u>, edited by Wilbur Scott,
     Collier Macmillan, New York, 1962, 316. The
     book is a useful survey of different English
     language views. On music criticism, see "Meta-
     music and Self-Meaning", chapter two of <u>The
     Shaping of the Foundations</u>.

74. J. R. Oppenheimer, <u>The Open Mind</u>, Simon and
     Schuster, New York, 1955, 88.

75. J. Haberer, "Politicalization in Science",
     <u>Science</u>, Vol. 178, 1972, (713-724), 713.

76. P. Berger, <u>op</u>. <u>cit</u>., xiv.

77. Herbert Butterfield, <u>The Origins of Modern
     Science</u>, Bell and Sons, London, 1965, vii; see
     also chapter X.

78. <u>Method in Theology</u>, 261-62.

79.   _Insight_, 72, 243.

80.   _Journal of Religion_, 1974, at footnote 14.

81.   _Ibid._   This point is central in dealing with
      Schubert Ogden's "Subjectivist Principle": see
      P. McShane, "The Core Psychological Present of
      the Contemporary Theologian", _Trinification of_
      the Word, eds. T. Dunne and J.-M. Laporte,
      Regis College Press, 1978, 84-96.

82.   The Donald Mathers Memorial Lectures, delivered
      by Fr. Lonergan in March 1976 at Queen's Univer-
      sity.   The first lecture, "Religious Experience"
      appeared in _Trinification of the Word_ (see prev-
      ious note), 71-83; the second lecture appeared
      in _Lonergan Workshop I_, ed. F. Lawrence, Scholars
      Press, 1978, 309-27; the third lecture appeared
      in _Studies in Religion_, 1977, 341-55.

83.   _Method in Theology_, 4.

84.   This, and the quotation to follow, are from the
      last of the three lectures.

85.   F. E. Crowe, "Dogma versus the Self-Correcting
      Process of Learning", _Foundations of Theology_,
      ed. P. McShane, Gill, Macmillan and Notre Dame,
      1971, 26.

86.   "B. Lonergan Responds", _Foundations of Theology_,
      224.

87.   I recall the parallel drawn in Part 1 between
      Beethoven's development and Lonergan's.   Pres-
      ent occasional lectures, like the last quartets,
      may be expected to go far beyond earlier sympho-
      nic volumes.

88.   The indices of _Method in Theology_, _A Second Coll-_
      ection, _Philosophy of God and Theology_.

89.   See, for example, the lecture "Aquinas Today:
      Tradition and Innovation, _Journal of Religion_,
      1975, and the lectures referred to in footnote 82
      above.

Notes: Chapter 1

90. P. McShane, Wealth of Self and Wealth of Nations,
     Exposition Press, New York, 1975, 96. The
     remark is made in the context of a discussion
     of "the menace of experiential conjugation".
     See Insight, 542.

91. I recall here Lonergan's metaphor of the rock on
     which one can build, including "the more import-
     ant part", Method in Theology, 19.

92. Insight, 227, provides an immediate context. The
     larger context is an understanding of the types
     of bias meshed into a grasp of the flow of mean-
     ings in history: see Method in Theology, 178.

93. Op. cit., n.85 above, 29.

94. I cannot enter here into the intricacies of its
     entry into the realms of feelings. "The prin-
     ciple of dynamic correspondence calls for a
     harmonious orientation on the psychic level, and
     from the nature of the case such an orientation
     would have to consist in some cosmic dimension,
     in some intimation of unplumbed depths that
     accrue to man's feelings, emotions, sentiments",
     Insight, 532. And there is the ongoing mediat-
     ion of sophistication in such intimations. See
     also notes 31 and 136.

95. See 47 above. There are also Jungian connot-
     ations: "This movement of the spiral - here
     reinforced by the dynamic action of the vortex -
     is characteristic of the 'indirect approach by
     means of the circumambulatio'. It is as if an
     unknown centre, which we can define only as the
     psychological self, produces a constant centri-
     petal movement, or in Jung's words 'acts like
     a magnet on the disparate materials and proc-
     esses of the unconscious ... Often one has
     the impression that the personal psyche is
     running round this central point like a shy
     animal, at once fascinated and frightened,
     always in flight, and yet steadily drawing
     nearer'", Gerhard Adler, The Living Symbol, A
     Case Study in the Process of Individuation,
     Pantheon, New York, 1961, 183. The inner quot-
     ation is from Jung's Alchemy.

96.   Section G, p.16 above.

97.   Insight, 393.

98.   See above, 14-15.

99.   The Shaping of the Foundations, chapter 1, at
      note 75.

100. Ibid., chapter 3, at note 50.

101. Ibid., chapter 2, the text after note 65,
      especially the quotation at note 80.

102. There is a problem here of concrete expectation:
      like suspecting that Finnegans Wake would emerge
      from the tail of Ulysses, or more precisely
      from the tail of "The Oxen of the Sun" episode.
      Not that Finnegans Wake is aggreformic express-
      ion, though it does open various Win-d-ohs!
      There is the wider problem of linguistic feed-
      back in the third stage of meaning: see Method
      in Theology, 88, note 34.   See also here notes
      94 and 136.

103. I recall here the basic text from Insight, sel-
      ected for this Part, and quoted on p.2 above.
      We are gradually recontextualizing the text and
      will return to it at the conclusion of the
      chapter.

104. "The culture becomes a slum", Method in Theology,
      99: the comment occurs in a discussion of
      undifferentiated consciousness in the later
      stages of meaning.

105. Insight, 735.

106. See note 94 above, and the citation there from
      Insight.   Note the ambiguity of the phrase "the
      conception was constitutive", and consider the
      meaning within later actual contexts, of the
      statement "self-transcendence is the eagerly
      sought goal not only of our sensitivity, not only
      of our intelligent and rational knowing, not
      only of our freedom and responsibility, but
      first of all of our flesh and blood that through
      nerves and brains have come spontaneously to live

Notes: Chapter 1

out symbolic meanings and to carry out symbolic
demands", from the second of the three lectures
cited in note 82, above.

107. Insight, 391.   It is perhaps significant that
     in the sublation of Insight into foundations
     Lonergan does not include the word implement-
     ation.   Embracing all heuristic structures is
     "the integral heuristic structure which is what
     I mean by a metaphysics".   This section can be
     seen as a case for its non-inclusion there.

108. Insight, 392-95.

109. Ibid., Epilogue.

110. Ibid., 530-31.

111. Ibid., 227.

112. On the latter point, Insight, 209-11; 226-27;
     698.

113. I am being both precise and cautious here.   Fr.
     Crowe remarks, at the beginning of a paper to
     which I will refer immediately, "it is possible
     that in some respects we are dealing, not with
     a development of Lonergan's thought, but with a
     further stage of its manifestation".   It is all
     too easy to latch on to such statements of Lon-
     ergan as "In Insight the good was the intellig-
     ent and reasonable.   In Method the good is a
     distinct notion", (A Second Collection, 263:
     Lonergan of 1972) as if Insight, the fruit of
     twenty-eight years of philosophy, had a fatal
     flaw.

     The paper of Fr. Crowe to which I refer, and to
     which I am deeply indebted, is his paper for the
     Boston Lonergan Workshop of 1974, "An Explorat-
     ion of Lonergan's New Notion of Value".   Need-
     less to say, the shift in the notion of value
     emerges with the more evidently illuminating
     shift to functional specialization.   The latter
     shift, and its interplay with the former, is a
     matter for detailed research.

114. "Authentic Subjectivity and International Growth:
Foundations", the Epilogue of The Shaping of the
Foundations, 127 ff.

115. A distinction is not a separation. What operates is the subject which I elsewhere speak of
as a notion of survival, "you at core and in
kilos", Wealth of Self and Wealth of Nations,
chapter 10, "The Notion of Survival".

116. Lonergan's view on finality has undergone an
enrichment which parallels the developments
indicated. In "Mission and Spirit", 1974, he
speaks of the passionateness of being as underpinning, accompanying, reaching beyond the
morally conscious. Lonergan's classic treat-
ments of finality are in "Finality Love Marriage",
1943, and in Insight, 442-51. I recall however
my cautionary comment in note 113.

117. B. Lonergan, "The Subject", A Second Collection,
81.

118. Ibid., 82.

119. I am indebted here to Fr. Crowe's paper for the
Boston Lonergan Workshop of 1974: "An Exploration of Lonergan's New Notion of Value".

120. Insight, 390.

121. Ibid., 396.

122. One might think of the meshing primarily in
terms of failure - the failure of Mandarinism
- but one can also think of it in terms of rip-
ening times, with hope and fantasy within the
praxis-mediation of which we are speaking. See
note 136 below.

123. "The concrete possibility of a scheme beginning
to function shifts the probability of the combination from the product of pqr, ..., to the
sum of p+q+r...." Insight, 121. I have discussed and illustrated this in Randomness,
Statistics and Emergence, chapter 11, "Probab-
ility-schedules of Emergence of Schemes". In

the present instance, a useful imaginative
crutch is the vortex. The structure of praxis
is a large vortex bringing together sets of
previously unintegrated ranges of macro- and
micro- vortex movements, with resultant dis-
continuities in angular velocities and accelerations. Since the vortices involve human
subjects and communities, the velocities and
accelerations involve six levels of change.

124. Insight, 119.

125. Method in Theology, 292.

126. M. Lamb, op.cit., note 72 above, 180-93, 514,
      speaks of a functional feedback model.

127. In The Donald Mathers Lectures, (see note 82
      above) Lonergan speaks of method as praxis and
      of praxis becoming an academic subject with the
      passing of the age of innocence. One cannot
      do brief justice to such points. A helpful
      illustration that Lonergan cites of the dynamic
      orientation in question is Heiler's view of the
      mission of the history of religions to lie in a
      preparation of the cooperation of religions.

128. B. Lonergan, "The Subject", A Second Collection,
      83.

129. Lonergan's brief expression of one of the issues
      raised in Fr. Tracy's article, "Lonergan's
      Foundational Theology: An Interpretation and a
      Critique", Foundations of Theology, 197-223.

130. "Bernard Lonergan Responds, Foundations of Theol-
      ogy, 230-31.

131. In the article already mentioned, (note 113
      above) Fr. Crowe spells out the analogy of quest-
      ioning and of criticism.

132. Op. cit., note 129, 214.

133. Insight, 332: this is the rock of Method in
      Theology, 19.

134. Method in Theology, 283-84:   this is "the more
      important part of the rock" of Method in Theology,
      19.

135. See note 123.   I refer here also to the large
      vortex of the interplay of functional specialties
      and to the set of turns of the subject involved
      in the practice of Method in Theology, 250,

136. "Without fantasy, all philosophic knowledge
      remains in the grip of the present or the past
      and severed from the future, which is the only
      link between philosophy and the real history of
      mankind".   (Herbert Marcuse, Negations: Essays
      in Critical Theory, translated, Jeremy J.
      Shapiro, Boston, 1968, 155).   In the third stage
      of meaning one must expect, hope for, envisage
      imaginatively, work to, new levels of humour,
      music, prayer, public kindliness and discourse.

137. The foundational theologian is committed to
      conceive of the invariants of progress and dec-
      line and of "our future destiny", Method in
      Theology, 291.

138. Method in Theology, xi.

139. Insight, 747.

140. Three points.   First of all, academic meaning
      ranges through all the types and functions of
      meaning outlined in Method in Theology, chapter
      3.   Secondly, one should note that adult growth
      in general heuristics involves an epiphanous
      reading stance towards words and things.
      "Incarnation" is more and more fully read in the
      clarity of the heuristic conception of the six-
      levelled hierarchy of aggregates which is man:
      $f(p_i, c_j, b_k, z_l, u_m, r_n)$, where for instance
      c_j connotes a subset of chemical conjugates.
      Other complexities emerge when one considers the
      heuristics of nerve and muscle, eye and brain.
      Thirdly, the above two points serve very clearly
      to bring out the need for generalized empirical
      method in human studies.

Notes: Chapter 1

141. Insight, 401.

142. The "opaqueness regarding truth" mentioned
      already in the centre of page 4 and at the end
      of page 13.   It is dealt with in a   theological
      context in the article cited in note 1, above.
      Chapter 4 below deals with it in the context of
      literary studies, 77 ff.

143. Method in Theology, 253.

144. In notes for lectures at the Thomas More Instit-
      ute in Montreal (unpublished).

145. This and the following two quotations are taken
      from a lecture Lonergan delivered at Hobart and
      William Smith Colleges (October 10th, 1974)
      entitled "Self-Transcendence: Intellectual,
      Moral, Religious".

Notes: Chapter 2

1.   Metamathematics may be said to have originated
      with David Hilbert's efforts to prove the con-
      sistency of classical mathematics by first
      expressing it in axiomatic form, making this
      formal system the object of a proof theory or
      metamathematics.   This theory was to use only
      intuitively convincing methods, called by Hilbert
      "finitary methods".   As the theory advanced,
      finitary methods were seen to be inadequate.

2.   For a general account of these subjects and their
      development, cf. E. T. Bell, The Development of
      Mathematics, McGraw Hill, New York, 1945.

3.   The Foundations of Arithmetic, translated by
      J. L. Austin, Basil Blackwell, Oxford, 1953, vi.

4.   Jacques Hadamard, The Psychology of Invention in
      the Mathematical Field, Princeton University
      Press, Princeton, 1945.

5.   J. L. Synge, Science, Sense and Nonsense, Cape,
      London, 1951, 112.

Notes: Chapter 2

6.   Georg Cantor, Contributions to the Founding of
     the Theory of Transfinite Numbers, Dover Pub-
     lications, New York, 105, 161, 204.

7.   Cf. E. W. Beth, The Foundations of Mathematics,
     North-Holland Pub. Co., Amsterdam, 1959, 376.
     I shall use this as a standard work of reference
     throughout, denoting it as "Beth".

8.   M. Pasch, Vorlesungen über neuere Geometrie,
     Teubner, Leipzig, 1882, 98-99.   For more detail
     on the nature of geometry see Randomness, Stat-
     istics and Emergence, the index under Geometry.

9.   G. Birkoff, Lattice Theory, New York, 1948.

10. H. S. M. Coxeter, Introduction to Geometry, Wiley
     & Sons, New York, 1961, 289.

11. Cf. note 1.

12. Beth, 593.

13. A general account of these three main approaches
     and their development is given in R. W. Wilder,
     Introduction to the Foundations of Mathematics,
     Wiley & Sons, New York, 1952.

14. Logicism may be traced to Gottlob Frege, who, in
     his Grundlagen der Arithmetic, Breslau, 1884,
     gave a summary reduction of arithmetic to logic.
     His work, however, was not widely known before
     Bertrand Russell arrived at some of his conclus-
     ions independently.   The latter advanced the
     program considerably.

15. Although L. E. J. Brouwer is considered to be
     the founder of intuitionism, he was preceeded
     by L. Kronecker, who insisted on the notion of
     mathematics as a construction on the basis of
     "intuitively given" natural numbers.   Kronecker
     is popularly remembered by his after-dinner-
     speech remark: "The integers were made by God,
     but everything else is the work of man".

16. The evidence for the thesis of Alonso Church,
     which may be considered as a generalization of

Notes: Chapter 2

that of Gödel, is fully discussed in S. C.
Kleene, Introduction to Metamathematics,
North-Holland Pub. Co., Amsterdam, 1952, 298-386.

17. For a discussion of the Skölem-Löwenheim paradox,
cf. Beth, 488-80, 513-16.

18. Ibid., 335-45.

19. B. Russell, The Principles of Mathematics, 2nd
ed., Allen & Unwin, London, 1935, chapter 10.

20. Beth, 381-408.

21. Cf. note 2.

22. B. Inhelder and Jean Piaget, The Growth of
Logical Thinking from Childhood to Adolescence,
Basic Books, New York, 1958. Also the many
independent works of Piaget such as The Child's
Conception of Number, Routledge & Kegan Paul,
London, 1952. One must take account, however,
of the influence of truncated subjectivity in
such works. See the concluding sections of
chapter 5, below.

23. Cf. note 4.

24. Insight, Longmans, Green & Co., London, 1957 and
various later editions.

25. Theological Studies, VII, 1946, 349-92; VIII,
1947, 35-79, 404-44; X, 1949, 3-40, 359-93.
Later published as Verbum: Word and Idea in
Aquinas, ed. D. Burrell, Notre Dame, 1967.

26. Theological Studies, VII, 1946, 386-88; Insight,
309-12, 395.

27. Insight, 490-97. De Deo Trini II, Gregorian
Press, Rome, 1964, 291-315.

28. Theological Studies, VIII, 36-46; Insight, 304-
16, passim; cf. also P. Hoenan,"De Origine Prim-
orum Principiorum Scientiae", Gregorianum, XIV,
1933, 153-84; XIX, 1938, 498-514; XX, 1939,
19-54, 321-50.

29. *Insight*, 58-62; *Randomness, Statistics and Emergence*, chapters 4 - 8.

30. *Insight*, chapters 1 and 2, *passim*; 146-47, 645-47.

31. *Ibid.*, 311-13.

32. *Metaphysics* I, 982a5-10.

33. *Critique of Pure Reason*, Introduction, Sec. 3.

Notes: Chapter 3

1. J. W. S. Pringle, *The Two Biologies*, Oxford, 1963, 25.

2. Cf., *Insight*, xx-xxi. Comparison of our initial example, the amoeba, with Lonergan's geometric example, the circle (7-13), will show how the mathematical example scores in precision. In *Insight*, Lonergan wisely postpones a discussion of the particular method of biology until chapter 15. The apparent folly of the present treatment has, however, other advantages.

3. Cf., Lonergan, *Insight*, 272-74; *De constitutione Christi ontologica et psychologica*, Rome, 1956, 92-95.

4. Lonergan, *Insight*, 320-21; *De constitutione Christi*, 87; *De Verbo Incarnato*, Rome, 1961, 276.

5. More properly *Chaos Chaos*, the Linnean classification of, most probably, *Proteus Amoeba*.

6. For a discussion of the meaning of these questions in an Aristotelian context, cf., Lonergan, *Verbum: Word and Idea in Aquinas*, 16 ff; *De Deo Trino* II, 1964, 280-85.

7. The comments on this example are representative of the first five canons of empirical method, *Insight*, chapter 3; the canon of statistical residues will be touched on later.

8. The image may be formal, virtual, or merely
    symbolic. Cf., Lonergan, "A Note on Geometric
    Possibility", Collection, 109-10; Insight,
    index under Image; "The Concept of Verbum",
    Theological Studies, VII, 1946, 372-79; De
    Constitutione Christi, 80.

9. C. H. Waddinton, The Strategy of the Genes,
    London, 1957, 30. Waddington goes on to con-
    sider the heuristic value of the model. It
    is perhaps worth noting that the stress on the
    heuristic role of images in Insight is not in
    contradiction to M. Beckner's insistence on
    explanatory models (The Biological Way of
    Thought, New York, 1959, chapter 3); it is
    mainly a difference in terminology: we would
    prefer to consider explanatory models as abstract
    systems.

10. Insight, index under Description; De Deo Trino
     II, 306-11.

11. Insight, 439-40; 480-81.

12. Biology indeed has already taken the road of
     modern physics. For a recent discussion of
     the nature of the gene, cf., R. B. Goldschmidt,
     Theoretical Genetics, University of California,
     1955, Part 1.

13. J. H. Woodger, Biological Principles, London,
     1948, 328.

14. Cf., Insight on the "already-out-there-now-real"
     and related notions.

15. Ibid., 269, 415, 432, 498.

16. Ibid., 37, 63-64.

17. Ibid., 78.

18. Ibid., 463-67. The very fact that our discuss-
     ion of the amoeba and the plant involves essential
     simplifications can be a help towards understand-
     ing not merely biological method but
     even the structure of the book, Insight.

19. Ibid., 63-66; 106-12. The experiment is des-
     cribed in detail in J. L. Harper and G. R.
     Sager, "Some aspects of the ecology of butter-
     cups in permanent grassland", Proc. British
     Weed Control Conference, (I), 1953, 256-63.
     and discussed further in Randomness, Statistics
     and Emergence, 77 ff.

20. Principles of Development, New York, 1939.

21. Ibid., 75.

22. Ibid., 108.

23. Ibid., 120.

24. Ibid., 237-46.

25. Ibid., 269-88.

26. Ibid., 289-435.

27. Ibid., 274.

28. Ibsight, 444-51.

29. Cf. "Finality Love Marriage", Theological Studies
     IV, 1943, 478-83; also a book review, ibid., 7,
     1946, 607-608; and "The Concept of Verbum",
     ibid., X, 1949, 378, note 89.

30. Insight, 33, 76, 128.

31. While Aristotle does not provide an analysis of
     development, the above point is made by him. Cf.,
     Physics, Bk.II, and St. Thomas' commentary.
     Relevant to the avoidance of the projection ment-
     ioned immediately in the text above is the
     distinction: "finis est principium, non quidem
     actionis sed ratiocinations, quia a fine incip-
     imus ratiocinari de iis quae sunt ad finem" (In
     II Phys., lecture 15, note 5).

32. British Journal for the Philosophy of Science,
     1950: "An Outline of General Systems Theory",
     159.

33. Ibid., 160.

34. Physics, II, 8, 198b, 21-34; Ross' translation.

35.   Cf., note 57 below and the text following it.

36.   Insight, 86-90.

37.   Ibid., 100-02; 491-94.

38.   Ibid., 46.

39.   Ibid., 48-50.

40.   Ibid., 93-96.

41.   Ibid., 54, 61-62.

42.   Ibid., 117 ff.

43.   Ibid., 259 ff.

44.   Ibid., 121-28.

45.   Ibid., 260.

46.   Ibid., 132-34.

47.   Cf., "Finality Love Marriage", Collection, 21.
      In note 16 Lonergan notes the affinity between
      modern statistical law and the contingens ut in
      maiori parte, between modern chance variations
      and the contingens ut in minore parte.

48.   Insight, 134.

49.   Ibid., 264-65.

50.   Ibid., 254-67;   437-42.

51.   Ibid., 451-58.

52.   Ibid., 465-67.

53.   Ibid., 463.

54.   For a survey of the complex data for which the
      answer must account, cf., R. B. Goldschmidt,
      Theoretical Genetics, Part III.

55.   Insight, 481-82;   458-63.

Notes: Chapter 3

56.   <u>Ibid</u>., 253-54;   484-85.

57.   <u>Ibid</u>., 205-06;   255-57;   439-40;   608.

58.   <u>Ibid</u>., 80;   334-35;   437.

59.   <u>Ibid</u>., 262-64.   It is as well to note here what
      we have ignored throughout the article: that
      the study of animals calls into play the auto-
      nomous science of animal psychology.   Cf.,
      <u>Insight</u>, 265.

60.   <u>Ibid</u>., 247-48;   435-36.

61.   For more detail, see <u>Randomness, Statistics and
      Emergence</u>, especially chapter 9.

62.   <u>Insight</u>, 398-99.

Notes: Chapter 4

1.   The elimination is that referred to in the foll-
     owing quotation from <u>Method in Theology</u>, 238:
     "Intellectual conversion is a radical clarific-
     ation and, consequently, the elimination of an
     exceedingly stubborn and misleading myth con-
     cerning reality, objectivity, and human know-
     ledge".

2.   From <u>Correspondence</u>, Conard, Paris, 1926-33, III,
     335, as cited in translation by R. K. Cross,
     <u>Flaubert and Joyce</u>, Princeton University Press,
     1971, 98.

3.   P. de Man, <u>Blindness and Insight</u>, Oxford Univ-
     ersity Press, 1971, 39.

4.   Briefly put, at this stage, it is a question of
     the personal intussusception of the program
     concretely intended by B. Lonergan and I. Progoff
     where "occupy us later" has the character of
     Bachelard's attitude: "Late in life, with
     indomitable courage, we continue to say that we
     are going to do what we have not yet done: we
     are going to build a house".   G. Bachelard,

Notes: Chapter 4

Poetics of Space, 61.

5.   Truth and Method, Seabury Press, N.Y. 1975.

6.   One may recognize here the principle of conflict
     between content and performance.   "To take the
     simplest instance, Hume thought the human mind
     to be a matter of impressions linked together
     by custom.   But Hume's own mind was quite orig-
     inal.   Therefore, Hume's own mind was not what
     Hume considered the human mind to be", Method
     in Theology, 21.

7.   P. de Man, op. cit., ix.

8.   Ibid., 29.

9.   Ibid., 11.

10. Ibid., 64-65.

11. Ibid., 77-78.

12. Ibid., 103.

13. Ibid., 82.

14. Ibid., 101.

15. Ibid., 114.

16. Ibid., 134.

17. On Context, see Method in Theology, 163; "cumul-
     ating" is relevantly ambivalent.

18. P. de Man, op. cit., 147.

19. Ibid., 159.

20. W. Iser (ed.), Immanente Aesthetik, Aesthetische
     Reflexion: Lyrik als Paradigma der Moderne,
     Munich, 1966.

21. P. de Man, op. cit., 171.

22. Ibid., 174.

Notes: Chapter 4

23. W. Benjamin, "Zwei Gedichte von Hölderin", in
     Schriften, II, Frankfurt am Main, 1955, 377.

24. More properly, a codetta, to complete the expos-
     ition: I am using the symbol of the beginning
     of an unwritten sonata, as I have done previously
     (The Shaping of the Foundations, 75). There is
     a need of symbols of where one stands in one's
     comprehension of being; the need of feeling,
     not like an oak but less than an acorn.

25. P. de Man, op. cit., 84.

26. I have discussed this at some length in chapter
     one, and will return to the topic in the foll-
     owing chapter.

27. P. de Man, op. cit., 88.

28. See McShane, Wealth of Self and Wealth of Nat-
     ions, 117.

29. R. Wellek and A. Warren, Theory of Literature,
     Harcourt, Brace and World, N.Y., 57-69.

30. Ibid., the earlier chapters of part 4.

31. Ibid., chapters 18, 19.

32. Ibid., chapters 8 - 11.

33. Method in Theology, 180.

34. Wellek and Warren, op. cit., chapter 17.

35. R. Crane's introduction notes the need for a
     general critique in a manner which could be made
     to parallel Lonergan's indications of a similar
     need in theology. I have noted the same need
     in the field of music, The Shaping of the Found-
     ations, 47-72.

36. In what sense is the specification meaningfully
     available? I would recall that naiveté's
     spontaneous philosophy is empiricism, and that
     "empiricism, idealism, and realism name three
     totally different horizons with no common ident-
     ical bjects. An idealist never means what an

Notes: Chapter 4

empiricist means, and a realist never means what
either of them mean", Method in Theology, 239.
However, the ambiguity of the word "spontaneous"
leaves a loophole for naiveté's hold on being.

37.   Method in Theology, 250 ff.   I would add the
context of Otto Rank, "Man is born beyond psychology and he dies beyond it but he can live
beyond it only through vital experience of his
own - in religious terms, through revelation,
conversions, or rebirth", Rank, 1932, 16.   The
critic is invited to live beyond criticism.

38.   See H. Kenner, The Pound Era, University of
California Press, 1971, 238-39;   the context may
be broadened from Kenner's index under Vortex,
Vorticism.

39.   The eight tasks are described in detail in
Method in Theology.

40.   R. Picard, New Criticism or New Fraud, Washington State University Press, 1969.

41.   W. Benjamin, Illuminations, edited with an
introduction by Hannah Arendt, translated by
Harry Zohn, New York, 1968, 258.

42.   S. Beckett, "Dante...Brune. Vico...Joyce",
Our Exagmination Round His Factification For
Incamination of Work in Progress.   A New
Direction Book, New York, 1972, 13 (first pub-
lished, 1929).

43.   Method in Theology, 260.

44.   R. Wellek contends that the history of modern
aesthetics is essentially a series of footnotes
to Kant ("Aesthetics and Criticism", The Philosophy of Kant and Our Modern World, C. Hendel,
ed., Liberal Arts Press, N.Y., 1957).   Paul
Bové has attacked the structuralists on the
grounds that their poetics are located within
a Kantian epistemology ("The Poetics of Coer-
cion: An Interpretation of Literary Competence",
Boundary (2), 1976, 263-84).   The second part
Of the present chapter (71 - 73) will note similar deficiencies in the British, the Hermeneutic
and the older Scholastic traditions.

45. On the varieties of differentiation of consciousness see Method in Theology, 258 ff., 272 ff.,
303 ff. My comments elsewhere (The Shaping of
the Foundations, 10 ff.) on the menace of experiential conjugation within the field of methodology are relevant here.

46. On constitutive meaning see Method in Theology,
78. On the dynamic resonances within subjectivity see Insight, 467-79; 546-49.

47. Insight, xxxviii.

48. My searchings for what I speak of here are docu-
mented in The Shaping of the Foundations. There
is the need for psychic liberation in the academic (40 ff.); there is Boulez' reaction to
Finnegans Wake looking to more complex mediations
(68 ff.); there is the delicacy of Lorenz' etho-
logical perception to be sublated into third-
stage meaning (79, 95); there is the need for
concrete fantasy (107 ff.); there is the relation to international growth of Yeats' challenge:
"Why should we honour those that die upon the
field of battle; a man may show as reckless a
courage in entering into the abyss of himself"
(104, 191 ff.) The writings of Ira Progoff put
such searchings in a new context: see his The
Death and Rebirth of Psychology, Julian Press,
N.Y., 1956; Depth Psychology and Modern Man,
Julian Press, N.Y., 1959; The Symbolic and the
Real, McGraw Hill, N.Y., 1973.

49. F. W. Bateson, "Linguistic and Literary Criticism",
The Discipline of Criticism, edited by P. Demetz,
T. Green and L. Nelson Jr., Yale University Press,
1968, 16.

50. The methodological notion is Lonergan's (Insight,
index under Aggregate), the terminology my own
(The Shaping of the Foundations, 113).

51. G. Durand, Les Structures Anthropologiques de
L'imaginaire, Paris, 1963. On Betcherev: 39.

52. S. Langer, Feeling and Form, Scribners, N.Y.,
1953, 258.

Notes: Chapter 4

53. G. Bachelard, The Poetics of Space, 1972, 91.

54. A dictum of R. W. Gerard, quoted in motto-
     fashion by R. S. de Ropp, Drugs and the Mind,
     N.Y., 1957, 203.

55. The Shaping of the Foundations, 78.

56. P. White's novel, The Eye of the Storm.

57. Langdon Gilkey, Naming the Whirlwind.

58. Maurice Nadeau, The Greatness of Flaubert, trans-
     lated by Barbara Bray, The Library Press, N.Y.,
     1972, 286.

59. G. Flaubert, Oeuvres complètes, XII, Club de
     l'Honnête homme, Paris, 1974, 229-32.

60. G. Adler, Pantheon, N.Y., 1961, 183.

61. See P. Ricoeur, The Symbolism of Evil, Beacon
     Press, Boston, 1967, 274.

62. Joyce, Ulysses, 182.

63. The Shaping of the Foundations, 106.

64. E. Voegelin, "Reason,: The Classical Experience",
     The Southern Review, July, 1974, 251.

65. I quote from the two-volume translation of
     Proust's great novel, Remembrance of Things Past,
     Random House, N.Y., Vol.I, 182. I recall
     Beckett's discussion of such turns in the work
     cited in the Introduction at note 10.

66. Insight, xxviii.

67. Truth and Method, xviii.

68. Sarah N. Lawall, Critics of Consciousness: The
     Existential Structures of Literature, Harvard
     University Press, 1968, 3.

69. Ibid., ix.

174

70. F. Jameson, <u>Marxism and Form</u>, Princeton University Press, 1971, 307-08. In this quotation, as in others, the reader may later detect, in the light of the personal discovery towards which this section points, the presence of dead metaphor.

71. P. Ricoeur, <u>La Métaphore vive</u>, Editions du Seuil, Paris, 1975.

72. M. B. Hester, <u>The Meaning of Poetic Metaphor</u>, Manton & Co., The Hague, 1967.

73. M. Blanchot, "La Question la plus profonde (I)", <u>Nouvelle Revue francaise</u>, 1960.

74. <u>Ibid.</u>, 1084.

75. S. Lawall, <u>op</u>. <u>cit</u>., note 68, 228.

76. See Method in Theology, 85-90, 302-20; also the works of B. Snell: <u>Der Aufbau der Sprache</u>; <u>The Discovery of Mind</u>, Harper Torchbooks, N.Y., 1960; <u>Poetry and Society</u>, Indiana University Press, 1961.

77. J. W. Yalton, "On Being Present to the Mind: A Sketch for the History of an Idea", <u>Dialogues</u> (14), 1975, 386.

78. Hoenan's articles are those referred to in note 28 of chapter 2.

79. A complete work, in process of publication runs to some 800 pages. A summary account is contained in F. Lawrence, "Self-knowledge in Gadamer and Lonergan", <u>Language Truth and Meaning</u>, ed. P. McShane, Gill and Macmillan, Dublin, 1972.

80. <u>Verbum: Word and Idea in Aquinas</u>, 25-6, note 122.

81. My comment above, 64, on <u>Insight</u> as allegory is related to this problem of actual philosophic context. See also the quotation from Lonergan, <u>Method in Theology</u>, 239 (below, 78 at note 117).

82. <u>Towards Deep Subjectivity</u>, Harper Torchbooks, N.Y., 1972, 132.

83.   See note 26 above.   I would recall Butterfield's
      remark that "since the rise of Christianity,
      there is no landmark in history that is worthy
      to be compared with "the seventeenth century
      revolutions in science", The Origins of Modern
      Science, G. Bell & Sons, London, 1965, 190.
      Theologians, Philosophers and Critics are reluct-
      ant to profit from personal reflection on the
      modern scientific achievement for a clarification
      of subjectivity: we return to this in the foll-
      owing chapter.

84.   More precisely, generalized empirical method:
      see above, 18 ff.

85.   Richard Ellman, Yeats: The Man and the Masks,
      Dutton, N.Y., 1948, 5.

86.   Cited in P. de Man, op. cit., 56.

87.   Erich Auerbach, Mimesis: The Representation of
      Reality in Western Literature, translated by W.
      R. Trask, Princeton University Press, 1953, 482.

88.   Ibid., 484.

89.   There are subtle difficulties in speaking of a
      'fictional person' which, however, will not, I
      think, trouble the non-theologian.   On the
      notion and constitution of person see Lonergan,
      De Constitutione Christi, Gregorian Press, Rome,
      1961, 9-41.

90.   G. Poulet, "The Circle and the Centre: Reality
      and Madame Bovary" (1955), reprinted in L. I.
      Lipking and W. A. Litz (eds.), Modern Literary
      Criticism, Atheneum, N.Y., 1972, 464.

91.   See Lawall, op. cit., note 68, p.76.

92.   G. Poulet, op. cit., 465.

93.   Ibid.

94.   An elimination of such dead metaphor would be
      facilitated by following leads regarding content
      and act in Insight, 81.

Notes: Chapter 4

95. "We place transcendence, not in going beyond a known knower, but in heading for being within which there are positive differences and, among such differences, the difference between object and subject", Insight, 377. The full argument spans pages 314-88 of this work. See also Method in Theology, 235-53.

96. G. Flaubert, Madame Bovary, translated by Alan Russell, Penguin Classics, 1977, 196.

97. Ibid., 103.

98. Ibid., 210.

99. Ibid., 236.

100. Ibid., 329.

101. Method in Theology, 265.

102. Cited, and discussed, by Poulet from a first draft of Madame Bovary, op. cit., note 90, 466.

103. From methodological reflection on the circle see Insight, 7-13; for similar reflections on the oval see McShane, Wealth of Self and Wealth of Nations, 22-23.

104. Madame Bovary, 91.

105. Lonergan, Verbum: Word and Idea in Aquinas, 7.

106. The issue here parallels that raised regarding the presence of a dog in Lonergan, Collection, 161. The entire discussion there is relevant here.

107. Lonergan, Collection, 163.

108. Ibid.

109. The conception of that complexity is spelled out in Lonergan, Insight, 375-84.

110. Collection, 162-63.

111. See note 83, above.

112. It is not easy to stretch the mind and imag-
     ination towards this transformation which I
     consider axial (the term is Jaspers', but it
     relates here to Lonergan's third stage of
     meaning). If, for instance, sculpture
     "effects the objectification of self and envir-
     onment for the sense of sight", S. Langer,
     Feeling and Form, Scribner, N.Y., 1953, 91,
     then one must expect a difference in object-
     ification and in the reception of all sculpture
     in history (consider a new Schiller's reaction
     to the bust of Juno Ludovisi), corresponding to
     the transformation of subjects. One might
     further envisage the transformation of such a
     work as Langer's Feeling and Form, liberated from
     dead metaphor.

113. R. Cross, Flaubert and Joyce, Princeton Univer-
     sity Press, 1971, 72.

114. Julian Press, N.Y., 1969.

115. Cited in Maurice Nadeau, The Greatness of Flau-
     bert, translated by B. Bray, The Library Press,
     N.Y., 1972, 123.

116. Joyce, Ulysses, conclusion.

117. Method in Theology, 239.

118. F. E. Crowe, "Christologies: How Up-to-date is
     Yours?", Theological Studies XXIX, 1968, 101.

119. A. Toynbee, Experiences, Oxford University Press,
     N.Y., 1969, 356.

120. Joyce, Finnegans Wake, 598.

Notes: Chapter 5

1.   A remark of W. B. Yeats quoted in Richard
     Ellman, Yeats: The Man and the Masks, Dutton,
     N.Y., 1948, 5.

2.   The paper mentioned immediately in the text
     was presented by Lonergan at the conference
     noted in the Introduction, vii.

3.   Method in Theology, 317.   See above vii, n.20.

4.   Heinrich Schenker, "Organic Structure in Sonata
     Form", Journal of Music Theory (12), 1968,
     194-95.

5.   Saul Bellow, Mr. Sammler's Planet, Penguin
     Books, 1970, 263.

6.   Ibid., 286.

7.   The title of an early book of K. Horney,
     published by W. W. Norton, N.Y., 1937.

8.   See The Shaping of the Foundations, 135 ff.,
     where I discuss in particular the bridge ment-
     ioned by Lonergan at the beginning of his
     discussion of space and time, Insight, 140.

9.   Method in Theology, 292.

10. From the Preface of the old Latin Mass for the
     Nativity.

11. The notion is an adaptation of suggestions by
     Eric Fromm, The Anatomy of Human Destructiveness,
     Fawcett Crest Books, N.Y., 1973, 27-31,
     ".... necrophilia, the passion to destroy life
     and the attraction to all that is dead, decay-
     ing, and purely mechanical....sensitivity towards
     destructiveness-cruelty is rapidly diminishing,
     and necrophilia,.... is increasing throughout
     our cybernetic industrial society".

12. See, for example, Theodore Roszak, The Dissent-
     ing Academy, Random House, N.Y., 1967.

13. I return to the topic of alienation in the
     next chapter, 106 ff.

14. J.-J. Rousseau, The First and Second Discourse, ed. Roger D. Masters, St. Martin, N.Y., 1964, 51.

15. Leo Strauss, "The Three Waves of Modernity", in Political Philosophy. Six Essays by Leo Strauss, ed. H. Gilden, Pegasus, Indianapolis, 1975.

16. F. Lawrence, "Political Theology and 'the longer cycle of decline'", Lonergan Workshop, Vol. I, ed. F. Lawrence, Scholars Press, 1978, 240.

17. Lonergan, Verbum: Word and Idea in Aquinas, 26, n.122. See also the work of P. Hoenan cited in chapter 2, n.28 (163, below), for a revelation of Scotus' influence on Thomism.

18. F. E. Crowe, "St. Thomas and the Concrete Operabile", Sciences Ecclésiastiques, 1955-56, rescues St. Thomas' meaning of application.

19. The monster, of course, is not simply an external thing. "If a man is a hero, he is a hero precisely because, in the final reckoning, he did not let the monster devour him, but subdued it, not once but many times. Victory over the collective psyche alone yields the true value - the capture of the hoard, the invincible weapon, the magic talisman....Anyone who identifies with the collective psyche - or, in mythological terms, lets himself be devoured by the monster - and vanishes in it, attains the treasure that the dragon guards, but he does so in spite of himself and to his own greatest harm". Cited from Jung's "The Relations between the Ego and the Unconscious", Two Essays in Analytic Psychology, tr. R.F.C. Hull, Collected Works, Princeton, 1966, VII, 173, by R. Doran, "Christ and the Psyche", Trinification of the World, eds. T. A. Dunne and J.-M. Laporte, Regis College Press, 1978, 116. Fr. Doran's work complements my own in emphasizing the need for an adequate modernity of a religious psychology. I am uncomfortable, however, about some of his basic strategies. So, for example, he suggests "The sublation of both psychology and

method by the process of the discernment of
spirits", (137: italics his).   This, it seems,
is to miss the point of method, and calls for
comments parallel to those made regarding Fr.
Tracy's work, above, 24-5.

20.   Of interest perhaps, Lonergan's review of
Plotinus: The Enneads, translated by Stephen
McKenna, revised by B. S. Page, Gregorianum
(40), 1959, 389-90.

21.   See B. Lonergan, Method in Theology, 40:   "Such
is the monster that has stood forth in our time;
90:    "....The culture has become a slum".

22.   E. G. Schachtel, "On Memory and Childhood
Amnesia", Psychiatry 10 (1947), 1-26;   cited
in R. M. Jones, The New Psychology of Dreaming,
Penguin, 1978, 136-37.

23.   Recall Yalton's comment on Locke's essay,
cited on page 72, above, at n. 77.   Also
Toulmin's remark in his book on Human Understanding (above, 6):   surely a self-condemnatory
remark.   See also T. Fenelhum, "Hume's Theory
of the Self Revisited", Dialogue, 1975, 389-409,
and the references there;   also Synthese (21),
1970:   Hilpinen, "Knowing that one Knows and the
Classical Definition of Knowledge", 109-32;
Ginet, "What Must be added to Knowing to Obtain
Knowing that one Knows?", 163-86.

24.   Method in Theology, 260.

25.   Op. cit., n.11, 110.

26.   Ibid., 27.

27.   Ibid.

28.   I have made a similar suggestion regarding
Piaget in chapter 2, n.22, 163 below.

29.   The shift is described succinctly in Insight,
464 ff.   On reductionism and language defects,
see above, 21, and the references there.   See
also n.140, of chapter 1, above, 160.

30. Recall the discussion in chapter 4 above, 76 ff.

31. The relevant text is cited in n.45, of chapter
     1, 151 above.

32. Above 9, and implicitly throughout the Introd-
     uction.

33. I am recalling here the first Vatican Council's
     view on mysteries (DS3016). I am not sugg-
     esting a clouding of natural understanding:
     on the contrary theology aims at systematically
     focusing the mystery through inverse insight.
     See Lonergan, De Deo Trino: Pars Dogmatica,
     1964, 274. See also above, 22-3.

34. See notes 102, 136 of chapter 1 (above, 156,
     160).

35. The Origins of Modern Science, G. Bell & Sons,
     London, 1965, 190.

36. I have discussed the methodological problems
     of zoology in "Zoology and the Future of
     Philosophy", The Shaping of the Foundations,
     79-95.

37. "Every person is an embodiment of natural right.
     Every person can reveal to any other his nat-
     ural propensity to seek understanding, to judge
     reasonably, to evaluate fairly, to be open to
     friendship. While the dialectic of history
     coldly relates our conflicts, dialogue adds
     the principle that prompts us to cure them, the
     natural right that is the inmost core of our
     being". Cited from the conclusion of a recent
     paper by Lonergan entitled "Natural Right and
     Historical Mindedness", a paper read to the
     American Catholic Philosophical Association,
     Easter 1977.

38. On technology, see notes 123 and 130 of the
     following chapter (195, 197, below).

39. Pierre Boulez, "Sonate, Que me veux-tu?"
     Perspectives of New Music (1), 1963, 32.

40.   Brian Moore, _An Answer from Limbo_, Paper Jacks,
      Canada, 1973, 269.

41.   The beginning of Brian Moore's novel, _I am Mary
      Dunne_, McClelland and Steward, Toronto, 1966.

42.   It is not easy to stretch the mind and imagin-
      ation to envisage this transformation of sens-
      ibility.   If, for instance, sculpture "effects
      the objectification of self and environment
      for the sense of sight", (S. Langer, _Feeling
      and Form_, London, 1953, 91), then one must
      expect a difference in objectification and in
      its reception corresponding to the transformed
      subjects.   One might further envisage a
      parallel difference of content and expression
      in a work such as _Feeling and Form._

43.   Recall here our discussion in the previous
      chapter of dead metaphor (above, 71 ff).

44.   E. Voegelin, _The Ecumenic Age_, Louisiana State
      University Press, 1974, 304.

45.   _Insight_, 185.

46.   _Method in Theology_.

47.   _Ibid._, 88, n.34.

48.   H. Hesse, _Narziss and Goldmund_, Penguin, 61.

Notes: Chapter 6

1.   _Method in Theology_, 55..

2.   I use the word in a Viconesque sense, and in a
      sense related to notes 47 and 95 of chapter 1
      (above 151, 155), as well as in the more evid-
      ent sense: that their content recurs in the
      list of general categories, _Method in Theology_,
      286-7.   The recurrence, obviously, must be in
      the subject seeking foundations.

3.   Method in Theology, 250.

4.   Oxford University Press, N.Y., 1954.

5.   This echoes August Boeckh's view of philology,
     as noted by Lonergan, Method in Theology, 210.

6.   I think here of actual context, interwoven
     questions and answers as constitutive of the
     subject. See Method in Theology, 163.

7.   The harmony calls for inner dialogue of the
     six-levelled subject, as well as a third-stage-
     of-meaning aesthetics of global transformation.
     Further pointers on this topic are given in
     section 5.

8.   Lonergan, "Philosophy and Theology", A Second
     Collection, 1974, 206.

9.   Ibid.

10. Method in Theology, 273-76;   303-05.

11. "The intelligibility....is immanent in world
     process....Emergent probability is a view of
     world order within the limits of empirical
     method", Insight, 128.   In what sense the form
     is normative will gradually emerge.   Praxis
     transforms the notion of empirical method: see
     above 18-25.

12. Method in Theology, 93-99.   Recall Insight,
     647:   "The intelligible in the ordinary sense
     can be understood without understanding what it
     is to understand;   but the intelligible in the
     profounder sense is identical with the under-
     standing, and so it cannot be understood without
     understanding what understanding is".

13. 1680, the beginnings of modern science and of
     the Enlightenment, is a relevant date.   See
     Lonergan, "Theology in its New Context",
     A Second Collection.

14. One should put Insight, 364-74, and Lonergan,
     De Constitutione Christi, Gregorian Press, Rome

1961, 9-13, into the context of E. Voegelin's
"Reason: The Classic Experience", The
Southern Review, July 1974, 245-64.

15. H. Butterfield, The Origins of Modern Science,
Bell, London, 1965, vii: the scientific revol-
ution "outshines everything since the rise of
Christianity and reduces the Renaissance and
Reformation to the rank of mere episodes".

16. "The Greeks needed an artistic, a rhetorical,
an argumentative development of language before
a Greek could set up a metaphysical account of
mind. The Greek achievement was needed to
expand the capacities of commonsense knowledge
and language before Augustine, Descartes, Pascal,
Newman could make their commonsense contributions
to our self-knowledge. The history of mathematics, natural science, and philosophy and,
as well, one's own personal reflective engagement in all three are needed if both commonsense
and theory are to construct the scaffolding for
an entry into the world of interiority", Method
in Theology, 261-62.

17. Lonergan, "Philosophy and Theology", A Second
Collection, 200. Illustrative of the attitude
is Lonergan's discussion of natural right in
"Natural Right and Historical Mindedness",
a paper read to the American Catholic Philosophical Association, Easter, 1977.

18. The precise meaning of "normative" here requires
the praxis view of the actual, probable and
possible seriations discussed in section two.

19. I have presented the case for this in "Image and
Emergence: Towards an Adequate Weltanschuung",
chapter 1 of The Shaping of the Foundations.

20. Lonergan, "Theology in its New Context", A
Second Collection, 60.

21. Method in Theology, 286-88, briefly lists these.
I must insist, however, on the difficulty of
this inclusion. "If one wants to know just what
forms are, the proper procedure is to give up

metaphysics and turn to the sciences", Insight, 498.   This page in Insight speaks of a division of labour.   In the third stage of meaning, with generalized empirical method as academic method, this division and a separate metaphysics become obsolete.

22.   Method in Theology, 292.

23.   "That notion of survival which is you at core but also you in kilos", McShane, Wealth of Self and Wealth of Nations, 95.   The particular chapter, "The Notion of Survival", raises a set of issues relevant to the present essay.

24.   See notes 47 and 95 of chapter 1 (above, 151,155).

25.   Lonergan, "The Origins of Christian Realism", A Second Collection, 239-62.   Relevant also is a history of the emergence of the vision in Lonergan.

26.   "Intus in nobis intelligibiliter secundum emanationem veritatis dicitur verbum nostrum verbi divini et secundum emanationem sanctitatis spiratur dilectio nostra divinae Dilectionis", Lonergan, De Deo Trino, Pars Systematica, Gregorian Press, Rome, 1964.   The present essay focuses on general categories.   But clearly Lonergan's transformation of Trinitarian theology is the centrepiece of the new Christian vision, I have tried to present it in popular form in Music That Is Soundless: An Introduction to God for the Graduate, University Press of America, Washington, 1977, chapters 5 - 7.

27.   On different degrees of sympathy see The Shaping of the Foundations, 105 ff.

28.   G. Bachelard, The Poetics of Space, Beacon. Press, Boston, 1970, 61.

29.   Central to the entire effort is a fundamental inverse insight.   One should link here Method in Theology, 341-42 with the treatment of mystery and inverse insight in De Deo Trino: Pars Dogmatica, 1964, 274.

30.   See _Insight_, 510.   _Praxisweltanschuung_,
      however, changes the meaning of the page - and
      indeed of the book as gesture.   One may speak
      of "the realization in accord with successive
      schedules of probabilities of the compound
      conditioned series of concretely possible solut-
      ions", but what does one mean by "realization"?
      One is not an observer.   By _Praxisweltanschuung_
      one is in ever more disturbing yet peaceful
      resonance with the finality of being.

31.   Lonergan, _De Constitutione Christi_, 80.

32.   _Insight_, 115-128, 259-62.

33.   Just what one means by, and can say about, such
      a symbolic indication helps to locate one's
      position with regard to the improbable vision.
      The animal is an integrated (zoological forms
      in the unity of a thing) aggregate of the three
      lower levels. p_i denotes forms of physics.
      How would one symbolise organs and neural net-
      works etc?   All this may seem farfetched, even
      foolish.   Yet the psychologists are hard at an
      equivalent, but largely reductionist, exterprize
      (see, for example, _Macromolecules and Behaviour_,
      edited by John Gaito, Appleton Century Crofts,
      N.Y., 1966).   Do the children of light have to
      always arrive "a little breathless and a little
      late"?   See the text at note 46, above 96.

34.   On the notion of collective responsibility, see
      the beginning of the paper by Lonergan, "Natural
      Right and Historicity" mentioned in note 17,
      above.

35.   A text I have found extremely helpful in opening
      up the explanatory perspective is _Insight_, 464-66,
      "Study of an organism begins from the thing-for-
      us...."   One can replace the word "organism" by
      plant, dog, man, Christ, universe and strain to
      reach the "world invisible" of explanation (see
      Insight, 394-95).   I may refer forward here also
      to the notion of transposition as discussed in
      section 5.   See note 40, below.

36.   _Insight_, 119.

37.   Ibid., 118.

38.   Selected from a table of business recessions
      in England (1790-1925), W. Mitchell, Business
      Cycles: The Problem and its Setting, National
      Bureau of Economic Research, New York, 1927,
      390.

39.   Insight, 119.

40.   Ibid. Perhaps at this stage I might indicate
      a diagrammatic underpinning that may help.
      One needs a solid global matrix, radius measuring
      time, each layer being a network of elements of
      schedules of probability at each corresponding
      point on earth. Six-levelled things within
      schemes become part of the actual series with
      the emergence of man. Obviously, one needs
      Toynbee and Voegelin and Lonergan's sets and
      sequences of differentiations of consciousness
      to fill this out. And one needs to complement
      and balance such diagramming with Method in
      Theology, 48 and Collection, 42; etc., etc.

41.   Method in Theology, 251.

42.   I refer to the two million copies sold of Samuel-
      son's famous text book. However, had Samuelson
      thought and written otherwise, the probability
      schedules would have shifted.

43.   Insight, 466.

44.   Ibid., 118.

45.   Ibid., 121. See also Randomness, Statistics
      and Emergence, 230-31.

46.   Insight, 733.

47.   Ibid., 119.

48.   Method in Theology, 40.

49.   See above, v, 84 ff.

50.   I refer to Voegelin's notion of the In-between.

See The Ecumenic Age, Lousiana State University
Press, 1974.

51.   Insight, 472-77.

52.   What is meant by "admission into consciousness"
       is discussed in the Epilogue of The Shaping of
       the Foundations, 124 ff.   "Hoping into consc-
       iousness" is related to the discussion of the
       Eschaton there.

53.   I recall the notion of self-inclusion from
       section 1.   Third stage meaning involves a
       discontinuity in instrumental acts of meaning.
       Is the component not the composer?

54.   Lonergan, Circulation Analysis, 2.   I am grate-
       ful to Fr. Lonergan for permission to quote from
       his unpublished work throughout this and later
       chapters.

55.   A. Toynbee, Mankind and Mother Earth, A Narrative
       History of the World, Oxford University Press,
       1976, 53-54.   The use of the word "surplus" in
       Lonergan's analysis relates more to Toynbee's
       usage than to that of Marx.

56.   J. Schumpeter, History of Economic Analysis,
       Oxford University Press, N.Y., 1954, 1135.

57.   Business Cycles.   A Theoretical, Historical and
       Statistical Analysis of the Capitalist Process,
       2 volumes, McGraw-Hill, N.Y., 1939.

58.   The analysis was probably completed in 1944.
       Lonergan's dependence on Schumpeter is not clear.
       Lonergan's notes include 25 pages of handwritten
       notes on, and extracts from, Schumpeter, some of
       which (like that cited shortly in the text)
       indicate that Lonergan had a developed view
       when reading Schumpeter.

59.   Schumpeter distinguishes these various sides of
       Marx in Capitalism, Socialism and Democracy,
       Harper and Row, 1942, Part One.   That Part is
       reprinted in Joseph Schumpeter, Ten Great Econ-
       omists from Marx to Keynes, Oxford University
       Press, N.Y., 1951.

60. H. Smith, "Marx and the Trade Cycle", The Review of Economic Studies (iv) 1936-37, 202.

61. J. Schumpeter, Ten Great Economists, 50-51.

62. Ibid., 7.

63. Wesley Mitchell's characterisation: op. cit., note 40, 11.

64. Apart from the Juglar, two other types of cycle have been named: the Kitchin, a short cycle of about three years, and the Kondratieff, a long cycle of about sixty years.

65. From handwritten notes, in a file labelled "Economic Analysis: notes Nov. 1942, no.60".

66. Schumpeter, Business Cycles, Vol.I, 140.

67. Ibid., 134. I would note that economic space requires the large six-levelled heuristic of sections 1 and 2. See also notes 128, 129 below, 196-97.

68. Lonergan, Circulation Analysis, 86.

69. Ibid., 19.

70. Lonergan, from an incomplete early typescript in a file "Econ. Spec. (2) No. 58". The type-script is entitled An Outline of Circulation Analysis, and the quotation is from section 1, "Viewpoint".

71. Lonergan, from the same file and typescript, as mentioned in note 70, section 2, "Method".

72. Clarendon Press, Oxford, 1950.

73. Arthur Burns, The Frontiers of Economic Knowledge, National Bureau of Economic Research, Princeton University Press, 1954, 267.

74. Ibid., 97. The comment occurs in the essay, "Wesley Mitchell and the National Bureau, 61-106.

75. The volume by Burns, just cited, is a good exam-ple. See, for instance, his essays "Economic

Research and the Keynesian Thinking of our Time",
26-45 and "Hicks and the Real Cycle", 236-67,
from which I have already quoted at note 73.
The British tradition, of course, that Robinson
represents, continues to call for serious theor-
etic effort: "The sad thing is that economists,
including many more eminent than Bober, continue
to be defeatist in this way about the possibility
of understanding the real world, and gladly
retreat into their warm, theoretical wombs,
where they are not threatened by facts.   What
is needed is a reallocation of economic brain-
power towards an analysis and interpretation of
the real world".   J. C. Odling-Smee, in a
review of S. Bober, The Economics of Cycles and
Growth, John Wiley, N.Y., and London, 1968, in
Economic Journal 79 (1969), 588.

76.   Op. cit., note 73, 175.

77.   Lonergan, Circulation Analysis, 73.

78.   Alvin Hansen, "Economic Progress and Declining
       Population Growth", American Economic Review,
       Vol. XXIX, No.1, (March 1939), 4.

79.   So titled in William Breit and Roger Ransom,
       The Academic Scribblers: American Economists
       in Collision, Holt Rinehart and Winston, N.Y.,
       1971.   This volume couples with Joan Robinson's
       Economic Heresies: Some Old-Fashioned Questions
       in Economic Theory, Basic Books, N.Y., 1973,
       provides a background to the present section.

80.   See the previous footnote.   Her recent text
       book, written with John Eatwell, An Introduction
       to Modern Economics, McGraw Hill, Maidenhead,
       England, 1973, complements this criticism.
       The next chapter will discuss this text book
       more fully.

81.   As I write, Time magazine surveys a new generat-
       ion of economists who are discontent with both
       Keynes and heavy government involvement.   But
       they give no indication of a large view of econ-
       omic dynamics.   So, for example, the following
       remark of Martin Feldstein may be greeted with
       the smile of the quotation at note 77, above,
       103:   "We know enough to move the economy out

of a trough but not enough to control the
business cycle".   (<u>Time</u>, August 27, 1979, 27).

82.   J. Robinson, in a review of C. E.
       Ferguson, <u>The Neo-classical Theory of Production and
       Distribution</u>, Cambridge University Press,
       London, 1969, in Economic Journal 80, 1970,
       337.   I am indebted to a set of more recent
       (1976) notes and extracts (pp.37) of Fr. Lonergan
       for this reference.

83.   <u>Method in Theology</u>, 11.   See also <u>Insight</u>, 30.
       There is a great deal more, of course, to be
       gleaned on abstraction and conception in
       Lonergan, <u>Verbum: Word and Idea in Aquinas</u>,
       University of Notre Dame Press, 1967; see the
       Index.

84.   <u>Insight</u>, 87-89.

85.   The paper continues to point to the necessity
       of the inner word of <u>Praxisweltanschuung</u>.   It
       is useful to recall here Lonergan's discussions
       of the necessity of inner words. <u>De Deo Trino,
       Pars Systematica</u>, 1964, 105, 290.   "Tertia
       autem verborum necessitas est ut scientias
       excolere possimus.   Nisi enim verba universalia
       formerentur, totum mundum aspectabilem nunquam
       scire possemus, sed ad particularia experta vel
       imaginata religaremur.   Item, nisi verba exacte
       definita formarentur, fluxu quoddam imagimum ad
       modum mentalitatis mythicae ferremur, cum
       nunquam clare et distincte constaret de quanam
       re ageretur", 105.

86.   One may note that the two difficulties are not
       unrelated.   See <u>Insight</u>, chapter 8, for the
       contrast between "body", which grounds confusion
       and blocks thought and "thing", which is the
       basis of a clear heuristic conception of change,
       genera and species, aggregates of events and
       the emergent probability of things.

87.   Leon Walras, <u>Elements of Pure Economics</u>, trans-
       lated by W. Jaffe, Richard Irwin, Inc., Illinois,
       1954.   Originally published in 1874.   "Samuel-
       son feels that Walras and Augustin Cournot

carried the development of mathematics in economics to a highly sophisticated level by the turn of the twentieth century. At that point, he claims the study was interrupted by the 'verbal' tradition of the English economists at Cambridge". (Breit and Ransom, The Academic Scribblers, 114, n).

88.   J. Schumpeter, History of Economic Analysis, 964, italics his.

89.   Ibid., 1160.

90.   Ibid., 1161.

91.   J. Robinson, Economic Heresies, XV.   The inner quotation is from J. M. Keynes, The General Theory of Employment, Interest and Money, Macmillan, London, 1936, 378-79.   Robinson seeks to rescue Keynes from the Keynesians, and even from himself.   She also draws on the Polish thinker, M. Kalecki, who independently arrived at a more coherent position than Keynes. We will refer to Kalecki later.   Schumpeter is, to say the least, not over-enthusiastic about Keynes' achievement.   I refer here to his essay on Keynes in Ten Great Economists, 260-91.   He even remarks that "Professor Myrdal's gentle sneer at 'that Anglo-Saxon kind of unnecessary originality' is amply justified", ibid., 277.

92.   Schumpeter, Ten Great Economists, 282.

93.   I pass over this topic entirely here.   There is a brief presentation of the theory as "The Hicks-Hansen Synthesis" in Breit and Ransom, The Academic Scribblers, 107-10.   It originated with Hicks' "Mr. Keynes and the 'Classics': A Suggested Interpretation", Econometrica 5 (1937), 147-59.   It is standard text book stuff.   It is bad statics.   J. Robinson gives it due treatment, Economic Heresies, 82-85.   In contrast with Hicks' simple relating of increasing interest rate to decreasing investment, there is the refreshingly realistic efforts of M. Kalecki, e.g., "Entrepreneurial Capital and Investment", "Determinants of Investment", both essays reprinted in his Selected Essays on the Dynamics

of the Capitalist Economy 1933-1970, Cambridge
University Press, 1971.

94. Breit and Ransom, The Academic Scribblers, 89.

95. Breit and Ransom, op. cit., tell the story at
     some length.

96. J. Robinson, Economic Heresies, 87.

97. The whirlpool contains the aggregate of six-
     levelled vortices of human aspiration and human
     desperation.

98. A Lowe, On Economic Knowledge. Towards a Science
     of Political Economics, Harper and Row, N.Y.,
     1965, discusses the problems of microautonomy
     and control. I have commented on his work in
     Wealth of Self and Wealth of Nations, chapter 10.

99. Lonergan, in a talk on art, during a workshop
     on the philosophy of education, 1959.

100. Method in Theology, 55, the last two paragraphs.

101. Lonergan, "Theology in its New Context", A
     Second Collection, 67.

102. Insight, 741-42.

103. I have treated the topic memory, re-membering,
     "boning up", in The Shaping of the Foundations,
     107 ff. Again, foundational shifts are normat-
     ively integral. One may recall, with symbolic
     value, Marcel's words: "the thinker is contin-
     ually on guard against the alienation (through
     inertia), the fossilization of his thought. He
     lives in a continual state of creativity and the
     whole of his thought is always called in question
     from one minute to the next", Being and Having,
     Fontana, 1965, 181.

104. The point was made by Lonergan in correspondence
     with me in the summer of 1968. He had been
     reading Metz' political theology at the time.
     It was then that he indicated the existence of
     his Circulation Analysis to me and was seeking an
     economist who would be interested in working on it.

105. F. E. Crowe, "Doctrines and Historicity in the
      Context of Lonergan's Method", Theological
      Studies, 38, 1977, 123.

106. Method in Theology, 286-88. A careful reading
      brings out the sublation.

107. Ibid., 298.

108. Ibid., 132-33.

109. Ibid., 142.

110. Ibid., 304. Recall the quotation on 94, above,
      at note 17.

111. Ibid., 319.

112. Ibid., 353.

113. Ibid., 317.

114. Insight, 504-06.

115. Ibid., 504.

116. Ibid., 506.

117. Ibid., 505.

118. The quotation is a comment of Lonergan's, from
      the 37 page set of 1976 notes already mentioned
      (note 82, above, 191). The comment is on an
      article by R. R. Nelson and S. G. Winter,
      "Neoclassical vs. Evolutionary Theories of
      Economic Growth: Critique and Prospectus",
      Economic Journal, 84, 1974, 886-905.

119. See note 110 above, the quotation at 108, and
      recall note 40, above, 187. The strategy I
      indicated in note 35 is useful here. Recall,
      for example, that the dog is studied by genetic
      method. An adequate account of the set of
      organic tracts within the dog's life requires
      that method and its context of emergent prob-
      ability. An account handling a "slice" of the
      dog's life falls far short of this. Think, now

of the larger problem that is associated with
the set of dogmatic tracts.

120.   In The Shaping of the Foundations, 116-17, I
discussed the problem of communication within
theology in terms of an 8 x 8 symmetrical matrix.
Unfortunately, contemporary theology, unlike
most other modern areas of inquiry, does not
have that problem in any acute fashion.

121.   The doctrine is associated with the Englishman
John A. Hobson, with Rosa Luxemburg, with Lenin.
It relates to the channeling of surplus wealth
abroad, to an economics of armament and war,
and to a theory of the instability of capitalism.
See M. Kalecki, "The Problem of Effective Demand
with Tugan-Baranovski and Rosa Luxemburg",
Selected Essays on the Dynamics of the Capitalist
Economy, 1933-1970, 146-55.   The problem is
popularly discussed in R. Heilbroner, "The
Victorian World and the Underworld of Economics",
The Worldly Philosophers, 164-204.

122.   See Nicholas Kaldor, "The Irrelevance of Equilibrium Economics", Economic Journal 82, 1972,
1237-1255; particularly the text cited later
in chapter 8, above 133-34; again I am indebted
here to Lonergan's 1976 notes for this reference.
Lonergan's analysis shows no hesitation about
the significance of prices: "prices cannot be
regarded as ultimate norms guiding strategic
economic decisions....the function of prices is
merely to provide a mechanism for overcoming the
divergence of strategically indifferent decisions...", Circulation Analysis, 1.   Also, internal to Lonergan's analysis is a theory of
distribution.

123.   The popular discontent with the quality of life
is regularly sublated by economists, without
much theoretical underpinning, and with little
suspicion of the large educational problem of a
microautonomic shift in values.   Again, it is
essential to locate the scientific and technological advances within the optimism of an emergent
probability which recognises the different sets
of statistics relating to the maturation of the
lower, middle and higher sciences and technologies
in the next 1,000 years.

124.   A context here is E. Voegelin, The Ecumenic Age,
       Lousiana State University Press, 1974.   Were
       the unifications of Italy, of Germany, of S.A.
       and of S.S.R. progress or decline?

125.   There is much that is suggestive in Lonergan's
       unpublished typescripts and handwritten notes.
       In a file, dating probably from the early forties,
       of economic notes and clippings, there is a
       brief scribble: "Either minimum taxes, free
       capitalist (machine?), violent cycles from above
       corrected by elimination or social welfare prog-
       rammes, high taxes, breakdown of capitalist
       motivation, socialism, or middle way - group
       economics".

126.   On the unhappy history of the Sherman Act and
       its reforms, see William Letwin, Law and Econ-
       omic Policy in America.   The Evolution of the
       Sherman Antitrust Act, Random House, N.Y., 1965.
       What can be noted throughout is "the relative
       lack of economic criteria in the formulation
       of....legislation", W. L. Baldwin, Antitrust and
       the Changing Corporation, Duke University Press,
       North Carolina, 1961, 282.   The United Kingdom
       started late (1948: Monopolies and Restrictive
       Trade Practices Act), but "have fallen into
       almost all the same pitfalls as their American
       counterparts", P. J. Curwen and A. H. Fowler,
       Economic Policy, Macmillan Press, 1976, Introd-
       uction.   There is required here an integration
       of Lonergan's analysis with contemporary discuss-
       ions of degrees of monopoly, both corporation
       and labour.

127.   "....the depression has notably augmented the
       numbers of the unemployed, and so the brilliant
       expedient of a steep income tax on the rich to
       provide a dole for the poor will effect the
       required....(adjustment); the upper leisure
       class of rentiers is recruited from a lower class
       of unemployed.   Obviously an economy that has
       worked itself into this impasse is not to be
       regarded as a model of enlightened legislation
       ....", Circulation Analysis, 125-26.

128.   I think here of an extension from house to city
       to environment to globe of G. Bachelard, The

Notes: Chapter 6

Poetics of Space, Beacon Bress, Boston, 1970.

129. Recall R. Poole on ethical space, Towards Deep Subjectivity, Harper Torchbook, 1972.

130. There is a large but somewhat stagnant literature on the relation of technology to human living. (For a survey see Bernard Gendron, Technology and the Human Condition, St. Martin's Press, N.Y., 1977). What is needed, however, is a reorientation of technological innovation within generalized empirical method. See note 124 above. E. F. Schumacher, Small is Beautiful: Economics as if People Mattered, Harper and Row, N.Y., 1975, is suggestive.

131. Henry C. Simons, Economic Policy for a Free Society, University of Chicago Press, 1948, 157.

132. Method in Theology, 320.

133. Insight, xxviii.

134. Method in Theology is method. But Method in Theology recurs in dialectic, and there it is to be faced incarnately.

135. Method in Theology, 317.

136. Lonergan, "Dimensions of Meaning", Collection, 266-67.

Notes: Chapter 7

1. Hywel Jones, An Introduction to Modern Theories of Growth, Nelson, London, 1978, 71.

2. A Lowe, The Path of Economic Growth, assisted by Stanford Pulrang with an appendix by E. J. Nell, Cambridge University Press, N.Y., 1976, ix.

3. Ibid., 7.

4. P. Sraffa, Production of Commodities by Means of Commodities, Cambridge University Press, 1960, 3-4; Lowe op. cit., 39.

5. Above, 104. For a summary account of the capital controversy, see Hywel Jones, op. cit., note 1, 127-142.

6. A. Lowe, op. cit., 44.

7. The book cited in note 1 above gives a convenient survey.

8. A. Burns, The Frontiers of Economic Knowledge, Princeton University Press, 1954, 267.

9. T. C. Koopmans, Readings in Business Cycles, eds. R. A. Gordon and L. A. Klein, Irwin, Homewood, Illinois, 1965, 192.

10. The Stages of Economic Growth, Cambridge University Press, 1960; Politics and the Stages of Growth, Cambridge University Press, 1971.

11. On the new economic history, see A. Fishlow, "The New Economic History Revisited", The Journal of European Economic History (3) 1974; M. Levy-Leboyer, "La 'New Economic History'", Annales (24) 1969. By the end of the essay the reader familiar with these traditions may be able to detect the relevance of Lonergan's functional analysis both to Rostow's view on take-off and to contra-factual historical analysis: indeed the adequate context for the latter analysis is Lonergan's view of emergent probability, with its series of actual, probable and possible schemes.

12. A recent substantial book by G. R. Feiwel, The Intellectual Capital of Michal Kalecki, University of Tennessee Press, 1975, puts Kalecki in a broad context. I would note that on page 458 Feiwel wrongly speculates that Schumpeter's omission of Kalecki's views from his History of Economic Analysis may have been due either to ignorance or to Schumpeter's lack of respect for Keynes. In fact, Schumpeter had considered

Kalecki's early work critically in his <u>Business
Cycles</u>, Vol.I, 1939, 185-89.

13. R. Frish, "Propagation Problems and Impulse
     Problems in Dynamic Economics", (first published
     in 1933), <u>Readings in Business Cycles</u>, R. A.
     and L. A. Klein, (eds.), Irwin, Homewood,
     Illinois, 1965, 155-56.

14. J. Schumpeter, <u>History of Economic Analysis</u>,
     Oxford University Press, New York, 1974,
     1160-61.

15. J. M. Keynes, <u>The General Theory of Employment,
     Interest and Money</u>, Macmillan, London, 1936,
     378-79; see Robinson, <u>Economic Heresies</u>,
     Basic Books, N.Y., 1973, xv.

16. Robinson and Eatwell, 51.

17. <u>Ibid.</u>, 89.

18. Below, 121.

19. William James, <u>Pragmatism</u>, Longmans, London,
     1912, 198.

20. See Schumpeter, <u>History of Economic Analysis</u>,
     1122-35; R. G. Link, <u>English Theories of
     Economic Fluctuations, 1815-1848</u>, Columbia
     University Press, 1959.

21. Neoclassical economics too has its islands with
     odd names like Solovia, Roswesri-Adelphi (see
     Hywel Jones, <u>op</u>. <u>cit</u>., note 1, 208) but on such
     islands it is not the people but the mathematical
     functions that are well-behaved. Our island,
     if you like, is in Lonergan's Cosmopolis (<u>Insight</u>,
     238): see also the following note.

22. I have discussed Lowe's view of control and
     microautonomy (expressed in his book <u>On Economic
     Knowledge</u>, Harper and Row, 1965) in chapter 10
     of <u>Wealth of Self and Wealth of Nations</u>, where
     I try to bring out the necessary dimensions of
     the required cultural shift. The issue of
     genuine political and economic liberty is funda-
     mentally the issue raised in the introduction,

the issue of education.   In a recent (1978)
revision of his economic manuscript Lonergan
has remarked: "coming to grasp what serious
education really is and, nonetheless, coming
to accept that challenge constitutes the
greatest challenge to the modern economy".

23.   Robinson, Economic Heresies, 39-40;   Robinson
and Eatwell, 183 ff.

24.   Robinson and Eatwell, 94.

25.   Robinson, Economic Heresies, 141.

26.   See Robinson, a review of C. E. Ferguson,
The Neo-classical Theory of Production and
Distribution, Economic Journal 80 (1970).

27.   Lonergan, "Theology and Praxis", Proceedings
of the Catholic Theological Society of America,
1977, 1.   Lonergan is here recalling the
Aristotelian position which is sublated in his
view of praxis.   I would note here that my
criticism of Robinson and Eatwell is not that
that they lack concern.   Their book springs from
concern about the inadequacy of present economics.

28.   Lonergan, Circulation Analysis, 97.

29.   Robinson and Eatwell, 183.

30.   Schumpeter, History of Economic Analysis, 963.

31.   In the previous chapter, especially in the footnotes of section 5 (196-97 above), I indicated
some wider political, legal and technological
implications of the analysis.   The reader no
doubt will arrive at further questions regarding
increasing and diminishing returns, monopoly
capital, and monopoly labour, welfare and
employment, the fundamental chasm between central
planning and the local subject's creative
insight, and so on.   These are legitimate
further questions.   I have insisted on focusing
on the central issue: the need of a functional
analysis of the productive process and its
correlated monetary flow.

1.   I have retained as much as possible the content
      and style of the original talk given in Loner-
      gan College, Concordia University, Montreal,
      March 1979.

2.   Insight, Harper and Row, N.Y., 1978 pb., 186.

3.   E. Voegelin, "Reason: The Classical Experience",
      The Southern Review, July 1974, 251.

4.   Insight, xv.

5.   F. E. Crowe has developed this notion in a
      number of unpublished treatises over the past
      twenty years. His most recent published work,
      Theology of the Christian Word: A Study in
      History, Paulist Press, N.Y., 1978, deals with
      aspects of it in the final chapters.

6.   N. Kaldor, "The Irrelevance of Equilibrium
      Economics", Economic Journal 82, 1972, 1240-41.

7.   Leon Walras, Elements of Pure Economics, trans-
      lated by W. Jaffe, Richard Irwin Inc., Illinois,
      1954. Originally published in 1874. "Samuelson
      feels that Walras and Augustin Cournot carried
      the development of mathematics in economics to
      a highly sophisticated level by the turn of the
      twentieth century. At that point, he claims
      the study was interrupted by the 'verbal' trad-
      ition of the English economists at Cambridge",
      W. Breit and R. Ransom, The Academic Scribblers:
      American Economists in Collision, Holt Reinhardt
      and Winston, New York, 1971, 114, n.

8.   See W. Jaffe, "A. N. Isnard, Progenitor of the
      Walrasian General Equilibrium Model", History
      of Political Economy, I, 1970.

9.   J. R. Hicks, "Mr. Keynes and the 'Classics': A
      Suggested Interpretation", Econometrica, 5, 1937,
      147-59. For a treatment which includes later
      views on the demand for money see F. R. Glahe,
      "A Permanent Restatement of the IS/LM Model",
      The American Economist XVII, 1973, 158-67.

10.   See W. Breit and R. Ransom, op. cit.

11.   C. Juglar, <u>Les Crises commerciales et leur</u>
      <u>retour periodique en France, en Angleterre et</u>
      <u>aux Etas Unis</u>, 1862, 1889.

12.   See H. Smith, "Marx and the Trade Cycle", <u>The</u>
      <u>Review of Economic Studies</u> (iv), 1936-37, $\overline{202}$.

13.   Mitchell was not given to theorizing but he
      kept the business cycle at the centre of his
      attention.   See, for example, Mitchell, <u>Business</u>
      <u>Cycles: The Problem of its Setting</u>, National
      Bureau of Economic Research, N.Y., 1927.

14.   His principal work on the subject is <u>Business</u>
      <u>Cycles, A Theoretical, Historical and Statis-</u>
      <u>tical Analysis of the Capitalist Process</u>, 2
      volumes, McGraw Hill, N.Y., 1939.

15.   Lowe's most up-to-date treatment is <u>The Path of</u>
      <u>Economic Growth</u>, Cambridge University Press,
      1976.

16.   <u>Grace and Freedom</u>, Darton Longman and Todd,
      London, 1970.

17.   Yale, 1961.

18.   See McShane, <u>Music That Is Soundless: An Introd-</u>
      <u>uction to God for the Graduate</u>, University Press
      of America, 1977;   the introduction and chapter
      five.

19.   <u>Insight</u>, 684.

20.   <u>The Lonely Crowd</u>, Yale, 1961, 307.

21.   Lonergan, "The Subject", <u>A Second Collection</u>, 73.

22.   <u>Method in Theology</u>, 261.

23.   <u>Insight</u>, 399.

24.   Hermann Hesse, <u>Narziss and Goldmund</u>, Penguin, 64.

25.   I have dealt with these issues at some length
      in <u>Randomness, Statistics and Emergence</u>.

26.   Discussed in Hugh Kenner, The Pound Era,
      University of California Press, 1971, where he
      quotes Pound, 238-39.

27.   Stuart Gilbert, "Prolegomena to Work in Progress",
      Samuel Beckett and others, Our Exagmination Round
      His Factification for Incamination of Work in
      Progress, London, 1961, 50, (first published in
      Paris, 1929).

28.   Lonergan, Gregorianum (40), 1959, 182-83.

29.   R. M. Kain, "Nothing Odd Will do Long: Some
      Thoughts on 'Finnegans Wake' Twenty-Five Years
      Later", Twelve and a Tilly.   Essays on the
      Occasion of the 25th Anniversary of Finnegans
      Wake, eds. J. P. Dalton and C. Hart, London,
      1966, 92.

30.   Chapter 4 here; chapter 2 of The Shaping of the
      Foundations.   I take advantage of this final
      reference to The Shaping of the Foundations to
      note a missing line on page 45 ; line 9 should
      conclude: "infinite intentionality, a dialogue
      which is the imaged hope of the ever-fuller
      emergence".

31.   David Lewin, "Behind the Beyond": A Response
      to E. T. Cone, Perspective of New Music (7),
      1969, 61.

32.   Paul de Man, Blindness and Insight, Oxford
      University Press, 1971, 39.

33.   G. R. Marek, Beethoven, Biography of a Genius,
      Kimber, London, 1970, 602.

34.   Leo Strauss, Liberalism: Ancient and Modern,
      N.Y., Basic Books, 1968, 3.